ARCHAEOLOGICAL EXPLORATION OF SARDIS

Fogg Art Museum of Harvard University—Cornell University
Corning Museum of Glass
Sponsored by the American Schools of Oriental Research

GENERAL EDITORS
George M. A. Hanfmann and Stephen W. Jacobs

MONOGRAPH 2

ARCHAEOLOGICAL EXPLORATION OF SARDIS

ANCIENT LITERARY SOURCES ON SARDIS

John Griffiths Pedley

HARVARD UNIVERSITY PRESS

CAMBRIDGE·MASSACHUSETTS
1972

© Copyright 1972 by the President and Fellows of
Harvard College

Library of Congress Catalog Card Number 72–172327
SBN 674–03375–2

Printed in the United States of America

Editors' Preface

The program known as the Archaeological Exploration of Sardis has been carried on since 1958 as a joint effort of the Fogg Art Museum of Harvard University and Cornell University; the Corning Museum of Glass has been a participant since 1960. The results of this collaborative project will be published in two series. The final *Reports* will contain the evidence from the excavations, accounts of conservation and restoration activities, and information on the major categories of excavated materials. The *Monographs* will include selected categories of objects suited to presentation in monograph form and special subjects supplementing the *Reports*.

In this second volume of the *Monographs*, we present the ancient literary sources on Sardis. The Sardis Expedition is greatly indebted to Professor John Griffiths Pedley of the University of Michigan, a member of the expedition for several seasons, for undertaking and most expeditiously completing this fundamental task. We join Professor Pedley in thanking the Loeb Classical Library Foundation for its grant of the fellowship which enabled him to work on this project at the Sardis research facility at Harvard.

On this occasion, we express our gratitude to the Government of the Republic of Turkey, and especially to the Ministry of National Education and (since 1971) the Ministry of Culture, as well as the Department of Antiquities and Museums, for extending their help and cooperation to the Archaeological Exploration of Sardis. We acknowledge gratefully the interest and support of the cooperating institutions whose presidents, deans, and other officers have made the program possible. Its development was greatly furthered by the sponsorship of the American Schools of Oriental Research.

Initial financial support came from the Bollingen Foundation (1957–1965) and the Old Dominion Foundation (1966–1968) of New York. Their grants set the Sardis expedition in motion and were a major factor in its progress. From 1962–1965 a grant made through Harvard University by the Department of State under Public Law 480 greatly enhanced the effectiveness of the research and training program. Since 1967, basic and matching grants made by the National Endowment for the Humanities through Harvard University have enabled the expedition to maintain momentum. Grateful acknowledgment is also made to the Ford Foundation for the grant of student traineeships through Cornell University from 1968 on, and to the Memorial Foundation of Jewish Culture, New York, for a grant for the publication of the synagogue. Generous assistance was also received from the Loeb Classical Library Foundation. Among the many individuals whose voluntary contributions have sustained the project through the years are: several well wishers who have made gifts through the American Schools of Oriental Research; donors of the Committee to Preserve the Ancient Synagogue of Sardis; and several hundred friends known as "Supporters of Sardis."

George M. A. Hanfmann
Harvard University
Stephen W. Jacobs
Cornell University

Author's Preface

In collecting the literary sources pertinent to Sardis, I found that the nature of the material itself dictated a historical rather than topographical approach. Accordingly, I have attempted to set out the sources which give us information on the careers of the city's kings as well as those that deal directly with the city itself. Sources which refer to Lydia have not been collected except insofar as they coincide with references to Sardis itself. I have not included either the inscriptions found at Sardis or those relating to Sardis but found elsewhere: these will be published by L. Robert in another volume in this series. To preserve a balanced view, the volume of inscriptions and this volume should be consulted together. Material which deals with Sardis in the Byzantine and Islamic period has been collected by Clive Foss and will appear in a subsequent monograph in this series. That volume will begin with an account of Diocletian's reorganization of the province and will also deal *in extenso* with early Christianity in the city, glancing backward to the references in this volume (*222, 223, 224*).

Problems of organization are almost overwhelming, and every method of arranging the material presented difficulties. For example, to set out the information chronologically according to the century or era in which the authors wrote would have given a certain coherence and social perspective. Yet it seemed better to keep bodies of information together, and hence the arrangement has been for the most part chronological, but from the point of view of the history of the city, not from that of the authority who is cited.

Again, in the topographical section, the question of geographical features presented itself—how far should geographical features be considered part and parcel of the topography of the city? Should Tmolus, Pactolus, Hermus, and so forth, be included? In the long run, but somewhat arbitrarily, I thought it best to include those features which were unique to Sardis, omitting others that were tangential to the city but which were not in any way salient or central. Thus, Pactolus and the Gygaean Lake, for instance, are included, while the Hermus is not.

The volume is divided historically into four principal chapters with a fifth devoted to topography and monuments and an appendix presenting some of the more important Near Eastern authorities. Within the historical chapters there is a further chronological or topical division, and within these again a further division by episode. The whole is arranged with emphasis on ease of consultation and access to bodies of information. Frequently, a long passage may be represented by only a small portion of the original text, followed by a translation of that portion and an English epitome of the rest of the text. For the sake of economy some less significant references appear only in the notes.

Authors are given in alphabetical order within each section, and when an author quotes another, the passage is given under the name of the quoting author.

When an item is of major relevance to more than one section, the serial number is repeated in parentheses in the other section and only the reference is given. When an item is of only minor relevance to another section, then the reference together with the serial number in parentheses is given in the annotations. For example, the item "Homer, *Iliad* 5.43" in the section "Homeric Lydians" is considered of major relevance to the section "The Name of Sardis"; hence, the serial number in parentheses and the reference are repeated there. By contrast, the item "Homer, *Iliad* 20.385" in "Homeric Lydians" is considered of only minor relevance to "The Name of Sardis." Accordingly, the reference with serial number in italic in parentheses is only mentioned in the note to the item "Strabo 13.4.6."

The notes are intended to explain the context of the passages and to point the reader in the direction of further relevant reading. They are hardly comprehensive, and while the reader may not always wish to be referred elsewhere, it is hoped that some notes, at any rate, may be stimulating if not enlightening.

I cannot claim to have collected all the sources relevant

to this vast topic. The problem, as Professor Wycherley was kind enough to write me, *solvitur ambulando*, but much strolling in the Widener Library may not necessarily have gathered all the appropriate material. One can only cast the net as wide as possible and hope that no big fish gets through; I do not doubt for a moment that several of the smaller fry may have escaped me.

The bulk of the translations are my own. In the appendix listing Near Eastern sources, I have, for obvious reasons, drawn on the work of other scholars. The translations from Assyrian texts are those of D. D. Luckenbill, *Ancient Records of Assyria and Babylonia* 2 (Chicago: University of Chicago Press, 1927) and A. C. Piepkorn, *Historical Prism Inscriptions of Assurbanipal* (Chicago: University of Chicago Press, 1933). The versions of the Babylonian texts cited here are those of S. Smith, *Babylonian Historical Texts* (London: Methuen & Co. Ltd., 1924), and the translations from Persian are those of R. G. Kent, *Old Persian* (New Haven: American Oriental Society, 1953) and R. T. Hallock, *Persepolis Fortification Tablets* (Chicago: University of Chicago Press, 1969). The version of the Arabic text of Polemo used here is that of G. Bowersock (hitherto unpublished). The use of all these translations is gratefully acknowledged.

Most of the work was done in the academic year 1969–1970 during the period of my tenure of the James Loeb Research Fellowship in Classical Archaeology at Harvard University. I should like to express my warmest thanks to the Loeb Classical Library Foundation, which was responsible for awarding me that Fellowship and

thus enabled me to take a leave of absence from The University of Michigan.

I am indebted to a great many colleagues for information and advice, and since to thank them all would be a very lengthy business, I want to thank them collectively, mentioning only a few. Professor George M. A. Hanfmann first suggested that I do this work, and throughout the whole project his knowledge and acuity were always generously available to me, providing enlightenment and numerous improvements. In the planning stage Professor Louis Robert provided many important answers with his usual cordiality and incisive thought. In Cambridge Professor Glen Bowersock was a constant source of support, and Mrs. Jane Scott and Mrs. Jane Waldbaum contributed invaluable help in my researches in the Sardis archives; it was a pleasure to work with them. In Ann Arbor Professor G. G. Cameron guided me to the most recent Near Eastern material, and in my own department I have been fortunate to be able to discuss a number of points with Professors Frank Copley, Bruce Frier, and Roger Pack. To all these colleagues and friends I extend my best thanks.

Finally I want to thank my wife, *unanima uxor*, without whose urgings and active assistance the work might never have been completed.

John Griffiths Pedley
The University of Michigan
Ann Arbor, Michigan

September 1971

Contents

Ancient Literary Sources on Sardis

Abbreviations

Abh	Abhandlungen (followed by name of academy, abbreviated)
AE	Ἀρχαιολογικὴ Ἐφημερίς
AJA	American Journal of Archaeology
AJP	American Journal of Philology
AM	Athenische Mitteilungen
AMIran	Archäologische Mitteilungen aus Iran
AnatSt	Anatolian Studies
AnzWien	Anzeiger der Akademie der Wissenschaften, Wien, Phil.-hist. Klasse.
AR	Annual Supplement to JHS Archaeological Reports
BASOR	Bulletin of the American Schools of Oriental Research
BCH	Bulletin de correspondance hellénique
BiblArch	The Biblical Archaeologist
BonnBeit	Bonner Beitrage
BSA	British School at Athens, Annual
CP	Classical Philology
CQ	Classical Quarterly
DOPapers	Dumbarton Oaks Papers
FGrHist	Jacoby, Fragmente der griechischen Historiker
FHG	Müller, Fragmenta Historicorum Graecorum
GRBS	Greek, Roman, and Byzantine Studies
HSCP	Harvard Studies in Classical Philology
InnsBeiKult	Innsbrucker beiträge zur Kulturwissenschaft
JCS	Journal of Cuneiform Studies
JEA	Journal of Egyptian Archaeology
JHS	Journal of Hellenic Studies
JNES	Journal of Near Eastern Studies
JOAI	Jahreshefte des oesterreichischen archäologischen Instituts
JRAS	Journal of the Royal Asiatic Society
JRS	Journal of Roman Studies
JWarb	Journal of the Warburg and Courtauld Institutes
KF	Kleinasiatische Forschungen
MDOG	Mitteilungen der deutschen Orient-Gesellschaft
MonPiot	Monuments et mémoires publ. par l'Académie des inscriptions et belles lettres, Fondation Piot
MusHelv	Museum Helveticum
NouvClio	La nouvelle Clio
NumChron	Numismatic Chronicle
RE	Pauly-Wissowa, Real-Encyclopädie der klassischen Altertumswissenschaft
REA	Revue des études anciennes
RhM	Rheinisches Museum für Philologie
WZKM	Wiener Zeitschrift für die Kunde des Morgenlandes
ZONF	Zeitschrift für Ortsnamenforschung

The reports of the first Sardis expedition (1910–1914 and 1922) are cited *Sardis* followed by volume number and year of publication. Seventeen volumes were planned by Howard Crosby Butler, Director of Excavations (*Sardis* I, p. viii); of these, nine were actually published under the general series title *Sardis, Publications of the American Society for the Excavation of Sardis*. They are: I—Howard Crosby Butler, *The Excavations*, pt. 1: *1910–1914* (Leyden: E. J. Brill, 1922). II—Howard Crosby Butler, *Architecture*, pt. 1: *The Temple of Artemis* (text and atlas of plates, Leyden: E. J. Brill, 1925). V—Charles Rufus Morey, *Roman and Christian Sculpture*, pt. 1: *The Sarcophagus of Claudia Antonia Sabina* (Princeton, New Jersey: Princeton University Press, 1924). VI—Enno Littmann, *Lydian Inscriptions*, pt. 1 (Leyden: E. J. Brill, 1916), William H. Buckler, *Lydian Inscriptions*, pt. 2 (Leyden: E. J. Brill, 1924). VII—William H. Buckler and David M. Robinson, *Greek and Latin Inscriptions*, pt. 1 (Leyden: E. J. Brill, 1932). X—T. Leslie Shear, *Terra-cottas*, pt. 1: *Architectural Terra-cottas* (Cambridge, England, 1926). XI—Harold W. Bell, *Coins*, pt. 1: *1910–1914* (Leyden: E. J. Brill, 1916). XIII—C. Densmore Curtis, *Jewelry and Gold Work*, pt. 1: *1910–1914* (Rome: Sindacato Italiano Arti Grafiche, 1925).

Introduction

Seventh and Sixth Centuries B.C.

Our sources for the history of the city and its kings begin in the Greek west almost with the dawn of literacy. Homer may not mention Sardis by name, but the homeland of his doughty Maeonians is never in doubt. They come from the region of the Gygaean Lake (see *238*), from the plain of Hermus (*239*), beneath Tmolus (*8*). Homer can mean no other domain for them than Sardis. It is still unclear whether the earliest township after the Bronze Age was called Sardis or Hyde (even Strabo [*17*] remained noncommittal), and another candidate, Tarne, was preferred by some (*7*), but Sardis it had become by the time of Alcman (*127*) and Sappho (*139*), mooning over her lost friend in the Lydian capital. Archilochus is the first Greek to refer to Gyges (*40*), the first Mermnad king; but the name was also known in the east in the Assyrian palaces where Assurbanipal talked of his relationship with Gyges (*293, 294, 295*) and complained effusively of Gyges' perfidy (*292*). Hipponax (*280*) gives us valuable topographical indications which include a mention of Gyges' tomb; Mimnermus (*44*) exhorts his contemporaries to remember their forefathers' valiance against the Lydian king; and Alcaeus (*73*) exclaims at the Lydians' financial meddling in the internal affairs of Lesbos, a reference perhaps to early largesse on the part of Croesus while his father's emissary in Adramytteium (*64*).

Fifth and Fourth Centuries B.C.

The Athenian tragedians are naturally not very interested in the history of a non-Greek city. For Aeschylus (*185*) Sardis was a contributor to the Persian war effort; for Euripides (*257*) she was the homeland of Dionysus; and for Sophocles (*189*) merely a source of gold. To Aristophanes (*187*) the city was a place where all things could be found.

Herodotus is the uniquely important source for us. He uses the story of the rise and fall of Croesus as the focus for the beginning of his *History*; and he uses it also as a stylistic paradigm, in terms of linearity punctuated by digressions, for the treatment of other sections of his work. In so doing he narrates the whole history of the Mermnad dynasty, fact and parable together. He articulates the Lydians' claim to the name Asia (*11*) and relates the story of the early Lydian emigration (*23*). He gives us a list of the Heraclid kings (*26*); he tells us his version of the Candaules story (*34*); he enumerates the deeds and doings of the early Mermnads, Gyges (*41, 43*), Ardys and Sadyattes (*52*), and Alyattes (*57, 59, 60, 62*). With the accession of Croesus he expands the narrative vastly, mingling historical facts with philosophical anecdotes in an episodic style. He sketches in the military campaigns westward (*71*) but reserves the bulk of his efforts for the exemplary material—Solon's visit to Sardis (*84*) and the Atys incident (*89*). He describes Croesus' preoccupation with the Greek oracles (*99, 100*) and his friendship with Sparta (*103, 104*). He tells us in detail of the expedition to the Halys (*111*) and of the fall of Sardis (*116*) of which Ctesias of Cnidus (*112*) among others gives us an implausible alternative account. There is a long description of Croesus on the pyre (*125*).

In the newly conquered Sardis we hear of Cyrus' negative reaction to the Ionians (*141*) and the Spartans (*142*), and subsequently we see the satrap Oroetes being overthrown (*145*). We are given a good picture of the Ionian revolt and the attack on Sardis (*150, 272, 282*), an impudent maneuver related for us also by Charon of Lampsacus (*149*) and referred to by Aristotle (*148*) and Plato (*153*). We witness the wily Histiaeus at work in the city (*151*). There is a vivid account of Xerxes' reviewing the troops in Sardis (*157*), and we find him returning there after his defeat in Greece (*158*), an episode of which we also catch a glimpse in Timotheus (*190*).

Herodotus' important account of the Ionian attack (*282*) enables us to visualize the agora of the city and the dwellings of the citizens, a picture which is now more fully documented by the archaeological evidence. He also mentions a temple of Cybele (*272*), a temple not yet located itself, but of which the recent excavations may well have given us an exact replica. He takes us around the walls of the acropolis with the negligent Meles and up them with the heroic Hyroeades (*116*). Of particular interest is the description of the tomb of Alyattes (*278*), penetrated centuries ago by Roman robbers and more recently (1857) by Spiegelthal. He provides us with information on the Royal Road which ran from Susa to Sardis (*191*).

His contemporary, Thucydides, was less interested in Asia Minor, mentioning Sardis only as a peripheral item related to the prosperity of the Ionians (*120*) and in connection with an alliance made by the Samians with the satrap Pissuthnes (*181*).

An author more concerned with Sardis and Lydian affairs was Xanthus, who, though a Lydian, wrote in Greek. He may have lived in Sardis, though Strabo (*216*) was unsure, and his name implies that he was a Hellenized Lydian or that his mother was a Greek. The Souda (s.v. Xanthus) tells us that his father was a Lydian. He was interested in early Lydia in a synoptic, comprehensive way, with something of the same anthropological slant as that of his great contemporary, Herodotus; but it is impossible to say how cohesive his *Lydiaka* was. What remains of his work is scattered through a good many later writers, in the form often of direct quotations, and it is Nicolas of Damascus who is thought to draw most heavily on him. Xanthus makes no mention of a Lydian emigration to Etruria, a fact of which Dionysius of Halicarnassus makes much (*21*). He was a student of geology (*19*) and mythology (*18*), and he gives us detailed if extraordinary stories about the early Lydian kings (*27, 28*). He describes the adventures of the shadowy Lydian Moxos (*9*) and gives Sardis the name Xuaris (*16*). He is one of the sources for some of Athenaeus' unflattering comments about the Lydians (*130*). His *Lydiaka* seems to have been a mélange of anecdote, etymology, myth, geology, and topography through which we are able to catch dim glimpses of political history and fact.

Of other fifth-century authors, Pindar (*101*) saw Croesus in a favorable light, doubtless drawing on a Delphic source for his *Pythian 1*. For Bacchylides (*124*) the downfall of Croesus and his plight on the pyre were a crucial metaphor. By the first quarter of the fifth century the pyre incident, resolved in Croesus' favor, was firmly entrenched in his biography, though the laconic sentences of the *Nabonidus Chronicle* (*296*) give us evidence to dispute the historicity of a life for Croesus beyond the pyre.

Parallel with our Greek authorities run sources from further east. The Persepolis fortification tablets tell us of craftsmen from Sardis working in Persia (*297, 300*) and

of travel rations issued to messengers journeying to and from Sardis (*298, 299*). Darius and Xerxes broadcast their control of the Lydian city (*301, 302, 304*), and the building inscription from Darius' palace at Susa (*303*) records the presence of masons and carpenters from Sardis in the work force. Gold also was brought from Sardis to Susa.

Aristotle (*107*) repeats for us the oracular response which (sources at Delphi said) predicted the overthrow of Sardis, while Plato (*86*) refers obliquely to the meeting between Solon and Croesus. And it is to Plato that we are indebted for the story of the ring of Gyges and another version of the death of Candaules (*36*).

Xenophon gives us an important account of the conflict between Cyrus and Croesus on the Hermus plain (*121*) and of the capture of the acropolis (*122*). In his narrative Croesus is spared and subsequently employed by Cyrus as an upper-level bureaucrat (*144*). To Xenophon we owe our evidence for the gallant death of the Persian prince Abradatas in the battle before Sardis (*276*). We witness the suicide of his wife, Panthea, and the construction of their tomb by the banks of the Pactolus (*277*), a tomb which we may well identify with that first excavated by the Princeton expedition and located on the south bank of a wadi leading westward to the Pactolus.

In later episodes we find Alcibiades a prisoner in Sardis (*162*) and Lysander a visitor there (*165*), admiring the gardens (*289*). It is to Sardis that Cyrus the Younger summoned his troops (*169*) at the outset of the *Anabasis* and thither that Xenophon went to join him (*170*). We are given important information about the altar of Artemis on which Orontas took oaths (*271*) and which may be identical with that which stood to the west of the later Artemis precinct. Agesilaus' maneuvers around Sardis are chronicled at length (*177, 178, 256*), and Xenophon's information is corroborated in part by the *Hellenica Oxyrhynchia* (*172*).

Hellenistic Writers

Among poets of the Hellenistic period, Dioskorides (*13*) offers a version of Atys' journey from Phrygia to Sardis, and Alexander of Aetolia (*39*) preserves a fragment of Alcman on which the claim that Alcman's native town was Sardis is based. In the mind of Callimachus (*188*) there is a clear echo of the long-time association of Ephesus with Sardis; and Nicander (*281*), discoursing on herbal remedies, gives us a flowery description of the tomb of Gyges which is more amusing and imaginative than topographical.

Polybius provides the bulk of the literary information we have on the career of the usurper Achaeus and the siege of Sardis by Antiochus. We see Achaeus warring on Attalus (*202*) and carrying all before him in Asia Minor. We get a vivid picture of him subsequently besieged in Sardis by Antiochus; and we are told of the feckless stratagems devised by either side and of the initiative of the enterprising Cretan, Lagoras (*203*). We are given a dramatic account of the scaling of the acropolis (*283, 284*) and of the capture and sack of the city (*285*). We hear of Achaeus' plan of escape and of his grisly end (*286*). Polybius had visited Sardis, where he would have gained some knowledge of the topography and monuments, and his narrative mentions the fortification walls, the theater, and two gates. The topography is reasonably clear, if imprecise. In later episodes we are told of the capture of the city by the Romans after Magnesia (*209*) and of the exploits of Gaius Gallus in the Hellenistic gymnasium (*210*).

The First Century B.C.

Cicero, in Laodicea in 50 B.C., wrote to the propraetor on behalf of a legate of his who was in dispute with the Sardians (*211*). He remembers Lysander's encounter with Cyrus (*287*) and the oracle which was Croesus' undoing (*108*); he was familiar with Plato's account of the ring of Gyges (*33*) and recalled a tradition about the precocious qualities of Croesus' son (*88*). Nepos tells us that Conon was imprisoned in Sardis by Tiribazus (*180*) and repeats Xenophon's narrative concerning Agesilaus' activities near Sardis (*173*). Pompeius Trogus informs us briefly of Alexander's capture of the city (*196, 197*), while Parthenius (*118*) gives a fanciful account of Cyrus' capture of the acropolis, involving Croesus' daughter, the treacherous Nanis, and her infatuation for Cyrus.

In the Latin poets the riches of Croesus are remembered (*74, 81*); and Horace (*229*), Ovid (*230, 231*), and Varro (*232*) make mention of Sardis itself. In most of these, however, it is not the city itself which attracts the poetic mind; and elsewhere, for Propertius (*249, 250*), Varro (*254*), and Virgil (*255*), it is the Pactolus alone which catches the imagination. Occasionally the Gygaean Lake (*240*) or Tmolus (*267*) becomes the focus.

In his *Library of History*, Diodorus Siculus gathered together information from earlier writers in a rather uncritical way. He seems to have followed his authorities quite closely, if in a capsulated style, and very often the source on which he draws is plain enough. He tells us of the events of Croesus' life (*70, 140*) and of his dedications at Delphi (*98*); we are told of Xerxes (*156*), Lysander (*163*), and Cyrus the Younger (*166*) in Sardis. Agesilaus' adventures are not omitted (*288*), and we see both Alexander (*192*) and his sister Cleopatra (*198*) in the Lydian capital.

Dionysius of Halicarnassus yields important information on the story of the Lydian migration to Italy. He gives us his version of events (*20*), quotes Xanthus as evidence for the story being more legend than fact (*21*), and states the reasons for his own belief that the Tyrrhenians did not come from Lydia (*22*).

Writers at the Turn of the Era

Of the authors at the turn of the era who contribute to our knowledge of Sardis, two are paramount: Strabo and Nicolas of Damascus. In a single passage Strabo gives us a detailed description of the city's geography with scraps of historical information here and there (*234*), and elsewhere he refers to some of the city's landmarks (*264, 265, 266*). He takes us to the tomb of Alyattes (*279*) which was built largely, according to him (and Herodotus), with contributions from the city's prostitutes. He participates in the discussion on the name of Sardis (*17*) and believes more strongly in geology than myth (*219*). He pays tribute to the authority of Xanthus (*19*), although he is unsure whether he lived in Sardis or not (*216*). In a passage crucial for the political history of the seventh century, he quotes Callinus and Archilochus on the subject of the Cimmerians and the destruction of Magnesia and Sardis (*51*). The Cimmerians and their leader, Lygdamis, appear in another historical episode where they overthrow Midas of Phrygia before taking Sardis. Lygdamis went on to his death in Cilicia (*49*). In another passage Strabo quotes Callisthenes and Callinus again as he lists the destruction which overtook the city in its early life (*50*). He tells us of two orators from Sardis, both named Diodorus, one of whom was a contemporary and friend of his (*216*); and he mentions Eumenes' victory over Antiochus near Sardis (*201*).

Nicolas of Damascus wrote a *Universal History*, fragments of which are preserved for us in excerpts made for the Byzantine emperor, Constantinus Porphyrogenitus, in the tenth century. In the Lydian portion of his history it is generally accepted that he is largely dependent on Xanthus, and he therefore is an authority of prime importance for us. He tells us of the early kings and heroes of Lydia: of Meles (*31*) who went into voluntary exile at the bidding of the soothsayers; of the intemperate glutton Camblitas (*29*) and his suicide; and of the Moxos who tangled with another Meles (*10*). We hear a long account of the twin kings, Cadys and Ardys (*30*), and of Myrsus, father of the Herodotean Candaules, the last of the Heraclid rulers in Sardis (*32*). To Nicolas, Candaules' name is Adyattes or Sadyattes; and in another lengthy account (*35*) he tells us of Gyges' return from exile, his affection for the Mysian princess Toudo, betrothed to Sadyattes, and of the murder of Sadyattes. Nicolas is our authority for a campaign waged by Gyges against Magnesia (*45*); he tells us of another Sadyattes (*53*); and in chronicling the events of the life of Alyattes (*58, 63*) he tells us of Croesus' spendthrift behavior while governor of Adramytteium and the plain of Thebe (*64*). Of great interest is his detailed treatment of the pyre incident (*126*), where some of the details are surely derived from sources other than Xanthus.

The architectural historian Vitruvius is an important source for what little we know of the Palace of Croesus (*291*) and, more concretely, for some of the information we have on construction techniques used in the Lydian capital (*134*). Livy describes Antiochus' maneuvers around Sardis (*205*) before the battle of Magnesia and his flight afterwards (*207*), an episode expanded by Appian (*206*). He also tells us of Eumenes' collecting an army at Sardis against the Gauls (*208*). Of the two Senecas, the Elder reflects on the inconstancy of fortune with Croesus in mind (*82*), while the Younger makes several mentions of the Pactolus and Tmolus (*251, 259, 260*) and tells us of Demaratus' request to ride into Sardis as a king (*160*).

The First and Second Centuries A.D.

Pliny (*233*) gives us a concise account of the geography around Sardis and pays special attention to the Pactolus (*248*). He tells us of the laurel trees at Sardis (*135*), of the yellow ochre used for painting (*136*), of the sards first discovered there (*137*), and of the invention of wool dyeing in the city (*133*). Following Vitruvius, he informs us that the Palace of Croesus was made of mudbrick and that it had seen use in Sardis as a senate house (*290*). He sheds interesting light on the artistic taste of Candaules, the last Heraclid king (*37*).

Plutarch's *Lives* and *Moralia* are a mine of information. If much is anecdote and biography rather than technical history, it is fascinating nonetheless, and any scrap of topographical background information has a good chance of being valid. Plutarch thought that Solon and Croesus actually met (*87*), in spite of the chronological difficulty of which he was well aware. He shows us Themistocles in Sardis examining the Metroon (*274*) and Alcibiades contriving his escape (*161*). We meet Lysander in the city (*164*); Agesilaus wreaking havoc in the environs (*175*); and Alexander in control of the area (*195*). We see Demetrius capturing Sardis (*200*) and Brutus and Cassius hailed as *Imperatores* in the city (*214*). Plutarch refers obliquely to early Lydian legend (*3, 24, 25*) and introduces us to Arselis of Mylasa, a champion of Gyges (*4*). He gives us information about a plot against the life of Croesus (*67, 68*) which, though its historical value may be questionable, should not be

ignored. If the details are inexact, the gist may well be true.

He has interesting ideas about the reasons for the Ionian attack on Sardis (*154*) and is critical of Herodotus' account of the adventure (*155*). In his own time, he addressed the *De exilio* to an exile from Sardis (*218*), probably the Menemachus to whom the *Praecepta gerendae reipublicae* was also addressed; and he tells us of personal hostilities and civil strife in Sardis somewhere around 100 A.D. (*227*).

Dio Chrysostom repeats from Herodotus the comic treatment of the endowment of the Alcmeonids (*75*) and was as impressed as anyone by the tales of Croesus' riches (*242*). Polyaenus gives us a dark explanation of Alyattes' defeat of the Cimmerians (*65*) and shows us Croesus besieging Ephesus (*72*). We are given another version of Cyrus' capture of the acropolis (*119*) and are again told of the shrewd deceptions of Agesilaus (*176*). We see the acropolis surrendered to Seleucus by a trembling Theodotus (*237*).

The traveler and geographer Pausanias was primarily concerned to take his readers around the world as he knew it, drawing their attention to the wonders and monuments which he encountered. There is much mythology and history in his many digressions, and for our purposes this is admirable. He implies that Gyges captured Smyrna but was subsequently driven out (*46*). He tells us of Croesus' generosity to the Spartans (*105*) and of his alliance with them (*106*). We see Cyrus in Sardis dispensing money to Lysander (*168*) and Agesilaus en route to Sardis undisturbed by an incomplete sacrifice (*174*). He mentions the sanctuary of Persian Artemis (*270*) and gives us a description of a Persian religious complex which included a fire altar similar to that recently excavated at Sardis (*273*).

In his *Antiquitates Judaicae*, Josephus (*275*) alludes to a synagogue in the city in the first century, a structure considerably earlier than the monumental building recovered by the recent excavators. A Jewish community had existed in Sardis for a long time (*305*). The presence of a Christian community in the city in the first century is attested by the *Revelation of St. John the Divine* (*223, 224*); and in the second century Melito, bishop of Sardis, was one of the leading figures of the church in Asia Minor (*222*).

No work adds more to our knowledge of the earthquake that destroyed Sardis and many other cities in Asia in 17 A.D. than the *Annales* of Tacitus (*220*), from whom we also learn of the Sardians' public claim to be kinsmen to the Romans (*221*). Valerius Maximus gives us a detail or two from an incident said to have taken place in the life of Gyges (*42*), and he drearily repeats Herodotus (*91, 92*).

Odd doings of men and animals are the stock in trade of Aelian, who narrates for us the mutual generosity of Pamphaes and Croesus (*66*), an episode which he may have gathered from Nicolas of Damascus, and the strange defensive measures taken by Pindarus of Ephesus in the face of Croesus' threats (*69*). He also quotes Autocrates telling of Lydian girls dancing for Artemis of Ephesus and bobbing up and down like wagtails (*184*).

The *Deipnosophistae* of Athenaeus is more of a guide to the good life, dining *comme il faut*, than it is a serious literary composition. But it does include many quotations culled from earlier writers whose works are lost and hence is valuable, if only as a repository of excerpts from lost works of others. Athenaeus quotes Mnaseas, in turn quoting Xanthus, on Moxos (*9*), and Phaenias of Eresus and Theopompus on the endowment of Delphi by the Lydian kings (*97*). We find Plato the comic poet referring to the popularity of blankets from Sardis (*128*) and Phylotimus discoursing on the quality of chestnuts from there (*129*). Athenaeus gives us the views of several poets on perfumes and baccaris from the Lydian capital (*131*). He cites Xanthus on the sterilization of women in Sardis and the sensational Clearchus of Soli, to be taken with a grain of salt, on some more extreme Sardian behavior (*130*).

In his *Anabasis*, a history of Alexander, Arrian of Bithynia gives us a full account of the Macedonian's visit to Sardis (*235*). He shows us the Persian commander and a delegation of citizens surrendering the city and Alexander pitching camp by the Hermus. He takes us up the acropolis with the conqueror; he tells us of Alexander's amazement at the defenses and of an inspirational thunderstorm and cloudburst directly over the palace of the Lydian kings.

To Lucian (*236*) the capture of the acropolis at Sardis was a symbol of the ultimate achievement, and Croesus (*79*) was a suitable companion for Midas and Sardanapalus.

Among the poets, Tmolus was still well known to Silius Italicus (*261, 262*) and Statius (*263*); and for Juvenal (*244*) and Lucan (*245*) the Pactolus remained the river of riches.

Later Roman Authors

Diogenes Laertius wrote in the first half of the third century and was a somewhat injudicious recipient of a great mass of folktale, biography, and philosophy from earlier authors. He informs us that Anaximenes flourished at the time of the taking of Sardis (*113*), records the story of the youths sent to Alyattes from Periander (*55*), and explains how Xenophon was introduced to Cyrus by the Boeotian friend of both, Proxenus (*167*). We follow the student career of Arcesilaus of Pitane, after a visit to Sardis, through the schools in Athens (*179*). We read letters from Pittacus (*93*) and Anacharsis (*94*) to Croesus, and from Periander to the Wise Men urging them to meet in Corinth now that they have tried Sardis (*56*). It is hard to believe that these letters are genuine.

Justin speaks of Croesus' defeat at Cyrus' hands (*117*) and of the presence of Cleopatra, sister of Alexander (*199*), in Sardis; Arnobius (*6*) makes indirect reference to the legend of Heracles in Sardis; and Lactantius (*78*), Arnobius' pupil, refers to Croesus and Crassus in the same breath.

In the fourth century Himerius extolled the Athenians for their part in the attack on Sardis in 499 B.C. (*152*), graphically outlined the reasons for Xerxes' hatred of Athens (*159*), and mentions Sardis in connection with Alexander's conquests (*193*).

Later and Byzantine Writers

Orosius gives a confused narrative of Alexander's progress through Asia Minor (*194*) and, describing the events of 86 B.C., declares that Sardis, following the example of Ephesus, shut its gates against Mithridates (*213*). Joannes Laurentius Lydus gives us two valuable pieces of information. Writing in the sixth century, he preserves an excerpt from Xanthus to the effect that Xuaris is an alternative term for Sardis (*16*). He also cites Eumelus, the Corinthian poet of perhaps the eighth century B.C., as saying that Zeus was born in Lydia (*14*).

Theophanes (*143*) claims—on what evidence is unclear—that the treasure of Croesus had been removed to Thybarmais, in Iran, while Tzetzes (*83*), the twelfth-century Byzantine scholar, concocted verse accounts of the biographies of Gyges and Croesus.

Such, then, are the literary sources for a city which in turn had been the capital of the Lydian empire, the seat of a Persian satrap, the administrative center of the Seleucids, and an important city in the Roman province. No ancient historian seems to have written a city chronicle of Sardis. Though our present sources are in some instances fragmentary, nevertheless, taken together, they suffice for an outline of the city's history and provide scattered information about its topography, monuments, industries, and manners. It is no surprise that the impact of sixth- and fifth-century Sardis on Greek authors was considerable, and it is obvious why, by the time of the establishment of the Roman province of Asia, the city attracted far less attention. By the turn of the era, Sardis and her kings are mentioned in the literary world more for their paradigmatic qualities, by those who praised or would learn from times gone by, than for contemporary events.

I. Early Sardis

This part of the volume contains a digest of sources which refer to the early history of Lydia, her kings and legendary sagas. Though Sardis itself is often not mentioned in connection with early Lydian events, the connection is often implied, and to include the material seems appropriate. At the same time I have frequently included only one or two passages on any one topic, reserving the bulk of the references for the annotations. Essentially this is a summary of the mythological traditions.

HEROES

Heracles and Omphale

1. (Apollodorus), *Bibliotheca* 2.6.3.   1st C. A.D.

τοῦ δὲ χρησμοῦ δοθέντος Ἑρμῆς Ἡρακλέα πιπράσκει· καὶ αὐτὸν ὠνεῖται Ὀμφάλη Ἰαρδάνου, βασιλεύουσα Λυδῶν, ᾗ τὴν ἡγεμονίαν τελευτῶν ὁ γήμας Τμῶλος κατέλιπε.

After the oracle Hermes sold Heracles. And Omphale, the daughter of Iardanus and queen of the Lydians, bought him; she to whom her husband Tmolus left the sovereignty at his death.

On Heracles and Omphale see also Diodorus Siculus 4.31.5; Schol. Homer, *Odyssey* 21.22; Sophocles, *Trachiniae* 247ff.
Pherecydes, cited by the scholiast on Homer (ibid.), says that Omphale bought Heracles from Hermes for three talents. Diodorus (ibid.) says that the money obtained by the purchase was to be paid to the sons of the murdered Iphitus as compensation. Sophocles (*Trachiniae* 252f) says that the period of Heracles' servitude was only one year; but Herodorus, cited by the scholiast on Sophocles (*Trachiniae* 253), claims that it was three years, which agrees with the account of Apollodorus.

Apollodorus lived in the second century B.C., but the *Bibliotheca* is usually thought to be at least a century later.

2. (Apollodorus), *Bibliotheca* 2.7.8.   1st C. A.D.

ἐξ Ὀμφάλης δὲ Ἀγέλαος, ὅθεν καὶ τὸ Κροίσου γένος.

Omphale bore Agelaus to him, from whom sprang the house of Croesus.

Diodorus Siculus (4.31.8) and Ovid (*Heroides* 9.53ff) say that Lamus was the name of the son whom Omphale bore to Heracles.
Herodotus (1.7) (see *26*) says that the dynasty which preceded the Mermnads in Sardis traced its descent from Alcaeus, the son of Heracles by a slave girl.

3. Plutarch, *An seni respublica gerenda sit* 4 (785E).

1st–2nd c. A.D.

οὐκ οἶδα ποτέρᾳ δυεῖν εἰκόνων αἰσχρῶν πρέπειν δόξει μᾶλλον ὁ βίος αὐτοῦ· πότερον ἀφροδίσια ναύταις ἄγουσι τὸν λοιπὸν ἤδη πάντα χρόνον, οὐκ ἐν λιμένι τὴν ναῦν ἔχουσιν ἀλλ' ἔτι πλέουσαν ἀπολιποῦσιν· ἢ καθάπερ ἔνιοι τὸν Ἡρακλέα παίζοντες οὐκ εὖ γράφουσιν ἐν Ὀμφάλης κροκωτοφόρον ἐνδιδόντα Λυδαῖς θεραπαινίσι ῥιπίζειν καὶ παραπλέκειν ἑαυτόν.

I do not know which of two shameful pictures his life will appear rather to be like; like that of sailors pursuing sexual pleasures without satisfaction when they have not brought their ship to harbor but have left it still under sail, or like that of Heracles as some paint him, jestingly but not well, wearing a yellow robe in Omphale's palace and surrendering himself to Lydian girls to fan him and curl his hair.

On Heracles and Omphale see also Hyginus, *Fabulae* 32; Joannes Lydus, *De magistratibus* 3.64; Lucian, *Dialogi deorum* 13.2; Ovid, *Heroides* 9.55; Schol. Homer, *Odyssey* 21.22; Seneca, *Hercules Oetaeus* 371ff (see *259*); Statius, *Thebais* 10.646–649; Tzetzes, *Historiarum variarum chiliades* 2.425ff.

4. Plutarch, *Quaestiones Graecae* 45 (302A).

1st–2nd c. A.D.

"Διὰ τί τοῦ Λαβρανδέως Διὸς ἐν Καρίᾳ τὸ ἄγαλμα πέλεκυν
ἠρμένον οὐχὶ δὲ σκῆπτρον ἢ κεραυνὸν πεποίηται;" ὅτι
'Ηρακλῆς 'Ιππολύτην ἀποκτείνας καὶ μετὰ τῶν ἄλλων
ὅπλων αὐτῆς λαβὼν τὸν πέλεκυν 'Ομφάλῃ δῶρον δέδωκεν.
οἱ δὲ μετ' 'Ομφάλην Λυδῶν βασιλεῖς ἐφόρουν αὐτὸν ὥς
τι τῶν ἄλλων ἱερῶν ἐκ διαδοχῆς παραλαμβάνοντες, ἄχρι
Κανδαύλης ἀπαξιώσας ἑνὶ τῶν ἑταίρων φορεῖν ἔδωκεν.
ἐπεὶ δὲ Γύγης ἀποστὰς ἐπολέμει πρὸς αὐτόν, ἦλθεν
"Αρσηλις ἐκ Μυλασέων ἐπίκουρος τῷ Γύγῃ μετὰ δυνάμεως, καὶ τόν τε Κανδαύλην καὶ τὸν ἑταῖρον αὐτοῦ
διαφθείρει, καὶ τὸν πέλεκυν εἰς Καρίαν ἐκόμισε μετὰ τῶν
ἄλλων λαφύρων. καὶ Διὸς ἄγαλμα κατασκευάσας τὸν
πέλεκυν ἐνεχείρισε, καὶ Λαβρανδέα τὸν θεὸν προσηγό-
ρευσε· Λυδοὶ γάρ "λάβρυν" τὸν πέλεκυν ὀνομάζουσι.

Q. For what reason was the statue of Zeus Labrandus
in Caria made equipped with an ax and not with a
scepter or a thunderbolt?
A. Because when Heracles killed Hippolyte he took
her ax with her other weapons and gave it to Omphale
as a gift. The Lydian rulers after Omphale used to
carry it like any of the other religious objects and they
handed it down in succession until the time of Candaules; he, however, despised it and gave it to one of
his companions to carry. But when Gyges revolted
and warred against Candaules, Arselis of Mylasa
came with an army as an ally of Gyges, and killed
Candaules and his companion, and carried off the ax
to Caria with the rest of the booty. And he built a
statue of Zeus and set the ax in its hand and called the
god Labrandeus: for the Lydians call the ax "Labrys."

The Heracles-Omphale love motif is perhaps derived from
Attic comedy's attacks on Pericles and Aspasia; on this,
Plutarch's other sources, and the explanation of the means
whereby a Lydian word was associated with a Carian god
and place-name, see W. R. Halliday, *The Greek Questions
of Plutarch* (Oxford 1928) 33–34, 185–189.

(**240**) Propertius 3.11.17–20.   1st c. B.C.

Heracles in Lydia

5. Schol. Apollonius Rhodius, *Argonautica* 4.1149

Πανύασις δὲ ἐν Λυδίᾳ τὸν 'Ηρακλέα νοσήσαντα τυχεῖν
ἰάσεως ὑπὸ "Υλλου τοῦ ποταμοῦ, ὅς ἐστι τῆς Λυδίας.

Panyassis says that in Lydia Heracles fell ill and
found a remedy from the river Hyllus, which is in
Lydia.

Panyassis, the epic poet, was kinsman to and possibly
uncle of Herodotus. He lived in Halicarnassus: on him see
Suidas, s.v. *Panyassis*; *FGrHist* 440; Kinkel, *EGF* 253–265;
G. L. Huxley, *Greek Epic Poetry: From Eumelos to Panyassis* (Cambridge, Mass. 1969) 177–190, 200.

On Heracles in Lydia see also Tacitus, *Annales* 3.61;
Schol. Homer, *Iliad* 24.616.

6. Arnobius, *Adversus nationes* 4.25.   3rd–4th c. A.D.
numquid aliquando a nobis conscriptum est mercen-
nariam deos seruitutem seruisse, ut Herculem Sardibus amoris et petulantiae causa.

Have we not sometimes written that the gods have
served a hired serfdom, as Hercules at Sardis, for the
sake of love and wantonness?

Arnobius was a Christian resident in North Africa. His
writings are to some degree dependent on Varro and
Lucretius.

Homeric Lydians

(**238**) Homer, *Iliad* 2.864–866.

7. Homer, *Iliad* 5.43–44.

'Ιδομενεὺς δ' ἄρα Φαῖστον ἐνήρατο Μήονος υἱὸν
Βώρου, ὃς ἐκ Τάρνης ἐριβώλακος εἰληλούθει.

Idomeneus killed Phaistus, son of Borus the Maeonian, who had come from Tarne rich in soil.

The scholiast *ad* 5.44 equates Tarne with Sardis.

8. Homer, *Iliad* 20.382–385.

πρῶτον δ' ἕλεν 'Ιφιτίωνα,
ἐσθλὸν 'Οτρυντεΐδην, πολέων ἡγήτορα λαῶν,
ὃν νύμφη τέκε νηῒς 'Οτρυντῆϊ πτολιπόρθῳ
Τμώλῳ ὕπο νιφόεντι, "Υδης ἐν πίονι δήμῳ.

First he killed Iphition, the noble son of Otrynteus,
leader of a great company, whom a naiad nymph bore
to Otrynteus, sacker of cities, beneath snowy Tmolus
in the rich land of Hyde.

On Hyde see Strabo 9.2.20; 13.4.6 (see *17*). The equation
between Hyde and Sardis is made, though Strabo is not
convinced.

(**239**) Homer, *Iliad* 20.389–392.

(**241**) Quintus Smyrnaeus, *Posthomerica* 11.67–69.

4th c. A.D.

Moxos

9. Athenaeus, *Deipnosophistae* 8.346 E, quoting Mnaseas.   2nd–3rd c. A.D.

ἡ δέ γε ᾽Αταργάτις, ὥσπερ Ξάνθος λέγει ὁ Λυδός, ὑπὸ Μόξου τοῦ Λυδοῦ ἁλοῦσα κατεποντίσθη μετὰ ᾽Ιχθύος τοῦ υἱοῦ ἐν τῇ περὶ ᾽Ασκάλωνα λίμνῃ διὰ τὴν ὕβριν, καὶ ὑπὸ τῶν ἰχθύων κατεβρώθη.

Atargatis, as Xanthus the Lydian says, was captured by Moxos the Lydian and with her son Ichthys was thrown into the lake near Ascalon because of her insolence and was devoured by the fish.

10. Nicolas of Damascus, *FGrHist* 90 F 16.
                    1st c. B.C.–A.D.

ὅτι Μόξος ὁ Λυδὸς πολλὰ καὶ καλὰ ἐργασάμενος καὶ τὸν Μήλην τῆς τυραννίδος καθελὼν τοῖς Λυδοῖς παρεκελεύσατο τὴν δεκάτην ἀποδοῦναι, καθὰ ηὔξατο, τοῖς θεοῖς. οἱ δὲ ἐπείθοντο καὶ ἀπαριθμοῦντες τὰ κτήματα ἐξῄρουν τὴν δεκάτην ἁπάντων καὶ κατέθυον. ἐπὶ τούτου μέγιστος αὐχμὸς καταλαμβάνει Λυδίαν, καὶ οἱ ἄνθρωποι ἐπὶ μαντείαν κατέφευγον * * πολλὰς δὲ στρατείας λέγεται πεποιῆσθαι οὗτος ὁ ἀνήρ, καὶ ἦν αὐτοῦ κλέος μέγιστον ἐν Λυδοῖς ἐπί τε ἀνδρείᾳ καὶ δικαιοσύνῃ. ταῦτα δὲ πράξας αὖθις ἐπὶ τὴν Κράβον (?) ἐστάλη, καὶ πολὺν χρόνον αὐτὴν πολιορκήσας εἷλε καὶ ἐπόρθησε, τοὺς δὲ ἀνθρώπους εἰς τὴν πλησίον λίμνην ἀγαγὼν οἷα ἀθέους ἐπόντωσεν.

Moxos the Lydian did many marvelous things. When he had driven Meles from the tyranny he urged the Lydians to surrender a tithe to the gods, as he had vowed. They agreed and reckoning up their goods they took a tenth part and dedicated it to the gods. In this man's time a great drought took hold of Lydia and the citizens took refuge in divination. This man is said to have made many campaigns, and his renown among the Lydians was paramount both for courage and justice. After this again he went against Krabos (?) and besieged it for a long time and took it and sacked it, and taking the men to a nearby lake he drowned them as godless folk.

For Moxos/Mopsos cf. Pausanias 7.3.1–2; Strabo 14.4.3 quoting Callinus; Xanthus *FGrHist* 765 F 17. And see R. D. Barnett, *AnatSt* 3 (1953) 83–84; P. Levy, *La Nouvelle Clio* 3 (1950) 188; H. Herter, *BonnBeit* 15 (1966) 33–35, 49.
On Meles and other early kings, see L. Alexander, *The Kings of Lydia* (Princeton 1913) 21–31, and passim.
For other lists of early Lydian kings cf. Herodotus 1.7 (see *26*) and Schol. Plato *Timaeus* 25 B.

OTHER TRADITIONS

Asios and Asia

11. Herodotus 4.45.   5th c. B.C.

ἤδη γὰρ Λιβύη μὲν ἐπὶ Λιβύης λέγεται ὑπὸ τῶν πολλῶν ῾Ελλήνων ἔχειν τὸ οὔνομα γυναικὸς αὐτόχθονος, ἡ δὲ ᾽Ασίη ἐπὶ τῆς Προμηθέος γυναικὸς τὴν ἐπωνυμίην. καὶ τούτου μὲν μεταλαμβάνονται τοῦ οὐνόματος Λυδοί, φάμενοι ἐπὶ ᾽Ασίεω τοῦ Κότυος τοῦ Μάνεω κεκλῆσθαι τὴν ᾽Ασίην, ἀλλ᾽ οὐκ ἐπὶ τῆς Προμηθέος ᾽Ασίης· ἐπ᾽ ὅτευ καὶ τὴν ἐν Σάρδισι φυλὴν κεκλῆσθαι ᾽Ασιάδα.

For many Greeks say that Libya is so called after a native woman, and that Asia has its name after the wife of Prometheus. But the Lydians have a share in this name saying that Asia was so named after Asies the son of Cotys who was the son of Manes, and not after Prometheus' wife, Asia. They declare that it is from this man that the tribe Asias in Sardis takes its name.

For linguistic similarity between the Hittite name Assuwa and the Greek name Asia see H. T. Bossert, *Asia* (Istanbul 1946).
For tribes in Sardis see *Sardis* VII:1 (1932) 179; cf. L. Robert, *Nouvelles inscriptions de Sardes* (Paris 1964) 46.
On Asies see also Dionysius of Halicarnassus, *Antiquitates Romanae* 1.27.1 (see *20*).
For the equation of Lydia with Asia see Schol. Apollonius Rhodius 2.777.

12. Schol. Homer, *Iliad* 2.461.

῎Ασιος υἱὸς Κότυος καὶ Μυιοῦς, Λυδῶν βασιλεύς, ὥς φησι Χριστόδωρος ἐν τοῖς Λυδιακοῖς "Κότυς λευκώλενον ἄλλην ἤγετο κουριδίην ὁμοδέμνιον, οὔνομα Μυιοῦν· ἡ δ᾽ ᾽Ασίην τέκε κοῦρον."

Asius was the son of Cotys and Muio, a king of the Lydians, as says Christodorus in his *Lydiaka*: "Cotys took another white-armed girl to wife whose name was Muio. And she bore a son Asius."

For Christodorus of Koptos (ca 491–518 A.D.) see Suidas s.v. *Christodorus*. See also *FGrHist* 283 and P. Friedlaender, *Hermes* 47 (1912) 57.
On *Asios* and *Asien* see *RE* II (1896) 1579–80, 1606.

Atys' Arrival

13. Dioskorides in *Anthologia Palatina* 6.220.
                    3rd c. B.C.

Σάρδις Πεσσινόεντος ἀπὸ Φρυγὸς ἤθελ' ἱκέσθαι,
 ἔκφρων μαινομένην δοὺς ἀνέμοισι τρίχα,
ἀγνὸς "Ατυς Κυβέλης θαλαμηπόλος.

From Pessinus in Phrygia he intended to journey to Sardis, giving his loosened hair to the winds in frenzied state, Atys chaste chamberlain of Cybele.

Cf. A. S. F. Gow and D. L. Page, *Hellenistic Epigrams* (Cambridge, Eng. 1965) I 85–86, II 246–248.

Pessinus was a chief seat of Cybele (cf., e.g., Cicero *De haruspicum responso* 28).

On Atys' journey to Sardis see Pausanias 7.17.9.

For a fraternity hall called "Attis" in Sardis see *Sardis* VII:1 (1932) 38, no. 17.6.

Lydian Zeus

14. Joannes Laurentius Lydus, *De mensibus* 4.71, quoting Eumelus.   6th c. A.D.

Εὔμηλος δὲ ὁ Κορίνθιος τὸν Δία ἐν τῇ καθ' ἡμᾶς Λυδίᾳ τεχθῆναι βούλεται, καὶ μᾶλλον ἀληθεύει ὅσον ἐν ἱστορίᾳ· ἔτι γὰρ καὶ νῦν πρὸς τῷ δυτικῷ τῆς Σαρδιανῶν πόλεως μέρει ἐπ' ἀκρωρείας τοῦ Τμώλου τόπος ἐστίν, ὃς πάλαι μὲν Γοναὶ Διὸς ὑετίου, νῦν δὲ παρατραπείσης τῷ χρόνῳ τῆς λέξεως Δεύσιον προσαγορεύεται.

Eumelus the Corinthian says that Zeus was born in what today we call Lydia, and he is as reliable as anyone: for still today on the western side of the city of Sardis, on the mountain ridge of Tmolus, there is a place which used to be called the Birth of Rain-bringing Zeus, and now with language altered by time is known as Deusion.

Cf. Lydus, *De mensibus* 3.30, and Kinkel, *EGF* frag. 18. See also A. B. Cook, *Zeus* II:2 (Cambridge, Eng. 1925) 957.

Eumelus perhaps wrote in the eighth century B.C.: cf. G. L. Huxley, *Greek Epic Poetry: From Eumelos to Panyassis* (Cambridge, Mass. 1969) 77.

The Name of Sardis

15. Eustathius, *Commentarii ad Homeri Iliadem* 366.15–20.   12th c. A.D.

καὶ μὴν ἕτεροι κατὰ τὸν γεωγράφον "Υδην τὴν τῶν Σάρδεων ἀκρόπολίν φασιν ἢ αὐτὰς τὰς Σάρδεις τὸ τῶν Λυδῶν βασίλειον, αἳ καὶ ὑπὸ Κιμμερίων ἑάλωσάν ποτε. Τμῶλος δέ, φησιν, ὄρος εὔδαιμον Λυδίας, ὑπερκείμενον Σάρδεων, ἔχον σκοπὴν ἐν τῇ ἀκρωρείᾳ, ἐξέδραν λευκοῦ λίθου, Περσῶν ἔργον.

According to the geographer some say that Hyde was the acropolis of Sardis rather than Sardis itself, the royal city of the Lydians which once was captured by the Cimmerians. Tmolus, he says, is the blessed mountain of Lydia, overlooking Sardis and having a vantage point on the summit, an exedra of white marble, the work of the Persians.

The description of the area continues following Strabo 13.4.5 (see *234*) and drawing on Sophocles (*Antigone* 1037ff) (see *189*) and Herodotus (7.27ff).

On Lydian extravagance see Eustathius 1144.14, and on campaigning practices see 1320.4.

(7) Homer, *Iliad* 5.43–44.

16. Joannes Laurentius Lydus, *De mensibus* 3.20, quoting Xanthus.   6th c. A.D.

"Οτι δὲ τὸν ἐνιαυτὸν ὡς θεὸν ἐτίμησαν, δῆλον ἐξ αὐτῆς τῆς Λυδῶν βασιλίδος πόλεως. Σάρδιν γὰρ αὐτὴν καὶ Ξυάριν ὁ Ξάνθος καλεῖ, τὸ δὲ Σάρδιν ὄνομα εἴ τις κατὰ ἀριθμὸν ἀπολογίσεται, πέντε καὶ ἑξήκοντα καὶ τριακοσίας εὑρήσει συνάγων μονάδας· ὡς κἀντεῦθεν εἶναι δῆλον, πρὸς τιμὴν ἡλίου τοῦ τοσαύταις ἡμέραις τὸν ἐνιαυτὸν συνάγοντος Σάρδιν ὠνομασθῆναι τὴν πόλιν. νέον δὲ σάρδιν τὸ νέον ἔτος ἔτι καὶ νῦν λέγεσθαι τῷ πλήθει συνομολογεῖται· εἰσὶ δὲ οἵ φασι, τῇ Λυδῶν ἀρχαίᾳ φωνῇ τὸν ἐνιαυτὸν καλεῖσθαι σάρδιν.

That they honored the year as a divinity is clear from the royal city of the Lydians. For Xanthus calls Sardis itself Xuaris, and if anyone analyses the name Sardis arithmetically, he will find that it contains three hundred and sixty-five units. From this then it is clear that the city was called Sardis to honor the sun that brings a year with just so many days. And it is agreed by many that the new year is still now the new sardis. There are those who say that in the ancient tongue of the Lydians the year was called sardis.

On Lydus' gloss Sardis-Xuaris see P. Kahle and F. Sommer, *KF* I/I (1927) 23, and W. Brandenstein, *WZKM* 36 (1929) 303 and *ZONF* 6 (1930) 239ff: less skeptically, R. Gusmani, *Lydisches Wörterbuch* (Heidelberg 1964) 202, 277, with Iranian linguistic analogy.

(233) Pliny, *Naturalis historia* 5.110.   1st c. A.D.

17. Strabo 13.4.6.   1st c. B.C.–1st c. A.D.

οἱ δὲ τὰς Σάρδεις "Υδην ὀνομάζουσιν, οἱ δὲ τὴν ἀκρόπολιν αὐτῆς.

Some name Sardis Hyde, others by Hyde mean only the citadel of Sardis.

Cf. Homer, *Iliad* 20.385 (see *8*).

Tylon

18. Pliny, *Naturalis historia* 25.14, quoting Xanthus.

1st c. A.D.

Xanthus historiarum auctor in prima earum tradit occisum draconis catulum revocatum ad vitam a parente herba, quam balim nominat, eademque Tylonem, quem draco occiderat, restitutum saluti.

Xanthus the author of histories says in the first of them that a young snake which was dead was brought back to life by its parent with a plant which Xanthus calls balis, and the same plant restored to life Tylon whom the snake had killed.

For Tylon see Nicolas of Damascus *FGrHist* 90 F 45 (see *31*), F 47 (see *35*); and cf. H. Herter, *RhM* 108 (1965) 189–212; G. M. A. Hanfmann, *HSCP* 63 (1958) 68–72.

Typhon

19. Strabo 12.8.19.

1st c. B.C.–1st c. A.D.

'Ακούειν δ' ἔστι καὶ τῶν παλαιῶν συγγραφέων, οἷά φησιν ὁ τὰ Λύδια συγγράψας Ξάνθος, διηγούμενος, οἷαι μεταβολαὶ κατέσχον πολλάκις τὴν χώραν ταύτην, ὧν ἐμνήσθημέν που καὶ ἐν τοῖς πρόσθεν. καὶ δὴ καὶ τὰ περὶ τὸν Τυφῶνα πάθη ἐνταῦθα μυθεύουσι καὶ τοὺς 'Αρίμους καὶ τὴν Κατακεκαυμένην ταύτην εἶναί φασιν.

We ought also to pay attention to the statements of the writers of old such as those made by Xanthus, the Lydian historian, when he discourses on the kind of changes which overtook this land frequently. These I have mentioned somewhere earlier in this treatise. But using myths they do say that Typhon's sufferings took place there and that the Arimi were there, and they call the place the Catacecaumene.

Cf. Strabo 1.3.4.
For Xanthus' comments see *FGrHist* 765 F 13 and cf. L. Pearson, *Early Ionian Historians* (Oxford 1939) 109–138.
On Xanthus see H. Herter *RE* 2:18 (1968) 1354–1374; H. Herter *RhM* 108 (1965) 189–212; H. Herter, *BonnBeit* 15 (1966) 31–60.
For the Arimi cf. Homer, *Iliad* 2.783; P. Pomtow, "De Xantho et Herodoto" (diss. Halle 1886) 13.
On Catacecaumene see Strabo 12.8.18; 13.4.11.

THE TYRRHENIAN MIGRATION

20. Dionysius of Halicarnassus, *Antiquitates Romanae* 1.27.1–2.

1st c. B.C.

Οἱ δὲ μετανάστας μυθολογοῦντες αὐτοὺς εἶναι Τυρρηνὸν ἀποφαίνουσιν ἡγεμόνα τῆς ἀποικίας γενόμενον ἀφ' ἑαυτοῦ θέσθαι τῷ ἔθνει τοὔνομα· τοῦτον δὲ Λυδὸν εἶναι τὸ γένος ἐκ τῆς πρότερον Μηονίας καλουμένης, παλαιὸν δή τινα μετανάστην ὄντα· εἶναι δ' αὐτὸν πέμπτον ἀπὸ Διός, λέγοντες ἐκ Διὸς καὶ Γῆς Μάνην γενέσθαι πρῶτον ἐν τῇ γῇ ταύτῃ βασιλέα· τούτου δὲ καὶ Καλλιρόης τῆς 'Ωκεανοῦ θυγατρὸς γεννηθῆναι Κότυν· τῷ δὲ Κότυϊ γήμαντι θυγατέρα Τύλλου τοῦ γηγενοῦς 'Αλίην δύο γενέσθαι παῖδας 'Ασίην καὶ "Ατυν· ἐκ δὲ "Ατυος καὶ Καλλιθέας τῆς Χωραίου Λυδὸν φῦναι καὶ Τυρρηνόν· καὶ τὸν μὲν Λυδὸν αὐτοῦ καταμείναντα τὴν πατρῴαν ἀρχὴν παραλαβεῖν καὶ ἀπ' αὐτοῦ Λυδίαν τὴν γῆν ὀνομασθῆναι· Τυρρηνὸν δὲ τῆς ἀποικίας ἡγησάμενον πολλὴν κτήσασθαι τῆς 'Ιταλίας καὶ τοῖς συναραμένοις τοῦ στόλου ταύτην θέσθαι τὴν ἐπωνυμίαν.

But those who tell a legendary tale that they came from a foreign land say that Tyrrhenus, the leader of the colony, gave his name to the nation, and that he was a Lydian by birth, from the area formerly called Maeonia, and that he emigrated long ago. He was fifth in line from Zeus, they say; and they claim that the son of Zeus and Ge was Manes, the first king in the land, and his son by Callirhoe, daughter of Oceanus, was Cotys. By Halie, daughter of earthborn Tyllus, Cotys had two sons, Asies and Atys; and by Callithea, daughter of Choraeus, Atys fathered two sons himself, Lydus and Tyrrhenus. Lydus remained there and took over his father's kingdom, and from him the land was called Lydia. Tyrrhenus, the leader of the colony, took a large part of Italy and gave his name to those who had participated in the enterprise.

For the migrations of the Tyrsenoi, cf. Thucydides 4.109.4 where they inhabit a promontory, Acte, in Chalcidice, after having been expelled from Attica and Lemnos (Herodotus 6.137ff).
For Cotys see Christodorus of Koptos (*FGrHist* 283). And cf. Herodotus 4.45 (see *11*); Schol. *Iliad* 2.461 (see *12*).

21. Dionysius of Halicarnassus, *Antiquitates Romanae* 1.28.2.

1st c. B.C.

Ξάνθος δὲ ὁ Λυδὸς ἱστορίας παλαιᾶς εἰ καί τις ἄλλος ἔμπειρος ὤν, τῆς δὲ πατρίου καὶ βεβαιωτὴς ἂν οὐδενὸς ὑποδεέστερος νομισθείς, οὔτε Τυρρηνὸν ὠνόμακεν οὐδαμοῦ τῆς γραφῆς δυνάστην Λυδῶν οὔτε ἀποικίαν Μηόνων εἰς 'Ιταλίαν κατασχοῦσαν ἐπίσταται Τυρρηνίας τε μνήμην ὡς Λυδῶν ἀποκτίσεως ταπεινοτέρων ἄλλων μεμνημένος οὐδεμίαν πεποίηται· "Ατυος δὲ παῖδας γενέσθαι λέγει Λυδὸν καὶ Τόρηβον, τούτους δὲ μερισαμένους τὴν πατρῴαν ἀρχὴν ἐν 'Ασίᾳ καταμεῖναι ἀμφοτέρους.

But Xanthus of Lydia, who was as well versed in ancient history as anyone and who may be considered a prime authority on the history of his own country, does not name Tyrrhenus in any part of his history as a prince of the Lydians nor is he aware of the landing of a colony of Maeonians in Italy. And though he is mindful of several less important matters, he does not make the least mention of Tyrrhenia as a Lydian foundation. He says that Lydus and Torebus were the sons of Atys, and that they divided the kingdom between them and both remained in Asia.

A contemporary of Herodotus, Xanthus—though a Lydian—wrote in Greek: evidently his work was intended for a larger public.

He may have lived in Sardis though Strabo (13.4.9) (see *216*) was unsure; his name suggests he was a Hellenized Lydian or that his mother was a Greek. His father was a Lydian, Candaules—see Suidas s.v. *Xanthus*.

22. Dionysius of Halicarnassus, *Antiquitates Romanae*
I.30.I. Ist c. B.C.

οὐ μὲν δὴ οὐδὲ Λυδῶν τοὺς Τυρρηνοὺς ἀποίκους οἶμαι γενέσθαι· οὐδὲ γὰρ ἐκείνοις ὁμόγλωσσοί εἰσιν, οὐδ' ἔστιν εἰπεῖν ὡς φωνῇ μὲν οὐκέτι χρῶνται παραπλησίᾳ, ἄλλα δέ τινα διασῴζουσι τῆς μητροπόλεως [γῆς] μηνύματα. οὔτε γὰρ θεοὺς Λυδοῖς τοὺς αὐτοὺς νομίζουσιν οὔτε νόμοις οὔτ' ἐπιτηδεύμασι κέχρηνται παραπλησίοις, ἀλλὰ κατά γε ταῦτα πλέον Λυδῶν διαφέρουσιν ἢ Πελασγῶν.

Nor do I believe that the Tyrrhenians were a colony of the Lydians; for they do not speak the same tongue, nor is it possible to say that, though they no longer speak a similar language, they retain other signs of their motherland. For they neither recognize the same deities as the Lydians nor have similar laws and institutions, but in these matters they are more different from the Lydians than from the Pelasgians.

For slim connection in Dionysius' mind between Lydia and Tyrrhenia cf. *Antiquitates Romanae* 3.61 where a purple robe worn by Tyrrhenian kings is said to resemble those of the kings of Lydia and Persia.

23. Herodotus I.94. 5th c. B.C.

ἐπὶ Ἄτυος τοῦ Μάνεω βασιλέος σιτοδείην ἰσχυρὴν ἀνὰ τὴν Λυδίην πᾶσαν γενέσθαι· καὶ τοὺς Λυδοὺς ἕως μὲν διάγειν λιπαρέοντας, μετὰ δέ, ὡς οὐ παύεσθαι, ἄκεα δίζησθαι, ἄλλον δὲ ἄλλο ἐπιμηχανᾶσθαι αὐτῶν. ἐξευρεθῆναι δὴ ὦν τότε καὶ τῶν κύβων καὶ τῶν ἀστραγάλων καὶ τῆς σφαίρης καὶ τῶν ἀλλέων πασέων παιγνιέων τὰ εἴδεα, πλὴν πεσσῶν· τούτων γὰρ ὦν τὴν ἐξεύρεσιν οὐκ

οἰκηιοῦνται Λυδοί. ποιέειν δὲ ὧδε πρὸς τὸν λιμὸν ἐξευρόντας· τὴν μὲν ἑτέρην τῶν ἡμερέων παίζειν πᾶσαν, ἵνα δὴ μὴ ζητέοιεν σιτία, τὴν δὲ ἑτέρην σιτέεσθαι παυομένους τῶν παιγνιέων. τοιούτῳ τρόπῳ διάγειν ἐπ' ἔτεα δυῶν δέοντα εἴκοσι. ἐπείτε δὲ οὐκ ἀνιέναι τὸ κακόν, ἀλλ' ἔτι ἐπὶ μᾶλλον βιάζεσθαι, οὕτω δὴ τὸν βασιλέα αὐτῶν δύο μοίρας διελόντα Λυδῶν πάντων κληρῶσαι τὴν μὲν ἐπὶ μονῇ, τὴν δ' ἐπὶ ἐξόδῳ ἐκ τῆς χώρης, καὶ ἐπὶ μὲν τῇ μένειν αὐτοῦ λαγχανούσῃ τῶν μοιρέων ἑωυτὸν τὸν βασιλέα προστάσσειν, ἐπὶ δὲ τῇ ἀπαλλασσομένῃ τὸν ἑωυτοῦ παῖδα, τῷ οὔνομα εἶναι Τυρσηνόν. λαχόντας δὲ αὐτῶν τοὺς ἑτέρους ἐξιέναι ἐκ τῆς χώρης [καὶ] καταβῆναι ἐς Σμύρνην καὶ μηχανήσασθαι πλοῖα, ἐς τὰ ἐσθεμένους τὰ πάντα, ὅσα σφι ἦν χρηστὰ ἐπίπλοα, ἀποπλέειν κατὰ βίου τε καὶ γῆς ζήτησιν, ἐς ὃ ἔθνεα πολλὰ παραμειψαμένους ἀπικέσθαι ἐς Ὀμβρικούς, ἔνθα σφέας ἐνιδρύσασθαι πόλιας καὶ οἰκέειν τὸ μέχρι τοῦδε. ἀντὶ δὲ Λυδῶν μετονομασθῆναι αὐτοὺς ἐπὶ τοῦ βασιλέος τοῦ παιδός, ὅς σφεας ἀνήγαγε· ἐπὶ τούτου τὴν ἐπωνυμίην ποιευμένους ὀνομασθῆναι Τυρσηνούς.

In the reign of Atys, son of Manes, there was a great famine up and down Lydia, and for a time the Lydians endured this patiently. Soon, however, when there was no respite from the famine, they looked for remedies, one contriving one thing and another another. Then were invented the games of dice and knuckle-bones and ball and all other forms of pastime, except draughts, the discovery of which the Lydians do not claim. They applied their inventions against the famine in the following way: they used to play for the whole of every other day so that they would not have to hunt food, and the next day they stopped their diversions and ate. In this way eighteen years passed. When the evil did not let up but the people were still further oppressed, the king finally divided them into two groups and made them draw lots so that one group should remain and the other leave the country. He himself was to be the leader of those who drew the lot to remain there, and his son, Tyrrhenus, of those who departed. Then one group drew the lot and left the country: they went down to Smyrna and built ships in which they put all their belongings which were transportable, and sailed away to search for a livelihood and a country, until finally after they had stayed with many nations in turn, they came to the land of the Ombrici where they founded cities and have lived ever since. Instead of Lydians they called themselves Tyrrhenians after the name of the king's son who led them.

For famine in western Asia Minor recorded in late Hittite texts shortly before 1200 B.C. and for Egyptian accounts of grain sent to the Hittites in the time of Merneptah, see G. A. Wainwright, *JEA* 46 (1960) 24–28.

For Tyrsenoi as sea peoples (Teresh) see G. A. Wainwright, *AnatSt* 9 (1959) 197–213.

For the whole problem of Etruscan origins see F. Schachermeyr, *Etruskische Frühgeschichte* (Berlin 1929). Cf. also M. Pallottino, *The Etruscans* (1955) 46–73, and J. Bérard, *La Colonisation grecque de l'Italie méridionale et de la Sicile dans l'antiquité* (1957) 499.

For allusion to Herodotus' Lydian origin of the Etruscans see Horace, *Odes* 3, 29.1.

For equation of Tyrsenoi with migratory European Villanovans see H. Hencken, *Tarquinia, Villanovans and Early Etruscans* (Peabody Museum, Cambridge, Mass. 1968) 607–618.

24. Plutarch, *De tuenda sanitate praecepta* 20 (132 F).

1st–2nd c. A.D.

Τοὺς μὲν οὖν Λυδοὺς ἐν τῷ λιμῷ λέγουσι διαγαγεῖν παρ' ἡμέραν τρεφομένους, εἶτα παίζοντας καὶ κυβεύοντας.

They say that during the famine the Lydians passed the time day after day one day feeding themselves and the next playing and gambling.

25. Plutarch, *Quaestiones Romanae* 53 (277D).

1st–2nd c. A.D.

ἐπεὶ δὲ Λυδοὶ μὲν ἦσαν οἱ Τυρρηνοὶ ἐξ ἀρχῆς Λυδῶν δὲ μητρόπολις αἱ Σάρδεις, οὕτω τοὺς Οὐηίους ἀπεκήρυττον· καὶ μέχρι νῦν ἐν παιδιᾷ τὸ ἔθος διαφυλάττουσι.

Now the Etruscans are Lydians in origin, and Sardis was the metropolis of the Lydians, so they offered the Veians for sale under that name; and even nowadays they keep the custom in jest.

The question was: why did they proclaim Sardians for sale?

See also Plutarch, *Romulus* 25 and cf. H. J. Rose, *The Roman Questions of Plutarch* (New York 1924) 194.

(261) Silius Italicus, *Punica* 5.9–11.   1st c. A.D.

(221) Tacitus, *Annales* 4.55.   1st–2nd c. A.D.

HERACLID KINGS

Chronology

26. Herodotus 1.7.   5th c. B.C.

ἡ δὲ ἡγεμονίη οὕτω περιῆλθε, ἐοῦσα Ἡρακλειδέων, ἐς τὸ γένος τὸ Κροίσου, καλεομένους δὲ Μερμνάδας. ἦν

Κανδαύλης, τὸν οἱ Ἕλληνες Μυρσίλον ὀνομάζουσι, τύραννος Σαρδίων, ἀπόγονος δὲ Ἀλκαίου τοῦ Ἡρακλέος. Ἄγρων μὲν γὰρ ὁ Νίνου τοῦ Βήλου τοῦ Ἀλκαίου πρῶτος Ἡρακλειδέων βασιλεὺς ἐγένετο Σαρδίων, Κανδαύλης δὲ ὁ Μύρσου ὕστατος. οἱ δὲ πρότερον Ἄγρωνος βασιλεύσαντες ταύτης τῆς χώρης ἦσαν ἀπόγονοι Λυδοῦ τοῦ Ἄτυος, ἀπ' ὅτευ ὁ δῆμος Λύδιος ἐκλήθη ὁ πᾶς οὗτος, πρότερον Μηίων καλεόμενος. παρὰ τούτων Ἡρακλεῖδαι ἐπιτραφθέντες ἔσχον τὴν ἀρχὴν ἐκ θεοπροπίου, ἐκ δούλης τε τῆς Ἰαρδάνου γεγονότες καὶ Ἡρακλέος, ἄρξαντες [μὲν] ἐπὶ δύο τε καὶ εἴκοσι γενεὰς ἀνδρῶν, ἔτεα πέντε τε καὶ πεντακόσια, παῖς παρὰ πατρὸς ἐκδεκόμενος τὴν ἀρχήν, μέχρι Κανδαύλεω τοῦ Μύρσου.

The family of Croesus was called the Mermnadae, and the empire passed to them from the Heraclidae in the following manner. Candaules, whom the Greeks call Myrsilus, was king of Sardis and from the family of Alcaeus, the son of Heracles. Agron, the son of Ninus and grandson of Belus, the son of Alcaeus, was the first Heraclid king of Sardis, and Candaules, the son of Myrsus, was the last. Those who ruled this land before Agron were descendants of Lydus, the son of Atys, from whom the whole Lydian people took their name, though formerly they had been termed Maeonians. The Heraclidae, born from Heracles and a female slave of Iardanus, received the empire from these people and held it as a result of an oracle. And they ruled for twenty-two generations, five hundred and five years, son succeeding father from generation to generation till the time of Candaules, son of Myrsus.

Hesychius, *Candaulas*, says that Candaulas equals Hermes or Heracles, with which cf. Hipponax fr. 3 (Masson) and the unusual assemblages of Lydian pottery and their contents (G. M. A. Hanfmann, *BASOR* 170 [1963] 10).

Nicolas of Damascus (*FGrHist* 90 F 47) (see *35*) refers to Candaules as Sadyattes.

Myrsilus is the name of a Hittite king (Hugo Winckler, *MDOG* 35 [1907] 18ff) as well as that of Pelops' charioteer and a tyrant of Lesbos.

Herodotus alone makes an Alcaeus son of Heracles, though both the grandfather of Heracles and Heracles himself (Diodorus 1.24) are sometimes called Alcaeus.

Ctesias (*FGrHist* 688) says that Ninus was the founder of Nineveh. Belus is a common name but became identified with the Babylonian deity. Evidently Herodotus has confused his genealogy.

For King Atys, cf. Herodotus 1.94 (see *23*); Dionysius of Halicarnassus, *Antiquitates Romanae* 1.27.1 (see *20*).

For Heracles and Iardanus cf. (Apollodorus) *Bibliotheca* 2.6.3 (see *1*); Dio Chrysostom, *Orationes* 15.6.

Aciamus

27. Stephanus of Byzantium, s.v. *Askalon*, quoting
Xanthus.   6th c. A.D.

πόλις Συρίας πρὸς τῇ Ἰουδαίᾳ. Ξάνθος ἐν δ̄ Λυδιακῶν
φησιν, ὅτι Τάνταλος καὶ Ἄσκαλος παῖδες ⟨Τ⟩υμεναίου·
τὸν δὲ Ἄσκαλον ὑπὸ Ἀκιαμοῦ τοῦ Λυδῶν βασιλέως
αἱρεθέντα στρατηγὸν εἰς Συρίαν στρατεῦσαι, κἀκεῖ παρ-
θένου ἐρασθέντα πόλιν κτίσαι, ἣν ἀφ' ἑαυτοῦ οὕτως
ὠνόμασε. τὰ αὐτὰ καὶ Νικόλαος ἐν δ̄ ἱστορίᾳ.

. . . a Syrian city near Judaea. Xanthus in Book 4 of
his *Lydiaka* says that Tantalus and Ascalus were sons
of Tymenaeus. Ascalus, captured by the Lydian king,
Aciamus, campaigned into Syria and there fell in
love with a girl and founded a city which was named
after him. The same material appears in Nicolas'
Book 4.

See also Nicolas of Damascus *FGrHist* 90 F 18; and for
Tantalus see Nicolas *FGrHist* 90 F 10.

Aciamus should not be identified with the Acimius of
Nicolas (*FGrHist* 90 F 44 [10]), (see *30*).

Cambles/Camblitas

28. Athenaeus, *Deipnosophistae* 10.415 CD, quoting
Xanthus.   2nd–3rd c. A.D.

Ξάνθος δ' ἐν τοῖς Λυδιακοῖς Κάμβλητά φησι τὸν βασιλε-
ύσαντα Λυδῶν πολυφάγον γενέσθαι καὶ πολυπότην, ἔτι
δὲ γαστρίμαργον. τοῦτον οὖν ποτε νυκτὸς τὴν ἑαυτοῦ
γυναῖκα κατακρεουργήσαντα καταφαγεῖν, ἔπειτα πρωὶ
εὑρόντα τὴν χεῖρα τῆς γυναικὸς ἐνοῦσαν ἐν τῷ στόματι
ἑαυτὸν ἀποσφάξαι, περιβοήτου τῆς πράξεως γενομένης.

In his *Lydiaka* Xanthus says that Cambles the king
of Lydia was quite a trencherman and a heavy
drinker to the point of gluttony. One night he
slaughtered his wife and ate her but when he found
her hand in his mouth the next morning he killed
himself since the murder was made common knowledge.

29. Nicolas of Damascus, *FGrHist* 90 F 22.
                                              Ist c. B.C.–Ist c. A.D.

ὅτι Καμβλίτας βασιλεὺς Λυδίας. τοῦτον λέγεται οὕτω
γαστρίμαργον σφόδρα γενέσθαι, ὥστε καὶ τὴν αὐτοῦ
γυναῖκα ἐπιθυμήσαντα καταφαγεῖν. αὐτός γε μὴν ἑαυτὸν
δόξας ὑπὸ φαρμάκων βεβλάφθαι, περιβοήτου τοῦ πράγ-
ματος γενομένου ξίφος ἔχων πληθυούσης ἀγορᾶς ἐν
μέσῳ στὰς εἶπεν· 'ὦ Ζεῦ, εἰ μὲν ἀπ' ἐμαυτοῦ δέδρακα
ταῦτα ἃ δέδρακα, τίσαιμι ἐν ἐμαυτῷ τὰς δίκας· εἰ δὲ

ὑπὸ φαρμάκων διαφθαρείς, οἱ ἐμὲ φαρμάξαντες πάθοιεν.'
ταῦτα εἶπε καὶ ὁρώντων πάντων ἑαυτὸν ἀπέσφαξεν. καὶ
οἱ μὲν τοῦτον ἐκερτόμουν ὡς γαστρίμαργον, οἱ δὲ ᾤκ-
τειρον ὡς φρενοβλαβῆ ὑπὸ φαρμάκων· ἐδόξαζον δὲ τὸν
Ἰάρδανον ταῦτα πεποιηκέναι διὰ τὸ ἔχθος.

It is said that the Lydian king Camblitas became so
much of a glutton that he took a fancy to his wife
and ate her. He thought that he had been influenced
by drugs, and when the matter became common
knowledge, he stood in the middle of the crowded
agora with a sword in hand and said, "O Zeus, if I
did what I did of my own volition, let me impose the
punishment on myself; but if I acted distraught with
drugs, let those who drugged me suffer." Whereupon
in everybody's sight he killed himself. Some sneered
at him as a gluttonous man, and others pitied him
as one deranged by drugs: and they thought that
Iardanus had done this in hatred.

Nicolas lived at the turn of the era; for him see B. Z.
Wacholder, *Nicolaus of Damascus* (Berkeley 1962).

For Iardanus cf. Herodotus 1.7 (see *26*) and (Apollodorus), *Bibliotheca* 2.6.3 (see *1*).

Cadys and Ardys

30. Nicolas of Damascus *FGrHist* 90 F 44.
                                              Ist c. B.C.–Ist c. A.D.

ὅτι Ἀδυάττεω τοῦ Λυδῶν βασιλέως παῖδες δίδυμοι,
Καδὺς καὶ Ἄρδυς· τούτοις κατέλιπε τὴν ἀρχήν, καὶ
ὁμοῦ ἐβασίλευον ἀμφότεροι στέργοντες ἀλλήλους καὶ
αὐτοὶ ὑπὸ τοῦ πλήθους στεργόμενοι. καὶ πως ἡ τοῦ
Καδύος γυνὴ Δαμοννὼ λεγομένη ὑπό τινος ἀνεψιοῦ τοῦ
ἀνδρὸς εὐπρεποῦς Σπέρμου ὄνομα μοιχευθεῖσα σὺν
ἐκείνῳ θάνατον ἐβουλεύετο τῷ ἀνδρί· δοῦσα δὲ αὐτῷ
φάρμακον ἔκτεινε μὲν οὔ, εἰς νόσον δ' ἐνέβαλεν. θερα-
πευθεὶς δ' ὑπὸ ἰατροῦ ὁ Καδὺς ῥᾷον ἔσχεν. ἐκ τούτου
τὸν ἰατρὸν ἀνελεῖν βουλομένη ἡ γυνὴ φάρμακα μὲν
αὐτῷ οὐκ ἔκρινε διδόναι διὰ τὴν τέχνην, βόθρον δ' ἐν
τῇ οἰκίᾳ ὀρύξασα καὶ ἐπιπολῆς αὐτὸν ἄδηλον ποιήσασα
κλίνην καθύπερθεν ἔστρωσεν καὶ ἄλλας ἐφεξῆς. καλέσασα
δ' αὐτὸν ἐπὶ δεῖπνον ἐλθόντα κατέκλινεν ἵναπερ ὁ
βόθρος ἦν. οἰχομένου δὲ κάτω, ἐπαμησαμένη τὴν γῆν
ἄδηλον ἐποίησεν.

Adyattes king of the Lydians left his kingdom to his
twin sons, Cadys and Ardys, who then ruled together
in mutual harmony and the affection of the people.
But Cadys' wife, Damonno, took a handsome cousin
of her husband's, Spermes, as a lover and with him
plotted the death of her husband. She gave a poison
to him and though he did not die, she made him

very poorly. Treated by a doctor, Cadys improved. Wishing to get rid of the doctor because of this, the woman decided cunningly not to give him poison. Instead she dug a pit in her house and hid it by placing a couch above it and others nearby. Summoning the doctor when he had arrived for dinner, she bade him sit down where the pit was. When he had fallen in, she piled in the earth and buried him.

Not much later Cadys died. Damonno and her lover then exiled Ardys and seized the kingdom; Ardys escaped with his family to Kyme (3). Spermes sent a brigand, Cerses, to kill Ardys with the promise of his daughter in marriage and a thousand staters (4). Cerses found Ardys living as an innkeeper in Kyme, fell in love with his daughter, and told him the whole story (5). By agreement with Ardys, Cerses returned to Sardis, deceived Spermes with a ruse, and chopped off his head (6). The Lydians were not unduly upset since Spermes had been a villain and there had been a drought during his reign. He had ruled for two years but he does not appear in the king lists (7). Cerses returned to Kyme in good spirits, got drunk in a shop where he stopped, told the tradesman the story, and was in turn beheaded (8). The tradesman, named Thuessus, took both the heads to Ardys who in gratitude agreed to allow him to conduct business without taxes in future. As a result Thuessus became rich and set up a market, named after him, and a temple of Hermes. The Lydians sent envoys, among whom were some of the Heraclidae, to recall Ardys (9). Ardys ruled best of all the kings after Acimius, being highly esteemed by the Lydians and the just. He numbered the Lydian army, which was mainly horsemen, and reportedly counted 30,000 cavalry (10). As Ardys grew old, Dascylus son of Gyges the Mermnad became very close to him and held practically all governmental power. Ardys' son Adyattes, in fear that when his father died Dascylus would seize the throne, killed him surreptitiously. Dascylus' pregnant wife fled to Phrygia, her homeland, in fear of her husband's murderers. The bedridden king was overcome with grief, denounced the killers, and cursed them, giving anyone who found them the authority to kill them. He died after a reign of 70 years (11).

For Ardys in Kyme see Aristotle F 611, 36 (Rose) and cf. H. Herter *BonnBeit* 15 (1966) 31–60.

For the temple of Hermes see Pliny, *Naturalis historia* 5.126.

For Lydian cavalry and horsemanship see Nicolas of Damascus *FGrHist* 90 F 62 (see *45*); Mimnermus F 13 (see *44*); Herodotus 1.79.

For Dascylus see Herodotus 1.8 (see *34*); Pausanias

4.21.5 (see *46*); Alexander, *Anthologia Palatina* 7.709; Herodorus, *FGrHist* 31 F 49.

Meles

31. Nicolas of Damascus, *FGrHist* 90 F 45.

1st c. B.C.–1st c. A.D.

ἐπὶ Μήλεω δὲ βασιλεύοντος Λυδῶν σφόδρα ἐλίμνε ⟨ἡ⟩ Λυδία, καὶ οἱ ἄνθρωποι ἐπὶ μαντείας ἐτράποντο. τοῖς δ' ἐσήμαινε τὸ δαιμόνιον δίκας πράττεσθαι τοῦ Δασκύλου φόνου παρὰ τῶν βασιλέων. ταῦτα ἀκούσας παρὰ τῶν χρησμολόγων, καὶ ὅτι δεῖ φεύγοντα ἐπὶ γ̄ ἔτη καθήρασθαι τὸν φόνον, ἔφυγεν ἐθελουσίως εἰς Βαβυλῶνα. ἔπεμψε δὲ καὶ εἰς Φρυγίαν παρὰ τὸν Δασκύλου παῖδα, Δάσκυλον καὶ αὐτὸν ὄνομα, ὅντινα ἡ μήτηρ ἐν γαστρὶ ἔχουσα ἔφυγε, κελεύων εἰς Σάρδεις ἀφικνεῖσθαι καὶ δίκας δέχεσθαι τοῦ πατρῴου φόνου παρ' αὐτῶν· οὕτως γὰρ ἐθέσπιζον οἱ μάντεις. ὁ δ' οὐκ ἐπείσθη, λέγων μὴ ἑωρακέναι τὸν πατέρα· κυεῖσθαι γὰρ ἔτι ὅτε ἀνῄρητο· οὔκουν προσήκειν αὐτῷ ταῦτα πολυπραγμονεῖν. Μήλης δὲ φεύγων τὴν ἀρχὴν ἐπίστευσε Σαδυάττῃ τῷ Καδύος γένος ὄντι τὸ ἀνέκαθεν ἀπὸ Τύλων⟨ος⟩, ὅστις φεύγοντα ἐπετρόπευσε καὶ κατιόντα ἐκ Βαβυλῶνος ἐδέξατο μετὰ τρία ἔτη καὶ τὴν βασιλείαν οἱ ἀπέδωκε πιστῶς.

In the reign of Meles there was a great famine in Lydia and the people turned to auguries. The deity decreed that they should exact penalties from the royal house for the murder of Dascylus. When he heard this from the interpreters, and was told that he ought to go away for three years to expiate the murder, Meles departed to Babylon of his own accord. He also sent to Phrygia to Dascylus, son of the murdered Dascylus, who was not yet born when his mother fled from Sardis, and summoned him to Sardis to receive recompense for his father's murder; for this is what the soothsayers decreed. But Dascylus refused to come saying that he had never seen his father, that he was not yet born when he had been taken away, and that therefore it was not seemly for him to meddle in these matters. On his departure Meles entrusted the realm to Sadyattes, son of Cadys, whose ancestor was Tylon. Sadyattes administered the kingdom for him while he was away, welcomed him when he returned from Babylon three years later, and loyally gave him back the throne.

On other Meles see Herodotus 1.84 (see *116*); Nicolas of Damascus, *FGrHist* 90 F 16 (see *10*).

On Cadys cf. Nicolas of Damascus *FGrHist* 90 F 44 (see *30*).

Sadyattes seems a common Lydian name (Herodotus 1.16 [see *52*]); Nicolas of Damascus 90 F 46 (see *32*), F 47 (see *35*).

On Tylon see Pliny, *Naturalis historia* 25.14.

Myrsus

32. Nicolas of Damascus, *FGrHist* 90 F 46.

ist c. B.C.–ist c. A.D.

βασιλεύοντος δὲ Μύρσου Δάσκυλος ὁ Δασκύλου τοῦ σφαγέντος ὑπὸ Σαδυάττεω, μὴ τὴν ἐπιβουλὴν εἰς ἑαυτὸν ἐπισπάσηται ὑπὸ τῶν Ἡρακλειδῶν φοβηθείς, ἐκ Φρυγίας φεύγων ᾤχετο εἰς Σύρους τοὺς ἐν τῷ Πόντῳ ὑπὲρ Σινώπης οἰκοῦντας· ἐκεῖ δὲ καταμείνας γυναῖκα τῶν ἐγχωρίων ἔγημε Σύραν, ἐξ ἧς αὐτῷ γίνεται Γύγης.

In the reign of Myrsus, Dascylus, son of the Dascylus murdered by Sadyattes, fearing that some plot was hatched against him by the Heraclids, left Phrygia and fled to the Syrians who live in Pontus above Sinope. There he settled and married a Syrian woman of the local populace and had a son by her, Gyges.

On Myrsus see Herodotus 1.7 (see *26*).

On the name Gyges, see Hesychius *gugai* and cf. A. Heubeck, *Lydiaka* (Erlangen 1959) 62–63.

Candaules

33. Cicero, *De officiis* 3.9.   ist c. B.C.

hinc ille Gyges inducitur a Platone, qui cum terra discessisset magnis quibusdam imbribus, descendit in illum hiatum aeneumque equum, ut ferunt fabulae, animadvertit, cuius in lateribus fores essent; quibus apertis corpus hominis mortui vidit magnitudine invisitata anulumque aureum in digito; quem ut detraxit, ipse induit—erat autem regius pastor—, tum in concilium se pastorum recepit.

Hereupon the story of Gyges is introduced by Plato. When the earth had opened after numerous rainstorms, he descended into the chasm and came upon a bronze horse, so the tales tell, in the flanks of which there was a door. He opened the door and saw the body of a dead man of unusual size and a gold ring on his finger. After he had taken this ring, he put it on (though he was one of the king's shepherds) and betook himself to a meeting of shepherds.

The quotation from Plato (*Republic* 2.359d) (see *36*) continues. See also Herodotus 1.10ff (see *34*).

34. Herodotus 1.8ff.   5th c. B.C.

οὗτος δὴ ὦν ὁ Κανδαύλης ἠράσθη τῆς ἑωυτοῦ γυναικός, ἐρασθεὶς δὲ ἐνόμιζέ οἱ εἶναι γυναῖκα πολλὸν πασέων

καλλίστην. ὥστε δὲ ταῦτα νομίζων, ἦν γάρ οἱ τῶν αἰχμοφόρων Γύγης ὁ Δασκύλου ἀρεσκόμενος μάλιστα, τούτῳ τῷ Γύγῃ καὶ τὰ σπουδαιέστερα τῶν πρηγμάτων ὑπερετίθετο ὁ Κανδαύλης καὶ δὴ καὶ τὸ εἶδος τῆς γυναικὸς ὑπερεπαινέων. χρόνου δὲ οὐ πολλοῦ διελθόντος, χρῆν γὰρ Κανδαύλῃ γενέσθαι κακῶς, ἔλεγε πρὸς τὸν Γύγην τοιάδε· "Γύγη, οὐ γάρ σε δοκέω πείθεσθαί μοι λέγοντι περὶ τοῦ εἴδεος τῆς γυναικός (ὦτα γὰρ τυγχάνει ἀνθρώποισι ἐόντα ἀπιστότερα ὀφθαλμῶν), ποίει ὅκως ἐκείνην θεήσεαι γυμνήν·" ὁ δὲ μέγα ἀμβώσας εἶπε· "Δέσποτα, τίνα λέγεις λόγον οὐκ ὑγιέα, κελεύων με δέσποιναν τὴν ἐμὴν θεήσασθαι γυμνήν; ἅμα δὲ κιθῶνι ἐκδυομένῳ συνεκδύεται καὶ τὴν αἰδῶ γυνή. πάλαι δὲ τὰ καλὰ ἀνθρώποισι ἐξεύρηται, ἐκ τῶν μανθάνειν δεῖ· ἐν τοῖσι ἐν τόδε ἐστί, σκοπέειν τινὰ τὰ ἑωυτοῦ. ἐγὼ δὲ πείθομαι ἐκείνην εἶναι πασέων γυναικῶν καλλίστην, καί σεο δέομαι μὴ δέεσθαι ἀνόμων."

This Candaules was very much in love with his wife and in his passion he believed her to be by far the most beautiful of women. With this in mind, since he confided the more important of his affairs to Gyges, son of Dascylus, who was his favorite among his bodyguards, he bragged to him about his wife's beauty also. Not much later Candaules, who was destined to meet an evil fate, spoke to Gyges as follows: "Gyges, I do not think that you believe me when I speak of my wife's beauty; but since men trust their ears less than their eyes, arrange things so that you may see her naked." Gyges protested and said, "Master, this is an unwholesome demand you make, bidding me see the queen naked. When a lady takes off her chiton, her honor also is exposed. We must learn rather from the wise precepts articulated by men long ago, one of which is that each should regard his own. I believe that she is the most beautiful woman alive; and I beg you not to ask unlawful things of me."

Gyges declined, afraid of what might befall him, but Candaules explained an arrangement whereby Gyges could see the queen and remain undetected (9). At a loss Gyges agreed to the plan, but was seen by the queen as he slipped out of the bedroom (10). The queen summoned Gyges the next day and gave him the choice of taking her and the kingdom after killing Candaules or death (11). Unable to avoid the choice Gyges murdered Candaules from the same spot where he had hidden before (12).

On Candaules as paradigm see Alexander of Aetolia in *Anthologia Palatina* 7.709 (see *39*).

On Candaules' aesthetic predilections see Pliny, *Naturalis historia* 35.55 (see *37*). On those of Gyges see Nicolas of Damascus *FGrHist* 90 F 62 (see *45*).

On the story of Gyges' accession see K. F. Smith, *AJP* 23 (1902) 261–282, 362–387; G. M. A. Hanfmann, *HSCP* 63 (1958) 76–80; H. Herter, *BonnBeit* 15 (1966) 51–60.

For the literary tradition of Gyges and Candaules see K. F. Smith, *AJP* 41 (1920) 1–37.

On the Gyges-Candaules story and the Herodotean account of Mermnad history see Tzetzes *Historiarum variarum chiliades* I 137–166; on Gyges' ring see Tzetzes, *Chiliades* VII 195–202; see also *Chiliades* VI 481–484 on Candaules.

35. Nicolas of Damascus, *FGrHist* 90 F 47.

1st c. B.C.–1st c. A.D.

ὅτι Ἀδυάττης ὁ ἔσχατος βασιλεὺς Λυδῶν κατελύθη τρόπῳ τοιούτῳ. ἦν τις ἐν Σάρδεσι Δασκύλου θεῖος τοῦ εἰς Πόντον ἀποχωρήσαντος Ἄρδυς ὄνομα, Γύγεω παῖς· οὗτος Ἀδυάττῃ τῷ βασιλεῖ ἐνέτυχεν ἀχθόμενος ἀτεκνίᾳ δοῦναί οἱ μεταπεμψαμένῳ Δάσκυλον ἐκ τοῦ Πόντου θέσθαι παῖδα, ὡς μὴ ἔρημος αὐτοῖς ὁ οἶκος γένοιτο, αὐτοῦ μὲν ὄντος ἄπαιδος, ἐκείνων δὲ οἰχομένων· ἐπιεικὲς δὲ ἤδη εἶναι σπένδεσθαι τοῖς Δασκυλίοις· καὶ γὰρ τοὺς τοῦ βασιλέως προπάτορας ἔφη καλεῖν αὐτοὺς εἰς Λυδίαν ἀπὸ τῆς φυγῆς.

Adyattes, the last king of the Lydians, was destroyed in the following way. In Sardis an uncle of the Dascylus who went to Pontus, named Ardys, son of Gyges, being disappointed in his childlessness, appealed to the king to allow him to send for Dascylus from Pontus and adopt him. In this way his house would not be empty though he himself was childless and they [Dascylus and his mother] had gone away. Ardys further argued that it was right to make up the arguments with the Dascylii since the king's ancestors had already recalled them to Lydia from exile. *Ardys' request was granted, but Dascylus was settled in Pontus and did not come. He sent instead his son Gyges, who was about 18 years old (2). Gyges was an outstanding fellow, and soon word of his prowess and appearance reached the king (3). The king sent for Gyges and made him a member of his bodyguard. Shortly after he began to suspect Gyges' nobility and gave him the most difficult and dangerous assignments. All these Gyges accomplished; then Sadyattes changed his opinion of him (4). The king began to honor Gyges above all others, and this roused the envy of many including Lixus of the family of Tylon, who made remonstrations to the king, and subsequently in public (5). Sadyattes was going to marry Toudo, daughter of Arnossus, king of the Mysians, and sent Gyges to fetch the bride (6). Gyges fell in love with Toudo, lost his head, and tried to force his attentions on her. She declined his advances, threatened him, and told all when she reached the king's presence. He swore to kill*

Gyges the following day (7). A female slave who was in love with Gyges and present in the room told Gyges. He hurried to his friends, told them what had happened and asked them to help him kill the king. He reminded them of the curses Ardys had sworn against the murderers of Dascylus. Judging that it was better to remove (S)adyattes rather than die at his hands, Gyges went with sword in hand into the royal bedchamber. The slave had opened the doors of the room, and Gyges killed Sadyattes while he slept. He had reigned three years (8). Gyges took possession of the kingdom after some initial uproar in the city. He killed some of his enemies and won over others with gifts (9). The Sardians sent to Delphi to inquire whether they should keep Gyges as their king. The oracle replied that vengeance on the Mermnads should come for the Heraclids in the fifth generation (10). Gyges married Toudo and forbade Lixus to appear in his sight (11), a judgment subsequently revoked by Gyges himself (14).

For a papyrus of the second century A.D. from Oxyrhynchus in which the story of Gyges and Candaules is partially recorded in Greek verse see D. L. Page, *A New Chapter in the History of Greek Tragedy* (Cambridge, Eng. 1951); and cf. K. Latte, *Eranos* 48 (1950) 136–141; V. Martin, *MusHelv* 9 (1952) 1–9; J. C. Ramerbeek, *Mnemosyne* ser. 4:5 (1952) 108–115.

Telmessus (Herodotus 1.78 [see *111*], 1.84 [see *116*]) was also popular as an oracular source with the Lydian kings; cf. Nicolas of Damascus, *FGrHist* 90 F 16 (see *10*), F 45 (see *31*).

Nicolas' Adyattes-Sadyattes is identical with Herodotus' Candaules. Adyattes-Sadyattes may have been a Lydian title (cf. Nicolas of Damascus, *FGrHist* 90 F 44 [see *30*]) as well as a common name (cf. Nicolas of Damascus, *FGrHist* 90 F 45 [31] with note).

36. Plato, *Republic* 2.359c–e.

4th c. B.C.

εἴη δ' ἂν ἡ ἐξουσία ἣν λέγω τοιάδε μάλιστα, εἰ αὐτοῖς γένοιτο οἵαν ποτέ φασιν δύναμιν τῷ [Γύγου] τοῦ Λυδοῦ προγόνῳ γενέσθαι. εἶναι μὲν γὰρ αὐτὸν ποιμένα θητεύοντα παρὰ τῷ τότε Λυδίας ἄρχοντι, ὄμβρου δὲ πολλοῦ γενομένου καὶ σεισμοῦ ῥαγῆναί τι τῆς γῆς καὶ γενέσθαι χάσμα κατὰ τὸν τόπον ᾗ ἔνεμεν. ἰδόντα δὲ καὶ θαυμάσαντα καταβῆναι καὶ ἰδεῖν ἄλλα τε δὴ ἃ μυθολογοῦσιν θαυμαστὰ καὶ ἵππον χαλκοῦν, κοῖλον, θυρίδας ἔχοντα, καθ' ἃς ἐγκύψαντα ἰδεῖν ἐνόντα νεκρόν, ὡς φαίνεσθαι μείζω ἢ κατ' ἄνθρωπον, τοῦτον δὲ ἄλλο μὲν οὐδέν, περὶ δὲ τῇ χειρὶ χρυσοῦν δακτύλιον ὄν⟨τα⟩ περιελόμενον ἐκβῆναι.

The kind of freedom which I mention would probably be realized if they had obtained the sort of

power which they say the ancestor of Gyges the Lydian acquired. For it is said that he was a shepherd working for the king of Lydia at that time and that after a great storm and earthquake the earth was split and a chasm appeared in the place where he was. When he saw this he was astonished and descended into the chasm: and he saw other amazing things, so they say, and a hollow bronze horse with little doors through which he looked inside and saw a dead body within, larger than life-size apparently. There was nothing else, they say, but a gold ring on the corpse's hand which he took and went away.
At a meeting of the shepherds he inadvertently twisted the hoop of the ring and became invisible (359e). He discovered the ring's properties and arranged to be a delegate to the king (360a). He seduced the queen and took the kingdom (360b).

That Plato means Gyges himself is evident from *Republic* 10.612b. Cf. Frazer's *Pausanias* 3.417 with reference to E. B. Cowell. *Journal of the Asiatic Society of Bengal* 30 (1861) 151–157.
For allusion to this early "invisibility" folklore see *Iliad* 5.845; Hesiod, *Scutum* 227; Aristophanes, *Acharnians* 390.
On the ring of Gyges see Diogenianus 2.20; Apostolius 15.85; Suidas, s.v. *Gygou Daktylios.*

37. Pliny, *Naturalis historia* 35.55.   1st c. A.D.

quid? quod in confesso perinde est Bularchi pictoris tabulam, in qua erat Magnetum proelium, a Candaule, rege Lydiae Heraclidarum novissimo, qui et Myrsilus vocitatus est, repensam auro? tanta iam dignatio picturae erat.

Moreover is it not commonly accepted that a painting of the battle of the Magnetes by the painter Bularchus was purchased with its weight in gold by Candaules, also called Myrsilus, the last Heraclid king of Lydia? So great was the importance already attached to painting.

Pliny discourses on the earliness of the value attached to painting.
For this particular painting see *Naturalis historia* 7.126; the battle depicted may have been between the Magnesians and the Treres, for which see Strabo 14.1.40 (see *51*) with notes.

38. Plutarch, *Adversus Coloten* 3 (1108D).
                                                    1st–2nd c. A.D.

ἐμοὶ δὲ δοκεῖ καθάπερ ὁ Λυδὸς ἐφ' αὑτὸν ἀνοίγειν οὐ θύραν μίαν, ἀλλὰ ταῖς πλείσταις τῶν ἀποριῶν καὶ μεγίσταις περιβάλλειν τὸν Ἐπίκουρον.

It seems to me that like the Lydian he opens the door upon himself, and not just one door; but most of his accusations, and the most serious, destroy Epicurus.

The Lydian is Candaules.

(4) Plutarch, *Quaestiones Graecae* 45 (302A).
                                                    1st–2nd c. A.D.

II. From the Accession of Gyges to the Fall of Sardis

This second chapter embraces the sources which refer to the history of the city during the period of the Mermnad dynasty, from ca. 680 B.C. to ca. 547 B.C. All the significant passages which mention Sardis herself have been included, and most of those which describe the careers of the city's royal family. For the sake of economy, certain episodes or topics have been limited to a few entries with other references listed in the notations. Frequently, as in Chapter I, when the narrative is lengthy, much of the substance is given in an English epitome.

GYGES

Gyges as Paradigm

39. Alexander of Aetolia in *Anthologia Palatina* 7.709.
3rd c. B.C.

Σάρδιες, ἀρχαῖος πατέρων νομός, εἰ μὲν ἐν ὑμῖν
  ἐτρεφόμαν, κέρνας ἦν τις ἂν ἢ βακέλας
χρυσοφόρος ῥήσσων λάλα τύμπανα, νῦν δέ μοι Ἀλκμάν
  οὔνομα καὶ Σπάρτας εἰμὶ πολυτρίποδος,
καὶ Μούσας ἐδάην Ἑλικωνίδας αἵ με τυράννων
  θῆκαν Κανδαύλεω μείζονα καὶ Γύγεω.

Sardis, ancient habitation of my fathers, if I had been raised in you, clad in gold I should have been a priest or eunuch in the service of Cybele beating the chattering kettledrums. But now my name is Alcman and my home is Sparta rich in tripods; and I have learnt from the Muses of Helicon who have made me greater than the kings Candaules and Gyges.

This passage is recorded by Plutarch (*De exilio* 599E). Cf. A. S. F. Gow and D. L. Page, *Hellenistic Epigrams* (Cambridge, Eng. 1965) I 10, II 28.

Alcman's native town remains unclear; on this see D. L. Page, *Poetae melici Graeci* (Oxford 1962) 29ff.

See also Antipater of Thessalonika in *Anthologia Palatina* 7.18; Suidas, s.v. *Alcman*.

40. Archilochus, 15.   7th c. B.C.

Οὔ μοι τὰ Γύγεω τοῦ πολυχρύσου μέλει
οὐδ' εἶλέ πώ με ζῆλος, οὐδ' ἀγαίομαι
θεῶν ἔργα, μεγάλης δ' οὐκ ἐρέω τυραννίδος·
ἀπόπροθεν γάρ ἐστιν ὀφθαλμῶν ἐμῶν.

I do not care for the wealth of Gyges rich in gold. Envy has never taken hold of me. I am not vexed at the divine order nor do I long for a tyrant's power. These things are far from my eyes.

The first Mermnad ruler of Sardis, Gyges reigned from ca. 680 B.C. to ca. 645 B.C.

On Archilochus see *Archiloque*, Fondation Hardt *Entretiens* X (Vandoeuvres-Genève 1964) passim. For others more impressed with Gyges' wealth, see Hipponax (F 32 Masson); Pythermus of Teos (Ananius F 1 Diehl); Philostratus, *Vita Apollonii* 8.21; Alpheius of Mytilene, *Anthologia Palatina* 9.110; Leonidas of Tarentum in *Anthologia Palatina* 7.740.

Gyges and Candaules

(33) Cicero, *De officiis* 3.9.   1st c. B.C.

(34) Herodotus 1.8ff.   5th c. B.C.

(35) Nicolas of Damascus, *FGrHist* 90 F 47
1st c. B.C.–1st c. A.D.

(36) Plato, *Republic* 2.359d.   4th c. B.C.

(4) Plutarch, *Quaestiones Graecae* 45 (302A).
1st–2nd c. A.D.

Gyges and Delphi

41. Herodotus 1.13–14.   5th c. B.C.

ἀνεῖλέ τε δὴ τὸ χρηστήριον καὶ ἐβασίλευσε οὕτω Γύγης.
τοσόνδε μέντοι εἶπε ἡ Πυθίη, ὡς Ἡρακλείδησι τίσις
ἥξει ἐς τὸν πέμπτον ἀπόγονον Γύγεω· τούτου τοῦ ἔπεος
Λυδοί τε καὶ οἱ βασιλέες αὐτῶν λόγον οὐδένα ἐποιεῦντο,
πρὶν δὴ ἐπετελέσθη. τὴν μὲν δὴ τυραννίδα οὕτω ἔσχον
οἱ Μερμνάδαι τοὺς Ἡρακλείδας ἀπελόμενοι, Γύγης δὲ
τυραννεύσας ἀπέπεμψε ἀναθήματα ἐς Δελφοὺς οὐκ
ὀλίγα, ἀλλ' ὅσα μὲν ἀργύρου ἀναθήματα, ἔστι οἱ πλεῖστα
ἐν Δελφοῖσι, πάρεξ δὲ τοῦ ἀργύρου χρυσὸν ἄπλετον
ἀνέθηκε ἄλλον τε καὶ τοῦ μάλιστα μνήμην ἄξιον ἔχειν
ἐστί, κρητῆρές οἱ ἀριθμὸν ἓξ χρύσεοι ἀνακέαται. ἑστᾶσι
δὲ οὗτοι ἐν τῷ Κορινθίων θησαυρῷ σταθμὸν ἔχοντες
τριήκοντα τάλαντα· ἀληθέϊ δὲ λόγῳ χρεωμένῳ οὐ Κορινθίων τοῦ δημοσίου ἐστὶ ὁ θησαυρός, ἀλλὰ Κυψέλου τοῦ
Ἠετίωνος. οὗτος δὲ ὁ Γύγης πρῶτος βαρβάρων τῶν
ἡμεῖς ἴδμεν ἐς Δελφοὺς ἀνέθηκε ἀναθήματα μετὰ Μίδην
τὸν Γορδίεω, Φρυγίης βασιλέα. ἀνέθηκε γὰρ δὴ καὶ
Μίδης τὸν βασιλήιον θρόνον ἐς τὸν προκατίζων ἐδίκαζε,
ἐόντα ἀξιοθέητον· κεῖται δὲ ὁ θρόνος οὗτος ἔνθα περ οἱ
τοῦ Γύγεω κρητῆρες. ὁ δὲ χρυσὸς οὗτος καὶ ὁ ἄργυρος,
τὸν ὁ Γύγης ἀνέθηκε, ὑπὸ Δελφῶν καλέεται Γυγάδας
ἐπὶ τοῦ ἀναθέντος ἐπωνυμίην.

The oracle then gave its decree and thus Gyges became king. But the Pythian proclaimed that the
Heraclids should have vengeance on the fifth generation after Gyges, of which statement the Lydians and
their kings took no notice until it was fulfilled. Thus
the Mermnads took the kingdom depriving the
Heraclids, and Gyges the king sent many gifts to
Delphi. Most of his offerings there are silver, but as
well as the silver he dedicated a great quantity of
gold among which six golden mixing-bowls are most
worthy of mention. These stand in the treasury of
the Corinthians and weigh thirty talents, though in
actual fact the treasury does not belong to the people
of Corinth but to Cypselus the son of Eetion. This
Gyges was the first of the barbarians that I know of
who set up dedications at Delphi after Midas the
son of Gordias, king of Phrygia. For Midas dedicated
the royal throne seated on which he used to render
judgments, and it is spectacular; the throne is located
just where the mixing bowls of Gyges are. This gold
and silver which Gyges gave is called by the Delphians
Gygadas after the name of the dedicator.

Herodotus presents his history of Mermnad Sardis in the
ensuing chapters, 1.15–86 (see *52, 59*, also *57*, etc.). The
bias of his pro-Delphic source is clear (see 1.20).

For Gyges and oracles see Pliny, *Naturalis historia*
7.151.

Midas was husband to the daughter of Agamemnon,
king of Kyme (Aristotle, *Fragmenta* 611, 37 [Rose];
Pollux 9.83); his westward trade route doubtless led
through Kyme.

42. Valerius Maximus 7.1.2.   1st c. A.D.

cum enim Gyges regno Lydiae armis et divitiis
abundantissimo inflatus animo Apollinem Pythium
sciscitatum venisset an aliquis mortalium se esset
felicior, deus ex abdito sacrarii specu voce missa
Aglaum Psophidium ei praetulit.

For when Gyges became arrogant because of the
wealth and power of the Lydian empire and had
come to the Pythian Apollo to find out whether any
mortal was happier than he, the god from the hidden
recess of the sanctuary replied and preferred Aglaus
Psophidius to him.

Cf. Herodotus 1.30ff (see *84*) and the story of Croesus and
Solon.

Attacks on the Greek Cities

43. Herodotus 1.14.   5th c. B.C.

ἐσέβαλε μέν νυν στρατιὴν καὶ οὗτος, ἐπείτε ἦρξε, ἔς τε
Μίλητον καὶ ἐς Σμύρνην καὶ Κολοφῶνος τὸ ἄστυ εἷλε.

While he ruled, this man invaded Miletus and
Smyrna and took possession of the city of Colophon.

Events ca. 680–670 B.C.
Gyges may have destroyed Miletus (G. M. A. Hanfmann, *BASOR* 162 [1961] 12 n. 8 suggesting a Cimmerian
destruction); the fortification of Kalabaktepe was a
logical response. He allowed Miletus to found Abydos in
Lydian territory where Strabo (13.1.22) found a promontory named Gygas; cf. W. Leaf, *Strabo on the Troad*
(Cambridge 1923) 125–126.

At Smyrna he may have been repelled: J. M. Cook,
BSA 53–54 (1958–59) 28, though a destruction is reported
about this time (J. M. Cook, *AR* [1960] 49).

Xenophanes complains effusively of Lydian influence
(F 3 Diehl) in Colophon, where Lydian sherds have been
found (L. B. Holland, *Hesperia* 13 [1944] 140).

For Gyges and Lydia in the Assyrian sources see D. D.
Luckenbill, *Ancient Records of Assyria and Babylonia* II
(Chicago 1927) 290ff, 323ff, 346 (see *292, 293, 295*); A. C.
Piepkorn, *Historical Prism Inscriptions of Assurbanipal*
(Chicago 1933) 19ff, 8ff (see *294*).

44. Mimnermus F 13.   6th c. B.C.

οὐ μὲν δὴ κείνου γε μένος καὶ ἀγήνορα θυμὸν
τοῖον ἐμεῦ προτέρων πεύθομαι, οἵ μιν ἴδον

Λυδῶν ἱππομάχων πυκινὰς κλονέοντα φάλαγγας
Ἕρμιον ἂμ πεδίον, φῶτα φερεμμελίην.

His was not that kind of strength and fecklessness of spirit, as I gather from my forebears, who saw him drive the thick columns of Lydian cavalry into confusion along the plain of Hermus, and he a spear-bearing mortal.

Mimnermus refers to a battle between the Smyrnaeans and the army of Gyges. On this see also Schol. Pindar *Nemean Odes* 3.10.

45. Nicolas of Damascus, *FGrHist* 90 F 62.

1st c. B.C.–1st c. A.D.

τούτου δὲ πολλοὶ μὲν καὶ ἄλλοι ἤρων, Γύγης δὲ καὶ μᾶλλόν τι ἐφλέγετο καὶ αὐτὸν εἶχε παιδικά. γυναῖκάς γε μὴν πάσας ἐξέμηνεν, ἔνθα ἐγένετο ὁ Μάγνης, μάλιστα δὲ τὰς Μαγνήτων, καὶ συνῆν αὐταῖς. οἱ δὲ τούτων συγγενεῖς ἀχθόμενοι ἐπὶ τῇ αἰσχύνῃ, πρόφασιν ποιησάμενοι, ὅτι ἐν τοῖς ἔπεσιν ᾖσεν ὁ Μάγνης Λυδῶν ἀριστείαν ἐν ἱππομαχίᾳ πρὸς Ἀμαζόνας, αὐτῶν δὲ οὐδὲν ἐμνήσθη, ἐπαίξαντες περικατέρρηξάν τε τὴν ἐσθῆτα καὶ τὰς κόμας ἐξέκειραν καὶ πᾶσαν λώβην προσέθεσαν. ἐφ' οἷς ἤλγησε μάλιστα Γύγης καὶ πολλάκις μὲν εἰς τὴν Μαγνήτων γῆν ἐνέβαλεν, τέλος δὲ καὶ χειροῦται τὴν πόλιν· ἐπανελθὼν δὲ εἰς Σάρδεις πανηγύρεις ἐποιήσατο μεγαλοπρεπεῖς.

Many other people were taken by this fellow, but Gyges was especially attracted by him and kept him as his favorite. Wherever he was, Magnes maddened all the women, and especially those of the Magnesians, and he consorted with them. Their kinsmen were vexed at this disgrace and making the excuse that in his songs Magnes praised the courage of the Lydians in the cavalry battle with the Amazons but never made any mention of them, they rushed him, tore his clothes, and cut his hair and dealt him every humiliation. Because of this Gyges was angry and frequently invaded the territory of the Magnesians and finally mastered the city. On his return to Sardis he celebrated magnificent festivals.

Herodotus (1.14) (see *41*) makes no mention of an inherently likely campaign against Magnesia.

It is to the other Magnesia (on the Maeander) that Archilochus (Diehl F 19) and Strabo (14.1.40) (see *51*) refer.

46. Pausanias 4.21.5.   2nd c. A.D.

ἐπειδὴ δὲ ἡμέρα τε ἦν καὶ ἀλλήλους καθορᾶν ἐδύναντο, ἐνταῦθα Ἀριστομένης καὶ Θέοκλος ἐπειρῶντο ἐς πᾶσαν ἀπόνοιαν προάγειν τοὺς Μεσσηνίους, ἄλλα τε ὁπόσα

εἰκὸς ἦν διδάσκοντες καὶ Σμυρναίων τὰ τολμήματα ἀναμιμνήσκοντες, ὡς Ἰώνων μοῖρα ὄντες Γύγην τὸν Δασκύλου καὶ Λυδοὺς ἔχοντας σφῶν τὴν πόλιν ὑπὸ ἀρετῆς καὶ προθυμίας ἐκβάλοιεν.

At daybreak when they could see one another, Aristomenes and Theoclus tried to drive the Messenians to a desperate frenzy, making mention of every appropriate matter and reminding the Messenians of the courage of the Smyrnaeans, and how they, Ionians, by their zeal and their courage expelled Gyges, son of Dascylus, and the Lydians who had taken possession of their city.

For Gyges elsewhere in Pausanias see 4.24.2.

47. Pausanias 9.29.4.   2nd c. A.D.

Μίμνερμος δέ, ἐλεγεῖα ἐς τὴν μάχην ποιήσας τὴν Σμυρναίων πρὸς Γύγην τε καὶ Λυδούς, φησὶν ἐν τῷ προοιμίῳ θυγατέρας Οὐρανοῦ τὰς ἀρχαιοτέρας Μούσας, τούτων δὲ ἄλλας νεωτέρας εἶναι Διὸς παῖδας.

But Mimnermus, the writer of elegiacs on the topic of the battle between the Smyrnaeans and Gyges and his Lydians, says in the prologue that the elder Muses are the daughters of Uranus, and that the other younger ones are the children of Zeus.

48. (Plutarch) *Parallela minora* 30 (312 E, F).

Σαρδιανοὶ πρὸς Σμυρναίους πόλεμον ἔχοντες περὶ τὰ τείχη ἐστρατοπεδεύσαντο καὶ διὰ πρέσβεων ἔπεμψαν μὴ πρότερον ἀναχωρῆσαι, ἐὰν μὴ τὰς γυναῖκας συνελθεῖν αὐτοῖς συγχωρήσωσι. τῶν δὲ Σμυρναίων διὰ τὴν ἀνάγκην μελλόντων πάσχειν κακῶς, θεραπαινὶς ἦν μία τῶν εὐσχημόνων, ἣ προσδραμοῦσα ἔφη τῷ δεσπότῃ Φιλάρχῳ δεῖν τὰς θεραπαίνας κοσμήσαντας ἀντ' ἐλευθέρων πέμπειν. ὃ δὴ καὶ ἔδρασαν. οἱ δὲ κοπωθέντες ὑπὸ τῶν θεραπαινῶν ἑάλωσαν. ὅθεν καὶ νῦν παρὰ Σμυρναίοις ἑορτὴ λέγεται Ἐλευθέρια, ἐν ᾗ αἱ δοῦλαι τὸν κόσμον τῶν ἐλευθέρων φοροῦσιν· ὡς Δοσίθεος ἐν τρίτῳ Λυδιακῶν.

The Sardians made war on Smyrna and camped around the walls and through envoys sent to say they would not retire unless the Smyrnaeans agreed to send their women to them. When of necessity the people of Smyrna were thus about to suffer intolerably, there was a certain slave girl of the better classes who ran forward and suggested to the ruler Philarchus that they should dress the slave girls and send them instead of the free. Which they did. And they, wearied by the slave girls, were overcome. So that even today there is a festival among the Smyrnaeans called Eleutheria at which the slave girls dress as free women, as Dositheos says in the third book of his Lydiaka.

For early wars at Smyrna cf. C. J. Cadoux, *Ancient Smyrna* (Oxford 1938) 55–85.

For the Eleutheria see F. Bömer, *AbhMainz* (1957) no. 7 500ff.

For a history of old Smyrna see J. M. Cook, *BSA* 53–54 (1958–1959) 9–34.

The Cimmerian Assault

49. Strabo 1.3.21.   1st c. B.C.–1st c. A.D.

οἵ τε Κιμμέριοι οὓς καὶ Τρῆρας ὀνομάζουσιν, ἢ ἐκείνων τι ἔθνος, πολλάκις ἐπέδραμον τὰ δεξιὰ μέρη τοῦ Πόντου καὶ τὰ συνεχῆ αὐτοῖς, τοτὲ μὲν ἐπὶ Παφλαγόνας, τοτὲ δὲ καὶ Φρύγας ἐμβαλόντες, ἡνίκα Μίδαν αἷμα ταύρου πιόντα φασὶν ἀπελθεῖν εἰς τὸ χρεών. Λύγδαμις δὲ τοὺς αὑτοῦ ἄγων μέχρι Λυδίας καὶ Ἰωνίας ἤλασε καὶ Σάρδεις εἷλεν, ἐν Κιλικίᾳ δὲ διεφθάρη.

The Cimmerians whom they also call Treres, or some one of their tribes, often overran the areas on the right of the Pontus and the contiguous countries, at one time attacking the Paphlagonians and at another even the Phrygians; at which time they say Midas drank bull's blood and went to his fate. But Lygdamis led his troops and marched to Lydia and Ionia, and he took Sardis, but perished in Cilicia.

The death of Midas is reported as occurring in 696 B.C. (Jerome) or 676 B.C. (Africanus).

Lygdamis may be a Carian name (M. N. Tod, *A Selection of Greek Historical Inscriptions to the End of the Fifth Century B.C.* I [Oxford 1946] 25). On Lygdamis, chief of the Cimmerians, see Wilamowitz, *Kleine Schriften* 5:1 (Berlin 1937) 134 n. 2; A. T. Olmstead, *Anatolian Studies Presented to William M. Ramsay* (Manchester 1923) 296.

50. Strabo 13.4.8.   1st c. B.C.–1st c. A.D.

Φησὶ δὲ Καλλισθένης ἁλῶναι τὰς Σάρδεις ὑπὸ Κιμμερίων πρῶτον, εἶθ᾽ ὑπὸ Τρηρῶν καὶ Λυκίων, ὅπερ καὶ Καλλῖνον δηλοῦν, τὸν τῆς ἐλεγείας ποιητήν, ὕστατα δὲ τὴν ἐπὶ Κύρου καὶ Κροίσου γενέσθαι ἅλωσιν. λέγοντος δὲ τοῦ Καλλίνου τὴν ἔφοδον τῶν Κιμμερίων ἐπὶ τοὺς Ἠσιονῆας γεγονέναι, καθ᾽ ἢν αἱ Σάρδεις ἑάλωσαν, εἰκάζουσιν οἱ περὶ τὸν Σκήψιον ἰαστὶ λέγεσθαι Ἠσιονεῖς τοὺς Ἀσιονεῖς.

Callisthenes says that Sardis was first taken by the Cimmerians and subsequently by the Treres and the Lycians, as Callinus the elegiac poet makes plain; and finally a capture of the city took place in the time of Cyrus and Croesus. But when Callinus says

that the invasion of the Cimmerians, in the course of which Sardis was taken, was directed against the Esioneis, Demetrius of Scepsis and his circle conjecture that Esioneis is the Ionic equivalent of Asioneis.

For Callisthenes see *FGrHist* 124 F 29; for Callinus, Callinus F 3 (Diehl).

On the capture of Sardis see Herodotus 1.15 (see 52); for the archaeological evidence see G. M. A. Hanfmann, *BASOR* 177 (1965) 13, G. F. Swift, Jr., in Hanfmann, *BASOR* 182 (1966) 10, Hanfmann, *BASOR* 186 (1967) 32–33.

51. Strabo 14.1.40.   1st c. B.C.–1st c. A.D.

τοῖς Μάγνησιν ὑπὸ Τρηρῶν ἄρδην ἀναιρεθῆναι, Κιμμερικοῦ ἔθνους, εὐτυχήσαντας πολὺν χρόνον· τῷ δ᾽ ἑξῆς ἔτει Μιλησίους κατασχεῖν τὸν τόπον. Καλλῖνος μὲν οὖν ὡς εὐτυχούντων ἔτι τῶν Μαγνήτων μέμνηται καὶ κατορθούντων ἐν τῷ πρὸς τοὺς Ἐφεσίους πολέμῳ, Ἀρχίλοχος δὲ ἤδη φαίνεται γνωρίζων τὴν γενομένην αὐτοῖς συμφοράν·

κλαίειν τὰ Θασίων, οὐ τὰ Μαγνήτων κακά·

ἐξ οὗ καὶ αὐτὸν νεώτερον εἶναι τοῦ Καλλίνου τεκμαίρεσθαι πάρεστιν. ἄλλης δέ τινος ἐφόδου τῶν Κιμμερίων μέμνηται πρεσβυτέρας ὁ Καλλῖνος, ἐπὰν φῇ·

νῦν δ᾽ ἐπὶ Κιμμερίων στρατὸς ἔρχεται ὀβριμοεργῶν·

ἐν ᾗ τὴν Σάρδεων ἅλωσιν δηλοῖ.

[Long ago it happened that] the Magnesians, who had experienced good fortune for a long time, were devastated by the Treres, a Cimmerian tribe; and in the following year the Milesians took over the place. Callinus recalls the Magnesians as still being in good shape and victorious in their war with the Ephesians, but Archilochus is apparently cognizant of the disaster which overtook them—"to weep for the sorrows of the Thasians, not those of the Magnesians." From this it is possible to see that he was a more recent poet than Callinus. But Callinus remembers another earlier incursion of the Cimmerians when he says—"Now the army of the Cimmerians fearful in deeds is approaching"; in which he makes plain the capture of Sardis.

Callinus F 3 (Diehl).
Archilochus F 19 (Diehl).
This passage is crucial for the political history of the seventh century in Asia Minor. See also Herodotus 1.6, 1.15 (see 52), 1.16 (see 59), 1.103; Theognis 603, 1103–1104; Callisthenes, *FGrHist* 124 F 29; Aelian, *Varia historia* 14.46; Clemens Alexandrinus, *Stromateis* 1.131; Ps.-Scymnus 947ff; F. Jacoby, *CQ* 35 (1941) 97–109.

The Tomb of Gyges

(**280**) Hipponax F 42. 6th c. B.C.

(**281**) Nicander, *Theriaca* 630–635. 2nd c. B.C.

ARDYS AND SADYATTES

52. Herodotus 1.15–16. 5th c. B.C.

῎Αρδυος δὲ τοῦ Γύγεω μετὰ Γύγην βασιλεύσαντος μνήμην ποιήσομαι. οὗτος δὲ Πριηνέας τε εἷλε ἐς Μίλητόν τε ἐσέβαλε, ἐπὶ τούτου τε τυραννεύοντος Σαρδίων Κιμμέριοι ἐξ ἠθέων ὑπὸ Σκυθέων τῶν νομάδων ἐξανασ-τάντες ἀπίκοντο ἐς τὴν ᾿Ασίην καὶ Σάρδις πλὴν τῆς ἀκροπόλιος εἷλον.

῎Αρδυος δὲ βασιλεύσαντος ἑνὸς δέοντα πεντήκοντα ἔτεα ἐξεδέξατο Σαδυάττης ὁ ῎Αρδυος, καὶ ἐβασίλευσε ἔτεα δυώδεκα, Σαδυάττεω δὲ ᾿Αλυάττης.

I will sooner make mention of Ardys the son of Gyges who succeeded him. He captured Priene and attacked Miletus. During his reign at Sardis the Cimmerians, pushed out of their domain by the wandering Scythians, came into Asia and took Sardis, all except its citadel. After Ardys had reigned forty-nine years, Sadyattes his son succeeded him and reigned for twelve years. After Sadyattes came Alyattes.

Archaic Priene may be lost beneath the estuary of the Maeander.

On Cimmerian origins see H. Kothe, *Klio* 41 (1963) 5–37. They destroyed Gordion (R. S. Young, *AJA* 64 [1960] 227–243; E. Akurgal, *Phrygische Kunst* [Ankara 1955] 123–125) before approaching Sardis. The Assyrian records tell of Gyges weathering their first assault (L. Hartman, *JNES* 21 [1962] 25) but of being killed in the second (D. D. Luckenbill, *Ancient Records of Assyria and Babylonia* II [Chicago 1927] 298 [see *292*]) perhaps ca. 645 B.C. For Herodotus' view of the Cimmerian invasions see 1.6, 1.103, 4.11–12, and cf. Strabo 13.4.8 (see *50*); 14.1.40 (see *51*) with references.

On the chronology of Gyges, Ardys, and Sadyattes see H. Kaletsch, *Historia* 7 (1958) 25–39.

53. Nicolas of Damascus, *FGrHist* 90 F 63.
1st c. B.C.–1st c. A.D.

ὅτι Σαδυάττης ὁ Λυδῶν βασιλεύς, ᾿Αλυάττεω παῖς, ἦν μὲν τὰ πολέμια γενναῖος, ἄλλως δὲ ἀκόλαστος. καὶ γάρ ποτε τὴν ἑαυτοῦ ἀδελφήν, γυναῖκα Μιλήτου ἀνδρὸς δοκίμου, καλέσας ἐφ᾿ ἱερὰ βίᾳ ᾔσχυνεν καὶ τὸ λοιπὸν αὐτὴν ἴσχει γυναῖκα.

Sadyattes, king of the Lydians and son of Alyattes, was noble in war, but in other respects lacked control. For on one occasion he invited his sister, the wife of an illustrious fellow named Miletus, to a sacrifice, violated her, and kept her thereafter as his wife.

Miletus fled to Daskyleion and thence to Proconessus (2). Sadyattes married two other women, sisters, who gave him sons, Attales and Adramys; his own sister bore him Alyattes (3).

Attales and Adramys may be eponyms for Attaleia and Adramyteion, though cf. Stephanus of Byzantium.

Xenophilos (*FGrHist* 767 F 1) names Sadyattes' sister Lyde.

54. Pausanias 4.24.2. 2nd c. A.D.

᾿Αριστομένης δὲ ἐς μὲν τὴν ῾Ρόδον ἀφίκετο σὺν τῇ θυγατρί, ἐκεῖθεν δὲ ἔς τε Σάρδεις ἐνενόει παρὰ ῎Αρδυν τὸν Γύγου καὶ ἐς ᾿Εκβάτανα τὰ Μηδικὰ ἀναβῆναι παρὰ τὸν βασιλέα Φραόρτην.

Aristomenes came to Rhodes with his daughter and from there intended to travel to Sardis to Ardys, son of Gyges, and to Median Ecbatana to King Phraortes.

ALYATTES

Alyattes and Periander

55. Diogenes Laertius 1.95. 3rd c. A.D.

ὅθεν ὀργισθεὶς ἔπεμψε τοὺς παῖδας αὐτῶν πρὸς ᾿Αλυάτ-την ἐπ᾿ ἐκτομῇ· προσσχούσης δὲ τῆς νεὼς Σάμῳ, ἱκετεύσαντες τὴν ῞Ηραν ὑπὸ τῶν Σαμίων διεσώθησαν.

Καὶ ὃς ἀθυμήσας ἐτελεύτησεν, ἤδη γεγονὼς ἔτη ὀγδοήκοντα. Σωσικράτης δέ φησι πρότερον Κροίσου τελευτῆσαι αὐτὸν ἔτεσι τεσσαράκοντα καὶ ἑνί, πρὸ τῆς τεσσαρακοστῆς ἐνάτης ᾿Ολυμπιάδος.

Angered by this he sent their sons to Alyattes to be made eunuchs, but when the ship reached Samos, they took refuge in the Heraeum and were saved by the Samians.

Dispirited, Periander died at the age of eighty. Sosicrates says that he died forty-one years before Croesus before the forty-ninth Olympiad.

Cf. Apollodorus, *FGrHist* 244 F 332a. On Alyattes and Bias cf. Diogenes Laertius 1.83–84.

56. Diogenes Laertius 1.99.   3rd c. A.D.

Περίανδρος τοῖς Σοφοῖς

Πολλὰ χάρις τῷ Πυθοῖ ᾿Απόλλωνι τοῦ εἰς ἓν ἐλθόντας
εὑρεῖν. ἀξοῦντί τε καὶ ἐς Κόρινθον ταὶ ἐμαὶ ἐπιστολαί.
ἐγὼν δὲ ὑμᾶς ἀποδέχομαι, ὡς ἴστε αὐτοί, ὅτι δαμοτι-
κώτατα. πεύθομαι ὡς πέρυτι ἐγένετο ὑμῶν ἁλία παρὰ
τὸν Λυδὸν ἐς Σάρδεις. ἤδη ὦν μὴ ὀκνεῖτε καὶ παρ᾿ ἐμὲ
φοιτῆν τὸν Κορίνθου τύραννον. ὑμᾶς γὰρ καὶ ἄσμενοι
ὄψονται Κορίνθιοι φοιτεῦντας ἐς οἶκον τὸν Περιάνδρου.

Periander to the Wise Men

I am most grateful to Pythian Apollo for finding you
gathered together, and my letters will bring you to
Corinth. As you know very well, I shall receive you
in the most generous manner. I gather that last year
your meeting took place in Sardis with the Lydian
king. Do not then hesitate to come to me the tyrant
of Corinth, for the Corinthians will be delighted to
see you coming to the house of Periander.

On Periander see A. Andrewes, *Greek Tyrants* (London
1956) 43–53, 108–109.
On gatherings of the wise men see Diogenes Laertius
1.40–41.

57. Herodotus 3.48.   5th c. B.C.

Κερκυραίων γὰρ παῖδας τριηκοσίους ἀνδρῶν τῶν πρώτων
Περίανδρος ὁ Κυψέλου ἐς Σάρδις ἀπέπεμψε παρὰ
᾿Αλυάττεα ἐπ᾿ ἐκτομῇ· προσσχόντων δὲ ἐς τὴν Σάμον
τῶν ἀγόντων τοὺς παῖδας Κορινθίων, πυθόμενοι οἱ
Σάμιοι τὸν λόγον, ἐπ᾿ οἶσι ἀγοίατο ἐς Σάρδις, πρῶτα
μὲν τοὺς παῖδας ἐδίδαξαν ἱροῦ ἅψασθαι ᾿Αρτέμιδος,
μετὰ δὲ οὐ περιορῶντες ἀπέλκειν τοὺς ἱκέτας ἐκ τοῦ
ἱροῦ, σιτίων δὲ τοὺς παῖδας ἐργόντων τῶν Κορινθίων,
ἐποιήσαντο οἱ Σάμιοι ὀρτήν, τῇ καὶ νῦν ἔτι χρέωνται
κατὰ ταὐτά.

Periander son of Cypselus sent three hundred youths,
sons of the leading citizens of Corcyra, to Alyattes
in Sardis to be made eunuchs. When the Corinthians
who were taking the boys put in at Samos, the
Samians discovered why they were being taken to
Sardis. At first they instructed them to take sanctuary
in the temple of Artemis, and later did not allow the
suppliants to be wrested from the temple. And when
the Corinthians were starving the boys out, the
Samians held a festival which they keep to this day
in the same way. . . .
*The Samians saved the youths and returned them to
Corcyra.*

Plutarch (*De Herodoti malignitate* 22 859F), on the
authority of Dionysius of Chalcis and Antenor, claims

that it was the Cnidians who saved the youths on Samos
and returned them to Corcyra.
On starving out suppliants cf. Thucydides 1.134.

58. Nicolas of Damascus, *FGrHist* 90 F 59 (3).
   1st c. B.C.–1st c. A.D.

ὁ δὲ Περίανδρος ἀθροίσας στράτευμα ἐνέβαλεν εἰς
Κέρκυραν, καὶ τὴν πόλιν ἑλὼν ν̄ τοὺς αἰτίους τοῦ φόνου
ἀπέκτεινεν, τοὺς δὲ τούτων υἱέας πλείστους ὄντας
ἔπεμψε πρὸς ᾿Αλυάττην τὸν Λυδῶν βασιλέα ἐπ᾿ ἐκτομῇ.
οἱ δὲ προσσχόντες Σάμῳ ἱκέται τῆς ῞Ηρας ἐγένοντο,
καὶ αὐτοὺς Σάμιοι αἰσθόμενοι τὸ σύμπαν ἐρρύσαντο.

Periander mustered his army and invaded Corcyra.
After capturing the city he killed fifty who were
guilty of murder and he sent their sons, who were
numerous, to Alyattes the king of the Lydians to be
made eunuchs. But they put in at Samos and became
suppliants of Hera, and the Samians, who grasped
the whole situation, protected them.

Military Activities

59. Herodotus 1.16.   5th c. B.C.

οὗτος δὲ Κυαξάρῃ τε τῷ Δηιόκεω ἀπογόνῳ ἐπολέμησε
καὶ Μήδοισι, Κιμμερίους τε ἐκ τῆς ᾿Ασίης ἐξήλασε,
Σμύρνην τε τὴν ἀπὸ Κολοφῶνος κτισθεῖσαν εἷλε, ἐς
Κλαζομενάς τε ἐσέβαλε. ἀπὸ μέν νυν τούτων οὐκ ὡς
ἤθελε ἀπήλλαξε, ἀλλὰ προσπταίσας μεγάλως.

He made war on Kyaxares, the descendant of
Deioces and the Medes, drove the Cimmerians out
of Asia, took Smyrna, the city colonized from
Colophon, and invaded Clazomenae. He did not
depart from there as he wished, but badly bruised.

The five-year war with Kyaxares (Herodotus 1.74) was
terminated by the eclipse of May 28, 585 B.C., T. R. von
Oppolzer, *Canon of Eclipses* [Vienna 1887] 1489).
The Cimmerians Alyattes drove out were those at
Antandros (Stephanus of Byzantium, s.v. *Antandros*;
Aristotle F 478 [Rose]; Pliny *Naturalis historia* 5.123).
And cf. Arrian, *FGrHist* 156 F 76; Promathidas, *FGrHist*
430 F 1.
Smyrna was originally an Aeolic foundation (Herodotus
1.149; Pausanias 7.5.1).
Alyattes' reverse before Clazomenae is inexplicable; the
site identified as archaic Clazomenae (J. M. Cook, *AE*
1953–4: 2 [1958] 149–157) would have been no match for
Lydian siegecraft and cavalry. War dogs may have been
instrumental, for which see G. L. Huxley, *The Early
Ionians* (New York 1966) 77, 181.
For a chronology of Alyattes see the Marmor Parium
(*FGrHist* 239 F 35) and Kaletsch, *Historia* 7 (1958) 34–39.

He came to the throne ca. 610 B.C., reduced Smyrna ca. 600 B.C., harassed the other Ionians ca. 600–590 B.C., and died in 561/560 B.C.

The Eclipse and the Median Campaign

60. Herodotus 1.74.   5th c. B.C.

μετὰ δὲ ταῦτα, οὐ γὰρ δὴ ὁ ᾿Αλυάττης ἐξεδίδου τοὺς Σκύθας ἐξαιτέοντι Κυαξάρῃ, πόλεμος τοῖσι Λυδοῖσι καὶ τοῖσι Μήδοισι ἐγεγόνεε ἐπ᾿ ἔτεα πέντε, ἐν τοῖσι πολλάκις μὲν οἱ Μῆδοι τοὺς Λυδοὺς ἐνίκησαν, πολλάκις δὲ οἱ Λυδοὶ τοὺς Μήδους· ἐν δὲ καὶ νυκτομαχίην τινὰ ἐποιήσαντο· διαφέρουσι δέ σφι ἐπὶ ἴσης τὸν πόλεμον τῷ ἕκτῳ ἔτεϊ συμβολῆς γενομένης συνήνεικε ὥστε τῆς μάχης συνεστεώσης τὴν ἡμέρην ἐξαπίνης νύκτα γενέσθαι. τὴν δὲ μεταλλαγὴν ταύτην τῆς ἡμέρης Θαλῆς ὁ Μιλήσιος τοῖσι ῎Ιωσι προηγόρευσε ἔσεσθαι, οὖρον προθέμενος ἐνιαυτὸν τοῦτον ἐν τῷ δὴ καὶ ἐγένετο ἡ μεταβολή. οἱ δὲ Λυδοί τε καὶ οἱ Μῆδοι ἐπείτε εἶδον νύκτα ἀντὶ ἡμέρης γενομένην, τῆς μάχης τε ἐπαύσαντο καὶ μᾶλλόν τι ἔσπευσαν καὶ ἀμφότεροι εἰρήνην ἑωυτοῖσι γενέσθαι.

Later, because Alyattes did not surrender the Scythians to Cyaxares when he asked for them, a state of war existed between the Lydians and the Medes for five years. And in this period the Medes frequently defeated the Lydians and the Lydians the Medes, and on one occasion they engaged in battle at night. At a time when the outcome of the war was still equally balanced, in the sixth year, an engagement took place and it happened that during the fighting, suddenly the day became night. Thales of Miletus had predicted this disappearance of the daylight to the Ionians, setting it within the year in which the eclipse took place. When the Lydians and the Medes saw that the day had become night they stopped fighting and both were eager rather to make peace.

Cf. Cicero, *De divinatione* 1.49 and *Papyri Oxyrhynchus* 2506 F 98.

61. Pliny, *Naturalis historia* 2.53.   1st c. A.D.

apud Graecos autem investigavit primus omnium Thales Milesius Olumpiadis XLVIII anno quarto praedicto solis defectu qui Alyatte rege factus est urbis conditae anno CLXX.

Among the Greeks however the first person who scrutinized these matters was Thales of Miletus. In the fourth year of the forty-eighth Olympiad he predicted the eclipse which happened while Alyattes was king in the one hundred seventieth year after the foundation of Rome.

Pliny is discussing theories of eclipses. For this eclipse cf. O. Neugebauer, *The Exact Sciences in Antiquity* (Providence 1957) 142–143.

For Thales see Herodotus 1.170; Diogenes Laertius 1.22, 1.27.

Campaigns to the West

62. Herodotus 1.17ff.   5th c. B.C.

ἐπολέμησε Μιλησίοισι, παραδεξάμενος τὸν πόλεμον παρὰ τοῦ πατρός. ἐπελαύνων γὰρ ἐπολιόρκεε τὴν Μίλητον τρόπῳ τοιῷδε. ὅκως μὲν εἴη ἐν τῇ γῇ καρπὸς ἁδρός, τηνικαῦτα ἐσέβαλλε τὴν στρατιήν· ἐστρατεύετο δὲ ὑπὸ συρίγγων τε καὶ πηκτίδων καὶ αὐλοῦ γυναικηίου τε καὶ ἀνδρηίου. ὡς δὲ ἐς τὴν Μιλησίην ἀπίκοιτο, οἰκήματα μὲν τὰ ἐπὶ τῶν ἀγρῶν οὔτε κατέβαλλε οὔτε ἐνεπίμπρη οὔτε θύρας ἀπέσπα, ἔα δὲ κατὰ χώρην ἑστάναι· ὁ δὲ τά τε δένδρεα καὶ τὸν καρπὸν τὸν ἐν τῇ γῇ ὅκως διαφθείρειε, ἀπαλλάσσετο ὀπίσω. τῆς γὰρ θαλάσσης οἱ Μιλήσιοι ἐπεκράτεον, ὥστε ἐπέδρης μὴ εἶναι ἔργον τῇ στρατιῇ.

He [Alyattes] made war on the Milesians, taking over the conflict from his father. He attacked and besieged Miletus in the following way: whenever the crop was ready, then he used to send in his army; and they marched to the pipes and harps and bass and treble flutes. When he came to the Milesian land, he did not destroy or burn the country cottages or tear off their doors, but left them alone. But after he had destroyed the trees and the crops he returned home. For the Milesians ruled the seas, so that a siege was futile from the army's point of view.
The war lasted eleven years (six under Sadyattes) (18). In the twelfth year Alyattes fell ill and was instructed by Delphi to rebuild the temple of Athena at Assessos accidentally burnt by his troops (19). Periander informed Thrasybulus of the oracle's response (20). Alyattes proposed a truce while he rebuilt the temple and Thrasybulus planned a ruse (21). Peace was made and Alyattes built two temples of Athena at Assessos and recovered (22). He reigned fifty-seven years and was second in his family to make offerings to Delphi (25).

Events ca. 610–605 B.C.
For Lydian musical instruments see Athenaeus 14.634c, f, 14.635d; for military music see Athenaeus 12.517a; Thucydides 5.70.
The twin temples at Assessos await the spade.
For Periander and Thrasybulus see Herodotus 3.48

(see *57*) (with which cf. Nicolas of Damascus, *FGrHist* 90 F 59 [3] [see *58*]); 5.92.

Alyattes' offering was seen by Pausanias (10.16.1–2).

63. Nicolas of Damascus, *FGrHist* 90 F 64.

1st c. B.C.–1st c. A.D.

ὅτι Ἀλυάττης ὁ Σαδυάττεω υἱός, βασιλεὺς Λυδῶν, ἕως μὲν νέος ἦν ὑβριστὴς ἦν καὶ ἀκόλαστος, ἐκβὰς δὲ εἰς ἄνδρα σωφρονέστατος καὶ δικαιότατος. ἐπολέμησε δὲ Σμυρναίοις καὶ εἷλεν αὐτῶν τὸ ἄστυ.

Alyattes, the son of Sadyattes, king of the Lydians, was arrogant and undisciplined when young, but when grown to maturity he was most wise and just. He made war on the Smyrnaeans and captured their city.

On Alyattes' war against Smyrna see Herodotus 1.16; J. M. Cook, *BSA* 53–54 (1958–1959) 23–27; J. K. Anderson, ibid. 148.

64. Nicolas of Damascus, *FGrHist* 90 F 65.

1st c. B.C.–1st c. A.D.

ὅτι Ἀλυάττης ὁ Κροίσου πατὴρ τοῦ Λυδῶν βασιλέως ἐπὶ Καρίαν στρατεύων περιήγγειλε τοῖς ἑαυτοῦ στρατὸν ἄγειν εἰς Σάρδεις ἐν ἡμέρᾳ τακτῇ, ἐν οἷς καὶ Κροίσῳ, ὅστις ἦν αὐτοῦ πρεσβύτατος τῶν παίδων, ἄρχων ἀποδεδειγμένος Ἀδραμυττείου τε καὶ Θήβης πεδίου. ὁ δέ, ὥς φασιν, ὑπὸ ἀκολασίας οὐχ οἷός τε ἦν καὶ πως διεβέβλητο πρὸς τὸν πατέρα.

When Alyattes, father of Croesus the king of the Lydians, was campaigning against Caria, he instructed his generals to bring their forces to Sardis on a day which he appointed. Among these was Croesus, his eldest son, who had been designated governor of Adramytteion and the plain of Thebe. However, they say that he was without means on account of his reckless living and had been accused to his father's face.
Croesus asked a rich Lydian, Sadyattes, for money to hire mercenaries. Sadyattes refused on the grounds that Alyattes had many sons (2). Croesus went to Ephesus and vowed Sadyattes' estate to Artemis if he became king (3). He received money from an Ionian Pamphaes, whom he rewarded on his accession with a wagon full of gold, from the acropolis. Sadyattes' estate was consecrated to Artemis (4). Croesus appeared at Sardis with an army on the appointed day and campaigned against Caria with Alyattes. His accusers were refuted (5).

Croesus was born 596/595 B.C. The campaign against Caria took place ca. 570 B.C.

For another son of Alyattes, Pantaleon, see Herodotus 1.92 (see *100*) where other dedications of Croesus are enumerated.

For Pamphaes see Aelian, *Varia historia* 4.27 (see *66*).

The attack on Caria was foiled by Bias, like Pamphaes, of Priene (Diogenes Laertius 1.83).

65. Polyaenus 7.2.

2nd c. A.D.

Ἀλυάττης Κιμμερίων ἐπιστρατευσάντων ἀλλόκοτα καὶ θηριώδη σώματα ἐχόντων μετὰ τῆς ἄλλης δυνάμεως καὶ τοὺς ἀλκιμωτάτους κύνας ἐπὶ τὴν μάχην ἐξήγαγεν, οἳ προσπλακέντες τοῖς βαρβάροις ὡς θηρίοις πολλοὺς μὲν αὐτῶν διέφθειραν, τοὺς δὲ λοιποὺς φεύγειν αἰσχρῶς ἐβιάσαντο.

When the Cimmerians, who have strange and beastly physiques, campaigned against him, Alyattes with the rest of his army led out to battle the fiercest war-dogs. They fastened on the barbarians as if they were wild beasts, killed many of them, and compelled the remainder to flee shamefully.
Against the Colophonians the Lydian king used bribery and treachery (2).

For Alyattes and the Cimmerians see Herodotus 1.16 (see *59*), and cf. H. Kaletsch, *Historia* 7 (1958) 37.

For war-dogs see R. M. Cook, *Festschrift Rumpf* (Krefeld 1952) 38–42.

The Tomb of Alyattes

(278) Herodotus 1.93.

5th c. B.C.

(279) Strabo 13.4.7.

1st c. B.C.

CROESUS

The Accession

66. Aelian, *Varia historia* 4.27

2nd –3rd c. A.D.

Ὅτι Παμφάης ὁ Πριηνεὺς Κροίσῳ τῷ Λυδῷ, τοῦ πατρὸς αὐτοῦ περιόντος, τριάκοντα μνᾶς ἐδωρήσατο. παραλαβὼν δὲ τὴν ἀρχὴν μεστὴν ἅμαξαν ἀργυρίου ἀπέπεμψεν αὐτῷ.

Pamphaes of Priene gave Croesus the Lydian thirty mnai while his father was still alive, and when Croesus became king, he sent him a wagon full of silver.

On Pamphaes and the early life of Croesus see Nicolas of Damascus, *FGrHist* 90 F 65 (see *64*).

(100) Herodotus 1.92.

5th c. B.C.

67. Plutarch, *De Herodoti malignitate* 18 (858 E).

1st–2nd c. A.D.

ἀδελφὸν γὰρ αὐτῷ Πανταλέοντα περὶ τῆς βασιλείας
αὐτῷ διαφέρεσθαι, ζῶντος ἔτι τοῦ πατρός· τὸν οὖν
Κροῖσον, ὡς εἰς τὴν βασιλείαν κατέστη, τῶν ἑταίρων
καὶ φίλων τοῦ Πανταλέοντος ἕνα τῶν γνωρίμων ἐπὶ
γνάφου διαφθεῖραι καταξαινόμενον, ἐκ δὲ τῶν χρημάτων
αὐτοῦ ποιησάμενον ἀναθήματα τοῖς θεοῖς ἀποστεῖλαι.

For he says that his brother Pantaleon contended
for the kingship with him while their father was still
alive, and that when Croesus ascended the throne,
he killed one of the nobles, an associate and friend
of Pantaleon, by flaying him on a carding comb, and
that he made dedications to the gods out of his
property and sent them off.

> Panteleon's supporter was named Sadyattes (Nicolas of
> Damascus, *FGrHist* 90 F 65 [see *64*]).
> Evidently the accession was not troublefree: cf. G. L.
> Huxley, *The Early Ionians* (New York 1966) 109.

68. Plutarch, *De Pythiae oraculis* 16 (401 E).

1st–2nd c. A.D.

λέγεται γὰρ Ἀλυάττην τὸν πατέρα τοῦ Κροίσου δευτέραν
ἀγαγέσθαι γυναῖκα καὶ παῖδας ἑτέρους τρέφειν· ἐπιβου-
λεύουσαν οὖν τῷ Κροίσῳ τὴν ἄνθρωπον φάρμακον
δοῦναι τῇ ἀρτοποιῷ καὶ κελεῦσαι διαπλάσασαν ἄρτον
ἐξ αὐτοῦ τῷ Κροίσῳ παραδοῦναι· τὴν δ' ἀρτοποιὸν
κρύφα τῷ Κροίσῳ φράσαι, παραθεῖναι δὲ τοῖς ἐκείνης
παισὶ τὸν ἄρτον.

For it is said that Alyattes, father of Croesus, took a
second wife and was bringing up other children.
Plotting against Croesus, the woman gave poison to
his baker and told her to knead it into the bread and
give it to him. But the baker secretly told Croesus
and gave the bread to the woman's children.

> Hence Croesus dedicated a statue of his baker in Delphi
> (Herodotus 1.51 [see *99*]).
> Croesus' mother was a Carian (Herodotus 1.92 [see
> *100*]). On Carians in Sardis see G. M. A. Hanfmann and
> O. Masson, *Kadmos* 6 (1967) 123–134.

Westward Military Campaigns

69. Aelian, *Varia historia* 3.26.   2nd–3rd c. A.D.

Πίνδαρος ὁ Μέλανος υἱός, Ἀλυάττου δὲ θυγατριδοῦς
τοῦ Λυδοῦ, διαδεξάμενος τὴν Ἐφεσίων τυραννίδα πρὸς
μὲν τὰς τιμωρίας πικρὸς ἦν καὶ ἀπαραίτητος, τά γε
μὴν ἄλλα ἐδόκει φιλόπατρις εἶναι καὶ σώφρων, καὶ τοῦ
μὴ δουλεῦσαι τὴν πατρίδα τοῖς βαρβάροις πολλὴν

πρόνοιαν ἔθετο. ἔδειξε ταῦτα οὕτως ἔχειν ἐκεῖνα δήπου.
ἐπεὶ γὰρ Κροῖσος ὁ πρὸς μητρὸς αὐτοῦ θεῖος κατασ-
τρεφόμενος τὴν Ἰωνίαν καὶ πρὸς τὸν Πίνδαρον πρεσ-
βείαν ἀπέστειλεν, ἀξιῶν Ἐφεσίους ὑπ' αὐτῷ γενέσθαι,**
ὡς δ' οὐκ ἐπείσθη, ἐπολιόρκει τὴν πόλιν Κροῖσος.
ἐπεὶ δέ τις τῶν πύργων ἀνετράπη ὁ κληθεὶς ὕστερον
Προδότης, καὶ ἐν ὀφθαλμοῖς ἑωρᾶτο τὸ δεινόν, συνε-
βούλευεν ὁ Πίνδαρος Ἐφεσίοις ἐκδήσαντας ἐκ τῶν
πυλῶν καὶ τῶν τειχῶν θώμιγγας συνάψαι τοῖς κίοσι
τοῦ τῆς Ἀρτέμιδος νεώ, οἱονεὶ τὴν πόλιν ἀνάθημα
ἐῶντας εἶναι τῇ Ἀρτέμιδι, ἀσυλίαν διὰ τούτων ἐπινοῶν
τῇ Ἐφέσῳ.

Pindarus, the son of Melas and grandson of Alyattes
the Lydian, took over the tyranny in Ephesus and
though he was harsh and unrelenting as far as
punishment was concerned, in other respects he
seemed wise and devoted to the city; and he gave
much thought to preventing the city's subjection to
the barbarians. He demonstrated these qualities in
the following way. For when Croesus his uncle on
his mother's side conquered Ionia and sent a delegation to Pindarus with the claim that the Ephesians
were his, Pindarus did not listen to him and Croesus
besieged the city. And when one of the towers, later
named the Traitor, was overturned and the awful
event took place before his eyes, Pindarus advised the
Ephesians to stretch ropes from the gates and walls
and join them to the columns of the temple of
Artemis as if they were claiming that the city was an
offering to Artemis. This way Pindarus contrived to
render Ephesus inviolable.

> The attack on Ephesus took place ca. 560 B.C. Croesus
> reigned ca. 560–ca. 547 B.C.
> On the archaic Artemisia at Ephesus see D. H. Hogarth,
> *British Museum: Excavations at Ephesus, the Archaic
> Artemisia* (London 1908).
> On the topography of archaic Ephesus see A. Bammer,
> *JOAI* 46 (1961–1963) 136–157.

70. Diodorus Siculus 9.25.1–2.   1st c. B.C.

Ὅτι Κροῖσος ναυπηγῶν πλοῖα μακρά, φασίν, ἔμελλε
στρατεύειν ἐπὶ τὰς νήσους. παρεπιδημοῦντα δὲ Βίαντα
ἢ Πιττακὸν καὶ θεωροῦντα τὴν ναυπηγίαν, ὑπὸ τοῦ
βασιλέως ἐρωτηθῆναι μή τι νεώτερον ἀκηκοὼς εἴη παρὰ
τοῖς Ἕλλησι γινόμενον.

They say that Croesus was having warships built
intending to campaign against the islands. But Bias
or Pittacus, who was visiting him and saw the ship-
building, was asked by Croesus if he had heard any
news recently.

Croesus was told, to his amusement, that the islanders

were planning a cavalry campaign against him; but Bias (or Pittacus) declared that the islanders were as delighted at his campaign against them by sea as he was at the thought of their attacking him by land. Croesus changed his purpose.

For Diodorus' biography of Croesus cf. 9.2.1–4; 9.27.1–2 (Croesus and Solon); 9.12.2, 9.27.4 (Croesus and Pittacus); 9.25.1–2 (the projected campaign against the islands); 9.26.3–5 (and Anacharsis); 9.27.3 (Croesus and Bias); 9.29.1–2 (Croesus and Adrastus); 9.31.1–3, 9.33.2 (Croesus and the oracles); 9.31.3 (replies to Cyrus); 9.32.1 (Croesus and the Peloponnesian mercenaries); 13.22.2–3 (Croesus and the pyre).

71. Herodotus 1.26–27.   5th c. B.C.

Τελευτήσαντος δὲ Ἀλυάττεω ἐξεδέξατο τὴν βασιληίην Κροῖσος ὁ Ἀλυάττεω, ἐτέων ἐὼν ἡλικίην πέντε καὶ τριήκοντα, ὃς δὴ Ἑλλήνων πρώτοισι ἐπεθήκατο Ἐφεσίοισι. ἔνθα δὴ οἱ Ἐφέσιοι πολιορκεόμενοι ὑπ᾽ αὐτοῦ ἀνέθεσαν τὴν πόλιν τῇ Ἀρτέμιδι, ἐξάψαντες ἐκ τοῦ νηοῦ σχοινίον ἐς τὸ τεῖχος. ἔστι δὲ μεταξὺ τῆς τε παλαιῆς πόλιος, ἣ τότε ἐπολιορκέετο, καὶ τοῦ νηοῦ ἑπτὰ στάδιοι. πρώτοισι μὲν δὴ τούτοισι ἐπεχείρησε ὁ Κροῖσος, μετὰ δὲ ἐν μέρεϊ ἑκάστοισι Ἰώνων τε καὶ Αἰολέων, ἄλλοισι ἄλλας αἰτίας ἐπιφέρων, τῶν μὲν ἐδύνατο μέζονας παρευρίσκειν, μέζονα ἐπαιτιώμενος, τοῖσι δὲ αὐτῶν καὶ φαῦλα ἐπιφέρων. ὡς δὲ ἄρα οἱ ἐν τῇ Ἀσίῃ Ἕλληνες κατεστράφατο ἐς φόρου ἀπαγωγήν, τὸ ἐνθεῦτεν ἐπενόεε νέας ποιησάμενος ἐπιχειρέειν τοῖσι νησιώτῃσι.

On the death of Alyattes, his son Croesus came to the throne at the age of thirty-five. First of all the Greeks he attacked the Ephesians who dedicated their city to Artemis when they were besieged by him by stretching a rope to the city wall from the temple. Between the ancient city which was then besieged and the temple is a distance of seven stades. Croesus attacked them first and subsequently each of the Ionian and Aeolic cities one by one, bringing different accusations against every township. When he could he preferred significant grounds for intervention, but sometimes brought forward the most trivial charges. When the Greeks in Asia had been brought into a tributary status toward him, then he planned to build ships and attack the islanders. *Bias or Pittacus dissuaded him from this course of action (27).*

Croesus turned his attack from the islanders to the Troad (Strabo 13.1.42).

72. Polyaenus 6.50.   2nd c. A.D.

Κροίσου τοῦ Λυδοῦ πολιορκοῦντος Ἔφεσον, ἐπειδὴ τῶν πύργων τις, ὁ προδότης κληθεὶς, ἔπεσε καὶ τὸ

δεινὸν τῆς ἁλώσεως ἐν ὀφθαλμοῖς ἦν, Πίνδαρος ὁ τυραννεύων τῆς πόλεως συνεβούλευσε τοῖς Ἐφεσίοις ἐκ τῶν πυλῶν καὶ τῶν τειχῶν θώμιγγας συνάψαι τοῖς κίοσι τοῦ ἱεροῦ τῆς Ἀρτέμιδος ὥσπερ ἀνατιθέντας τῇ θεῷ τὴν πόλιν. Κροῖσος τιμῶν τὴν θεὸν ἐφείσατο τῆς πόλεως ὥσπερ ἀναθήματος καὶ πρὸς τοὺς Ἐφεσίους ἐπὶ ἐλευθερίᾳ συνθήκας ἐποιήσατο.

When Croesus the Lydian was besieging Ephesus and one of the towers, the one called the Traitor, fell and the terror of capture was imminent, the tyrant of the city, Pindarus, advised the Ephesians to tie ropes from their gates and walls to the columns of the temple of Artemis like citizens dedicating the city to the goddess. Since Croesus honored the goddess, he spared the city on the grounds that it was a dedication and made a treaty with the Ephesians granting them their freedom.

The Riches of Croesus

73. Alcaeus F 116 (69).   6th c. B.C.

Ζεῦ πάτερ, Λύδοι μὲν ἐπασχάλαντες
συμφόραισι δισχελίοις στά[τηρας
ἄμμ᾽ ἔδωκαν, αἴ κε δυνάμεθ᾽ ἴρ[αν
ἐς πόλιν ἔλθην.

Father Zeus, the Lydians distressed at these misfortunes gave us two thousand staters in the hope that we could get to the holy city.

Alcaeus' benefactor may well have been Croesus; see D. L. Page, *Sappho and Alcaeus* (Oxford 1955) 226–234, esp. 230.

For other Lydian offers of financial aid to Lesbos made by Croesus, see Diogenes Laertius, *Pittacus* 1.4.74.

74. Catullus 115.1–4.   1st c. B.C.

Mentula habet instar triginta jugera prati,
    quadraginta arvi: cetera sunt maria.
cur non divitiis Croesum superare potis sit,
    uno qui in saltu tot bona possideat?

Mentula has about thirty acres of grazing land and about forty of arable; the rest is the sea. Why will he not be able to exceed Croesus in wealth, who possesses so many good things in one estate?

Elsewhere (24.4) Catullus uses Midas as his paradigm of fabulous wealth.

For Croesus elsewhere in the Roman poets see Manilius, *Astronomica* 4.64; Propertius 2.26.23, 3.5.17, 3.18.28; Statius, *Silvae* 1.3.105; Silius Italicus, *Punica* 13.776.

75. Dio Chrysostom, *Orationes* 78.32.   1st–2nd c. A.D.

Οὐδέ γε τὸν λαβόντα παρὰ Κροίσου τὴν δωρεὰν ἐκείνην
Ἀλκμέωνα ἐζήλωσεν οὔτε Σόλων οὔτε ἄλλος οὐδεὶς
τῶν τότε σοφῶν ἀνδρῶν, ᾧ φασι τὸν Λυδὸν ἐπιτρέψαι
τοὺς θησαυροὺς ἀνοίξαντα φέρειν αὐτὸν ὁπόσον βούλεται τοῦ χρυσοῦ. καὶ τοῦτον εἰσελθόντα πάνυ ἀνδρείως
ἐμφορήσασθαι τῆς βασιλικῆς δωρεᾶς, χιτῶνά τε ποδήρη
καταζωσάμενον καὶ τὸν κόλπον ἐμπλήσαντα γυναικεῖον
καὶ βαθὺν καὶ τὰ ὑποδήματα ἐξεπίτηδες μεγάλα καὶ
κοῖλα ὑποδησάμενον, τέλος δὲ τὴν κόμην διαπάσαντα
καὶ τὰ γένεια τῷ ψήγματι καὶ τὸ στόμα ἐμπλήσαντα
καὶ τὰς γνάθους ἑκατέρας μόλις ἔξω βαδίζειν, ὥσπερ
αὐλοῦντα τὴν τῆς Σεμέλης ὠδῖνα, γέλωτα καὶ θέαν
Κροίσῳ παρέχοντα καὶ Λυδοῖς. καὶ ἦν τότε Ἀλκμέων
οὐδεμιᾶς ἄξιος δραχμῆς, ὡς εἶχεν ἱστάμενος.

Neither Solon nor any other wise man at that time
envied Alcmeon when he received that amazing gift
from Croesus. They say that the Lydian allowed him
to open his treasuries and carry off all the gold he
wanted. He, they say, went in and loaded himself
with the king's gift with a will, filling the deep
womanish folds of the lengthy tunic that he wore and
the large spacious boots which he had put on pur-
posely. Finally he sprinkled gold dust on his hair
and in his beard and stuffed it in his mouth and cheeks.
He scarcely managed to walk out, looking like a
fluteplayer playing "The Birth-Pangs of Semele"
and presenting a ludicrous spectacle to Croesus and
the Lydians. At that moment Alcmeon was not worth
a single drachma, standing there like that.

Dio is discussing envy. He may refer to Timotheus'
"Birth-Pangs of Semele" (Athenaeus, *Deipnosophistae*
8.352 A) or to a Semele pantomime.

For the political implications of the story see M. Miller,
Klio 41 (1963) 77–79, and cf. W. G. Forrest, *BCH* 80
(1958) 51.

76. Favorinus, *De Fortuna* 26–27.   1st–2nd c. A.D.

θησαυροὶ μὲν εἰς ἀνθρώπους οὗτοι παρὰ θεοῖς, ταμιεύει
δὲ αὐτῶν πρὸς τὸ ἐπιβάλλον ἡ Τύχη καὶ ῥήτορι καὶ
στρατηγῷ, καὶ πένητι καὶ πλουσίῳ, καὶ πρεσβύτῃ καὶ
νέῳ. Κροίσῳ δίδωσι χρυσόν, Κανδαύλῃ γυναῖκα, Πηλεῖ
ξίφος, Νέστορι ἀσπίδα, Πτερέλᾳ κόμην χρυσῆν, Νίσῳ
πλόκαμον πορφυροῦν, Ἀλκιβιάδῃ κάλλος, Σωκράτει
[δὲ] φρόνησιν, Ἀριστείδῃ δικαιοσύνην, Λακεδαιμονίοις
γῆν, Ἀθηναίοις θάλατταν.

These resources come to men from the gods, and
Fortune is steward of them as to their disposition,
for orator and general alike, for rich and poor, for
young and old. She gives gold to Croesus, a wife to
Candaules, a sword to Peleus, a shield to Nestor,
golden locks to Pterela, red hair to Nisus, beauty to
Alcibiades, wisdom to Socrates, justice to Aristides,
the land to Sparta, and the sea to Athens.

On Croesus cf. *De Fortuna* I, 5.

77. Herodotus 6.125.   5th c. B.C.

τοῦτο μὲν γὰρ Ἀλκμέων ὁ Μεγακλέος τοῖσι ἐκ Σαρδίων
Λυδοῖσι παρὰ Κροίσου ἀπικνεομένοισι ἐπὶ τὸ χρηστήριον τὸ ἐν Δελφοῖσι συμπρήκτωρ τε ἐγίνετο καὶ συνε-
λάμβανε προθύμως, καί μιν Κροῖσος πυθόμενος τῶν
Λυδῶν τῶν ἐς τὰ χρηστήρια φοιτεόντων ἑωυτοῦ εὖ
ποιέειν μεταπέμπεται ἐς Σάρδις, ἀπικόμενον δὲ δωρέεται χρυσῷ τὸν ἂν δύνηται τῷ ἑωυτοῦ σώματι ἐξενεί-
κασθαι ἐσάπαξ. ὁ δὲ Ἀλκμέων πρὸς τὴν δωρεήν, ἐοῦσαν
τοιαύτην, τοιάδε ἐπιτηδεύσας προσέφερε· ἐνδὺς κιθῶνα
μέγαν καὶ κόλπον βαθὺν καταλιπόμενος τοῦ κιθῶνος,
κοθόρνους τοὺς εὕρισκε εὐρυτάτους ἐόντας ὑποδησάμενος
ἤιε ἐς τὸν θησαυρὸν ἐς τόν οἱ κατηγέοντο. ἐσπεσὼν δὲ
ἐς σωρὸν ψήγματος πρῶτα μὲν παρέσαξε παρὰ τὰς
κνήμας τοῦ χρυσοῦ ὅσον ἐχώρεον οἱ κόθορνοι, μετὰ δὲ
τὸν κόλπον πάντα πλησάμενος χρυσοῦ καὶ ἐς τὰς τρίχας
τῆς κεφαλῆς διαπάσας τοῦ ψήγματος καὶ ἄλλο λαβὼν
ἐς τὸ στόμα ἐξήιε ἐκ τοῦ θησαυροῦ, ἕλκων μὲν μόγις
τοὺς κοθόρνους, παντὶ δέ τεῳ οἰκὼς μᾶλλον ἢ ἀνθρώπῳ·
τοῦ τό τε στόμα ἐβέβυστο καὶ πάντα ἐξώγκωτο. ἰδόντα
δὲ τὸν Κροῖσον γέλως ἐσῆλθε, καὶ οἱ πάντα τε ἐκεῖνα
διδοῖ καὶ πρὸς ἑτέροισι μιν δωρέεται οὐκ ἐλάσσοσι
ἐκείνων. οὕτω μὲν ἐπλούτησε ἡ οἰκίη αὕτη μεγάλως,
καὶ ὁ Ἀλκμέων οὗτος οὕτω τεθριπποτροφήσας Ὀλυ-
μπιάδα ἀναιρέεται.

When the Lydians sent by Croesus to the Delphic
oracle arrived from Sardis, Alcmeon son of Megacles
worked with them and assisted them zealously.
Hearing from the Lydians who frequented the oracle
that Alcmeon was his benefactor, Croesus sent for
him to Sardis and on his arrival rewarded him with a
gift—as much gold as he could carry off at one time
by himself. In the face of such a gift Alcmeon made
the following preparations. He put on a large chiton,
leaving a deep fold in it, and the largest boots he
could find. In this outfit he entered the treasury to
which guides took him. He dived headlong into a
pile of gold dust and first crammed alongside his
legs as much gold as the boots could hold; he next
filled all the fold of the chiton with gold and sprinkled
dust on the hair of his head and pushed more of it
into his mouth. Then he left the treasury, dragging
his boots along with difficulty. Since his mouth was
stuffed and his body all puffed out, the last thing he
resembled was a human. When Croesus saw him he
burst into laughter and gave him all he was carrying

and as much again at least on top. In this way that family became very rich and Alcmeon came to own four-horse chariots and win at Olympia.

A comic treatment of the endowment of the Alcmeonids.
On the Alcmeonids see the ensuing chapters of Herodotus (126–131) and cf. Pausanias 2.18.8.

78. Lactantius, *De vero cultu* 13.11.　　　3rd c. A.D.

unum est enim sapientis et justi et vitalis viri opus divitias suas in sola justitia conlocare: qua profecto qui eget, licet ille Croesum aut Crassum divitiis superet, hic pauper, hic nudus, hic mendicus putandus est.

The one task of a wise and just and generous man is to organize his riches in fairness, and in fairness alone. He who does not follow this course may directly surpass Croesus or Crassus in wealth, but he is to be considered a pauper and destitute and a beggar.

Lactantius was a pupil of Arnobius. Like him he was from Africa and became a Christian.

79. Lucian, *Dialogi mortuorum* 3 (2).　　　2nd c. A.D.

ΚΡΟΙΣΟΣ

Οὐ φέρομεν, ὦ Πλούτων, Μένιππον τουτονὶ τὸν κύνα παροικοῦντα· ὥστε ἢ ἐκεῖνόν ποι κατάστησον ἢ ἡμεῖς μετοικήσομεν εἰς ἕτερον τόπον.

ΠΛΟΥΤΩΝ

Τί δ᾽ ὑμᾶς δεινὸν ἐργάζεται ὁμόνεκρος ὤν;

ΚΡΟΙΣΟΣ

Ἐπειδὰν ἡμεῖς οἰμώζωμεν καὶ στένωμεν ἐκείνων μεμνημένοι τῶν ἄνω, Μίδας μὲν οὑτοσὶ τοῦ χρυσίου, Σαρδανάπαλλος δὲ τῆς πολλῆς τρυφῆς, ἐγὼ δὲ Κροῖσος τῶν θησαυρῶν, ἐπιγελᾷ καὶ ἐξονειδίζει ἀνδράποδα καὶ καθάρματα ἡμᾶς ἀποκαλῶν, ἐνίοτε δὲ καὶ ᾄδων ἐπιταράττει ἡμῶν τὰς οἰμωγάς, καὶ ὅλως λυπηρός ἐστιν.

Croesus: Pluto, we cannot stand this dog, Menippus, as our neighbor. Set him some place else or we shall move to another spot.
Pluto:　What ill does he do you, when he is a fellow spirit with you?
Croesus: Whenever we complain and moan remembering our lives above, Midas thinking about gold, Sardanapalus about his great luxury and I, Croesus, about my treasures, he laughs at us and reviles us calling us slaves and riffraff, and sometimes he sings and interrupts our lamentation. He is a quite noisome fellow.

On Croesus in Lucian see also *Hippias* 2 (and Thales); *Juppiter confutatus* 12 (and Adrastus); *Gallus* 25, *Vitarum auctio* 3, *Pro imaginibus* 20 (and the mute son); *Bis accusatus* 1, *Alexander* 48, *Philopatris* 5 (and oracles) ; *De mercede conductis* 20, *Apologia* 1 (and wealth); *Menippus* 16, *Navigium* 26 (and Fortune).

80. Pollux, *Onomasticon* 3.87.　　　2nd c. A.D.

εὐδόκιμος δὲ καὶ ὁ Γυγάδας χρυσὸς καὶ οἱ Κροίσειοι στατῆρες.

Highly prized is the Gygaean gold, as are the staters of Croesus.

On Gygaean gold see also Pollux 7.98, and on the staters of Croesus, Pollux 9.84.
On the creation of coinage see Pollux 9.83, and on other matters Lydian cf. Pollux 1.132; 4.65, 78; 7.93, 102.

81. Propertius 3.18.27–28.　　　1st c. B.C.

Nirea non facies, non vis exemit Achillem,
　　Croesum aut, Pactoli quas parit umor, opes.

Beauty did not help Nireus, nor did strength deliver Achilles; and the riches which flowing Pactolus provides did not save Croesus.

On Nireus see *Iliad* 2.673.
Other references to Lydia include 3.17.30 (with which cf. Euripides, *Bacchae* 494) and 4.7.62.

82. Seneca, *Controversiae* 2.1(9).7.
　　　1st c. B.C.–1st c. A.D.

ille Croesus inter reges opulentissimus, memento, post terga vinctis manibus ductus est.

The famous Croesus, the richest of kings, remember, was led away with hands bound behind his back.

See also, on the mute son, *Controversiae* 7.5(20).13.

83. Tzetzes, *Historiarum variarum chiliades* 1:1, 1–5.
　　　12th c. A.D.

Κροῖσος ὁ Ἀλυάττεω Λυδῶν ἦν βασιλεύων,
Μητρόπολιν ἀνάκτορον τὰς Σάρδεις κεκτημένος.
Τοῦ Πακτωλοῦ δὲ ῥέοντος ἐκεῖσε πρὶν χρυσίου
Ὄμβροις ἐκ Τμώλου ὄρεος τὸ ψῆγμα δεχομένου,
Πάντων πολυχρυσότερος γέγονε βασιλέων.

Croesus son of Alyattes was ruler of the Lydians and possessed the metropolis, Sardis, as his home. Because the river Pactolus, which formerly was golden and received the dust from Mount Tmolus during rain storms, flows through there, Croesus became richer in gold than any king.

Tzetzes' version of the biography of Croesus follows: *Historiarum variarum chiliades* 1:1, 6–102, 821–825; *Iambici* 29ff.

For Croesus' wealth see also Plutarch, *Praecepta gerendae reipublicae* 31 (823A); Diogenianus 8.53, with which cf. Apostolius 17.17.

Croesus and Solon

84. Herodotus 1.28ff.   5th c. B.C.

χρόνου δὲ ἐπιγενομένου καὶ κατεστραμμένων σχεδὸν πάντων τῶν ἐντὸς Ἅλυος ποταμοῦ οἰκημένων· πλὴν γὰρ Κιλίκων καὶ Λυκίων τοὺς ἄλλους πάντας ὑπ' ἑωυτῷ εἶχε καταστρεψάμενος ὁ Κροῖσος· εἰσὶ δὲ οἵδε, Λυδοί, Φρύγες, Μυσοί, Μαριανδυνοί, Χάλυβες, Παφλαγόνες, Θρήικες οἱ Θυνοί τε καὶ Βιθυνοί, Κᾶρες, Ἴωνες, Δωριέες, Αἰολέες, Πάμφυλοι· κατεστραμμένων δὲ τούτων καὶ προσεπικτωμένου Κροίσου Λυδοῖσι, ἀπικνέονται ἐς Σάρδις ἀκμαζούσας πλούτῳ ἄλλοι τε οἱ πάντες ἐκ τῆς Ἑλλάδος σοφισταί, οἳ τοῦτον τὸν χρόνον ἐτύγχανον ἐόντες, ὡς ἕκαστος αὐτῶν ἀπικνέοιτο, καὶ δὴ καὶ Σόλων ἀνὴρ Ἀθηναῖος, ὃς Ἀθηναίοισι νόμους κελεύσασι ποιήσας ἀπεδήμησε ἔτεα δέκα, κατὰ θεωρίης πρόφασιν ἐκπλώσας, ἵνα δὴ μή τινα τῶν νόμων ἀναγκασθῇ λῦσαι τῶν ἔθετο. αὐτοὶ γὰρ οὐκ οἷοί τε ἦσαν αὐτὸ ποιῆσαι Ἀθηναῖοι· ὁρκίοισι γὰρ μεγάλοισι κατείχοντο δέκα ἔτεα χρήσεσθαι νόμοισι τοὺς ἄν σφι Σόλων θῆται. αὐτῶν δὴ ὦν τούτων καὶ τῆς θεωρίης ἐκδημήσας ὁ Σόλων εἵνεκεν ἐς Αἴγυπτον ἀπίκετο παρὰ Ἄμασιν καὶ δὴ καὶ ἐς Σάρδις παρὰ Κροῖσον.

With the passage of time Croesus overcame almost all the peoples west of the Halys except the Cilicians and Lycians, and he kept them subject to him. These are the Lydians, Phrygians, Mysians, Mariandynians, Chalybes, Paphlagonians, Thracians, Thynians and Bithynians, Carians, Ionians, Dorians, Aeolians, and Pamphylians. All these were conquered and held like the Lydians in Croesus' power. Sardis was at the peak of her wealth. Whereupon all the teachers from Greece who then lived came to the city on whatever grounds they chose; and among them came Solon of Athens. At the Athenians' request this man had made laws for them, and he had subsequently left the city for ten years. Travel was the excuse he gave for his journeyings but in reality he left to avoid being obliged to change any of the laws he had made. For the Athenians could not change them since they were held by oaths to keep for ten years whatever laws Solon made. For these reasons then Solon left his homeland and went to Amasis in Egypt and Croesus at Sardis.

Croesus showed Solon his treasury and questioned him. Solon chose Tellus as the happiest of men (30). Croesus pursued his questioning and Solon told the story of Cleobis and Biton (31). Solon's philosophical statement: all situations contain seeds of self-destruction—man is contingency—call no man happy till he is dead (32).

If the meeting took place, it must have been at the beginning of Croesus' reign, ca. 560 B.C.

On Croesus' diplomatic activities see 1.46 (see *99*), 1.77 (see *111*).

On Herodotus' view of Croesus see M. Miller, *Klio* 41 (1963) 58–94. For his chronology see M. Miller, *Klio* 37 (1959) 29–52, and *Klio* 46 (1965) 109–128; and cf. M. White, *Phoenix* 23 (1969) 39–48. Plutarch (*Solon* 27 [see *87*]) thought that Croesus and Solon actually met.

85. Juvenal 10.273–275.   2nd c. A.D.

festino ad nostros et regem transeo Ponti
et Croesum, quem vox justi facunda Solonis
respicere ad longae jussit spatia ultima vitae.

I hurry on to our own citizens, omitting the king of Pontus and Croesus, whom the eloquent voice of wise Solon urged to consider the final moments of a long life.

The king of Pontus is Mithridates. See also Juvenal 14.328.

86. Plato, *Epistle* 2.311A.   4th c. B.C.

καὶ Περίανδρον τὸν Κορίνθιον καὶ Θαλῆν τὸν Μιλήσιον ὑμνεῖν εἰώθασιν ἅμα, καὶ Περικλέα καὶ Ἀναξαγόραν, καὶ Κροῖσον αὖ καὶ Σόλωνα ὡς σοφοὺς καὶ Κῦρον ὡς δυνάστην.

Men are accustomed to refer to Periander of Corinth and Thales of Miletus together, and Pericles and Anaxagoras, and Croesus too and Solon as wise men with Cyrus as a ruler.

On Croesus and Solon see also Plato Scholia on *Republic* 599e.

87. Plutarch, *Solon* 27.1ff.   1st–2nd c. A.D.

Τὴν δὲ πρὸς Κροῖσον ἔντευξιν αὐτοῦ δοκοῦσιν ἔνιοι τοῖς χρόνοις ὡς πεπλασμένην ἐξελέγχειν. ἐγὼ δὲ λόγον ἔνδοξον οὕτω καὶ τοσούτους μάρτυρας ἔχοντα καὶ (ὃ μεῖζόν ἐστι) πρέποντα τῷ Σόλωνος ἤθει καὶ τῆς ἐκείνου μεγαλοφροσύνης καὶ σοφίας ἄξιον, οὔ μοι δοκῶ προήσεσθαι χρονικοῖς τισι λεγομένοις κανόσιν, οὓς μυρίοι διορθοῦντες, ἄχρι σήμερον εἰς οὐδὲν αὐτοῖς ὁμολογούμενον δύνανται καταστῆσαι τὰς ἀντιλογίας.

Some think by means of chronology to refute the story of his meeting with Croesus as a concocted tale. But I do not think it right to reject by means of some chronological so-called canons a story so well known which has such significant witnesses and (what is most important) fits well with Solon's character and is worthy of his generosity and wisdom. Thousands are straightening out these canons, but up to this point they are not able to exchange their contradictions for any agreement.

Solon met Croesus (2) but was unimpressed (3). The interrogation of Solon (4, 5) and his homilies on moderation and unpredictability (6, 7).

Croesus' Sons

88. Cicero, *De divinatione* 1.53. 1st c. b.c.

et si mulier leonem peperisse visa esset, fore ut ab exteris gentibus vinceretur ea res publica in qua id contigisset.

Eiusdem generis etiam illud est, quod scribit Herodotus, Croesi filium, cum esset infans, locutum; quo ostento regnum patris et domum funditus concidisse.

And if a woman dreamed that she had given birth to a lion, this meant that the country in which she dreamt the dream would be overcome by foreign peoples. The story which Herodotus writes is of the same kind when he says that Croesus' son when an infant spoke; which portent meant that the child's father's kingdom and home was altogether ruined.

For Meles and the lion borne him in Sardis by a mistress see Herodotus 1.84 (see *116*), and cf. Herodotus 6.131; Plutarch, *Pericles* 3.

89. Herodotus 1.34ff. 5th c. b.c.

Μετὰ δὲ Σόλωνα οἰχόμενον ἔλαβε ἐκ θεοῦ νέμεσις μεγάλη Κροῖσον, ὡς εἰκάσαι, ὅτι ἐνόμισε ἑωυτὸν εἶναι ἀνθρώπων ἁπάντων ὀλβιώτατον. αὐτίκα δέ οἱ εὕδοντι ἐπέστη ὄνειρος, ὅς οἱ τὴν ἀληθείην ἔφαινε τῶν μελλόντων γενέσθαι κακῶν κατὰ τὸν παῖδα. ἦσαν δὲ τῷ Κροίσῳ δύο παῖδες, τῶν οὕτερος μὲν διέφθαρτο, ἦν γὰρ δὴ κωφός, ὁ δὲ ἕτερος τῶν ἡλίκων μακρῷ τὰ πάντα πρῶτος· οὔνομα δέ οἱ ἦν Ἄτυς. τοῦτον δὴ ὦν τὸν Ἄτυν σημαίνει τῷ Κροίσῳ ὁ ὄνειρος, ὡς ἀπολέει μιν αἰχμῇ σιδηρέῃ βληθέντα. ὁ δὲ ἐπείτε ἐξηγέρθη καὶ ἑωυτῷ λόγον ἔδωκε, καταρρωδήσας τὸν ὄνειρον ἄγεται μὲν τῷ παιδὶ γυναῖκα, ἐωθότα δὲ στρατηγέειν μιν τῶν Λυδῶν οὐδαμῇ ἔτι ἐπὶ τοιοῦτο πρῆγμα ἐξέπεμπε, ἀκόντια δὲ καὶ δοράτια καὶ τὰ τοιαῦτα πάντα τοῖσι χρέωνται ἐς πόλεμον ἄνθρωποι, ἐκ τῶν ἀνδρεώνων ἐκκομίσας ἐς τοὺς θαλάμους συνένησε, μή τί οἱ κρεμάμενον τῷ παιδὶ ἐμπέσῃ.

After Solon had left, the anger of the gods overtook Croesus because, as I think, he thought he was the happiest of men. Immediately a dream came to him while he was sleeping which revealed to him the truth about disasters impending for his son. He had two sons, of whom one was a complete wretch for he was deaf and dumb, but the other, named Atys, was by far outstanding among his peers. The dream revealed to Croesus that Atys should be struck by an iron spear and perish. When he awoke and thought the dream over, Croesus was very afraid, arranged a marriage for Atys, and no longer sent him, accustomed though he was to lead the Lydian armies, on military expeditions. And he removed the javelins and spears and all the weapons men use in war from their rooms and heaped them up in the women's quarters lest any of them suspended above Atys should fall on him.

Adrastus came to Sardis from Phrygia and was purified by Croesus (35). The Mysians begged Croesus' help in dealing with a gigantic boar (36). Atys requested permission, previously refused by Croesus, to go on the hunt (37). Croesus told Atys of the dream (38) but was won over by his son (39, 40). Croesus entrusted Atys to Adrastus (41) who reluctantly promised to help (42). Adrastus killed Atys accidentally (43) and Croesus was distraught (44). Adrastus committed suicide (45) and Croesus mourned his son for two years until roused by Cyrus' defeat of Astyages (46).

Herodotus has inserted a cult-myth into history. His purpose may be paradigmatic. Croesus may historically have had a son who died young; for his grandson see 7.27. Pliny (*Naturalis historia* 11.270) claims that one of Croesus' sons spoke at six months.

90. Herodotus 1.85. 5th c. b.c.

ὁ δὲ παῖς οὗτος ὁ ἄφωνος ὡς εἶδε ἐπιόντα τὸν Πέρσην, ὑπὸ δέους τε καὶ κακοῦ ἔρρηξε φωνήν, εἶπε δέ· Ὤνθρωπε, μὴ κτεῖνε Κροῖσον. οὗτος μὲν δὴ τοῦτο πρῶτον ἐφθέγξατο, μετὰ δὲ τοῦτο ἤδη ἐφώνεε τὸν πάντα χρόνον τῆς ζόης.

When this dumb son saw the Persian approaching, in fear and shock he broke into speech and said, "Man, do not kill Croesus." This son spoke then for the first time, and afterwards he was able to speak for the rest of his life.

On the sudden speech of the dumb son see also A. Gellius 5.9; Pliny, *Naturalis historia* 11.270; and cf. Apostolius 16.99; Solinus 1.112.

91. Valerius Maximus 1.7 Ext. 4.　　　　1st c. A.D.

Efficax et illa quietis imago, quae Croesi regis animum maximo prius metu, deinde etiam dolore confecit: nam e duobus filiis et ingeni agilitate et corporis dotibus praestantiorem imperiique succes-sioni destinatum Atym existimauit ferro sibi erep-tum.

That dream also was effective which filled the mind of Croesus the king at first with great alarm and subsequently with grief. For he believed that of his two sons the one that excelled in intellectual agility and physical prowess and was destined to succeed to the throne, Atys, would be stolen from him by iron.

The story is repeated from Herodotus 1.34ff (see *89*).

92. Valerius Maximus 5.4 Ext. 6.　　　　1st c. A.D.

captis enim a Cyro Sardibus, cum unus e numero Persarum ignarus viri in caedem eius concitato im-petu ferretur, velut oblitus quid sibi fortuna nascenti denegasset, ne Croesum regem occideret procla-mando paene iam inpressum iugulo mucronem revocauit.

For when Sardis had been taken by Cyrus and one of the Persians, ignorant of the identity of his victim, was rushing headlong to kill Croesus, his son, as if oblivious of the handicap with which Fortune had saddled him at birth, shouted that he should not kill king Croesus, and by so doing, checked the dagger at that moment poised at the king's throat.

Contemporaries of Croesus

93. Diogenes Laertius 1.81.　　　　3rd c. A.D.

Πιττακὸς Κροίσῳ

Κέλεαί με ἱκνέεσθαι ἐς Λυδίην, ὅπως σοι τὸν ὄλβον ἴδοιμι· ἐγὼ δὲ καὶ μὴ ὀρεὶς πέπεισμαι τὸν Ἀλυάττεω παῖδα τῶν βασιλήων πολυχρυσότατον πέλειν. οὐδέν τε πλέον ἄμμιν ἱκομένοις ἐς Σάρδις· χρυσοῦ γὰρ οὐ δεύμεθα, ἀλλὰ πέπαμαι ἄρκια καὶ τοῖς ἐμοῖς ἑτάροις. ἔμπας δ' ἵξομαι, ὡς ἀνδρὶ ξείνῳ γενοίμην τοι συνόμιλος.

Pittacus to Croesus

You urge me to come to Lydia to see your prosperity. But without seeing it I am persuaded that Alyattes'

son is the richest of kings. There is no point in my coming to Sardis, for I am not without gold and I have enough for myself and my friends. But I will come to get to know someone who wants to receive me.

After describing Pittacus in unflattering terms, Diogenes records this letter.

On Pittacus see A. Andrewes, *Greek Tyrants* (London 1956) 92–99, 117. On Pittacus and Croesus see also Diogenes Laertius 1.30, 1.75, 1.77.

94. Diogenes Laertius 1.105.　　　　3rd c. A.D.

Ἀνάχαρσις Κροίσῳ

Ἐγώ, βασιλεῦ Λυδῶν, ἀφῖγμαι εἰς τὴν τῶν Ἑλλήνων, διδαχθησόμενος ἤθη τὰ τούτων καὶ ἐπιτηδεύματα. χρυσοῦ δ' οὐδὲν δέομαι, ἀλλ' ἀπόχρη με ἐπανήκειν ἐς Σκύθας ἄνδρα ἀμείνονα. ἥκω γοῦν ἐς Σάρδεις, πρὸ μεγάλου ποιούμενος ἐν γνώμῃ τοι γενέσθαι.

Anacharsis to Croesus

O King of the Lydians, I have come to the land of the Greeks to learn their customs and habits. I do not want any gold but it is sufficient for me if I return to Scythia a better man. Anyway I have arrived in Sardis, most anxious to meet you.

On Anacharsis see Herodotus 4.46, 4.76ff. Among other achievements he invented the anchor.

On Croesus elsewhere in Diogenes Laertius see 1.25 (and Miletus); 1.29 (and the golden goblet); 1.50ff, 1.67 (and Solon).

95. Plutarch, *De fraterno amore* 12 (484C).

　　　　1st–2nd c. A.D.

χρήσθω δὲ καὶ παραδείγμασιν ἐνδόξοις οἷόν ἐστι καὶ τὸ τοῦ Πιττακοῦ πρὸς τὸν βασιλέα Λυδῶν πυνθανό-μενον εἰ χρήματ' ἔστιν αὐτῷ, "διπλάσι'" εἶπεν "ἢ ἐβουλόμην, τοῦ ἀδελφοῦ τεθνηκότος."

Let him use famous paradigms such as the statement of Pittacus to the king of Lydia when he asked whether Pittacus had money: "Double what I would wish, now my brother is dead."

The Lydian king is Croesus: cf. Diogenes Laertius 1.75. For Pittacus and Alyattes see *Septem sapientium convivium* 10 (153E).

96. Plutarch, *Septem sapientium convivium* 4 (150A).

　　　　1st–2nd c. A.D.

ὁ δ' Αἴσωπος (ἐτύγχανε γὰρ ὑπὸ Κροίσου νεωστὶ πρός τε Περίανδρον ἅμα καὶ πρὸς τὸν θεὸν εἰς Δελφοὺς ἀπε-σταλμένος καὶ παρῆν ἐπὶ δίφρου τινὸς χαμαιζήλου παρὰ τὸν Σόλωνα καθήμενος ἄνω κατακείμενον) . . .

Aesop happened lately to have been sent by Croesus
to Periander and to the god at Delphi, and he too
was present sitting on a low stool close by Solon
who was reclining just above . . .

Cf. Plutarch, *Solon* 28; *De sera numinis vindicta* 12
(556F). For Aesop ill-received in Delphi see Callimachus,
Iambi 172. On Aesop and Croesus see Zenobius 5.16;
Apostolius 11.3.

Croesus and Oracles

(**107**) Aristotle, *Rhetoric* 3.1407a (5.4).　　　4th c. B.C.

(**108**) Cicero, *Poetica fragmenta* 90.　　　1st c. B.C.

97. Athenaeus, *Deipnosophistae* 6.231e–232a.

2nd–3rd c. A.D.

καὶ τὰ ἐν Δελφοῖς δὲ ἀναθήματα τὰ ἀργυρᾶ καὶ τὰ
χρυσᾶ ὑπὸ πρώτου Γύγου τοῦ Λυδῶν βασιλέως ἀνετέθη·
καὶ πρὸ τῆς τούτου βασιλείας ἀνάργυρος, ἔτι δὲ ἄχρυσος
ἦν ὁ Πύθιος, ὡς Φαινίας τέ φησιν ὁ Ἐρέσιος καὶ Θεόπο-
μπος ἐν τῇ τεσσαρακοστῇ τῶν Φιλιππικῶν. ἱστοροῦσι
γὰρ οὗτοι κοσμηθῆναι τὸ Πυθικὸν ἱερὸν ὑπό τε τοῦ
Γύγου καὶ τοῦ μετὰ τοῦτον Κροίσου, μεθ' οὓς ὑπό τε
Γέλωνος καὶ Ἱέρωνος τῶν Σικελιωτῶν, τοῦ μὲν τρίποδα
καὶ Νίκην χρυσοῦ πεποιημένα ἀναθέντος καθ' οὓς
χρόνους Ξέρξης ἐπεστράτευε τῇ Ἑλλάδι, τοῦ δ' Ἱέρωνος
τὰ ὅμοια. λέγει δ' οὕτως ὁ Θεόπομπος· "ἦν γὰρ τὸ
παλαιὸν τὸ ἱερὸν κεκοσμημένον χαλκοῖς ἀναθήμασιν,
οὐκ ἀνδριᾶσιν ἀλλὰ λέβησι καὶ τρίποσι χαλκοῦ πεποιη-
μένοις. Λακεδαιμόνιοι οὖν χρυσῶσαι βουλόμενοι τὸ
πρόσωπον τοῦ ἐν Ἀμύκλαις Ἀπόλλωνος καὶ οὐχ εὑρίσ-
κοντες ἐν τῇ Ἑλλάδι χρυσίον πέμψαντες εἰς θεοῦ
ἐπηρώτων τὸν θεὸν παρ' οὗ χρυσίον πρίαιντο. ὁ δ'
αὐτοῖς ἀνεῖλεν παρὰ Κροίσου τοῦ Λυδοῦ πορευθέντας
ὠνεῖσθαι. καὶ οἱ πορευθέντες παρὰ Κροίσου ὠνήσαντο."

The silver and gold dedications in Delphi were set up
first by Gyges, king of the Lydians. Before him the
Pythian god was without silver, and gold for that
matter, as Phaenias of Eresus says and Theopompus
in the fortieth book of the *Philippika*. These historians tell us that the Pythian sanctuary was
adorned by Gyges and his successor Croesus, and
after them by Gelon and Hieron, the Sicilians. Gelon
set up a golden tripod and a Nike at the time when
Xerxes was invading Greece, and Hieron made
similar dedications. The following is what Theopompus says—"Long ago the sanctuary was adorned
with bronze gifts which were not statues but bronze
cauldrons and tripods. The Spartans who wanted to
gild the face of the Apollo of Amyclae, but who
could not find any gold in Greece, sent to Apollo's
oracle and asked where they might buy gold. He
told them to go and buy it from Croesus the Lydian;
and they went and bought it from him."

For Phaenias of Eresus see *FGrHist* IIIB 443, 658;
FHG 2.297. For Theopompus see *FGrHist* 115 F 193.

98. Diodorus Siculus 16.56.6.　　　1st c. B.C.

τὰς γὰρ ἀνατεθείσας ὑπὸ Κροίσου τοῦ Λυδῶν βασιλέως
χρυσᾶς πλίνθους, οὔσας ἑκατὸν καὶ εἴκοσι διταλάντους,
κατέκοψεν εἰς νόμισμα, φιάλας δὲ χρυσᾶς τριακοσίας καὶ
ἑξήκοντα διμναίους καὶ λέοντα χρυσοῦν καὶ γυναῖκα,
τριάκοντα ταλάντων χρυσοῦ σταθμὸν ἀγόντων τῶν πάντων. ὥστε τὸ πᾶν κατακοπὲν χρυσίον εἰς ἀργυρίου
λόγον ἀναγομένων τῶν χρημάτων εὑρίσκεσθαι τάλαντα
τετρακισχίλια· τῶν δ' ἀργυρῶν ἀναθημάτων τῶν τε
ὑπὸ Κροίσου καὶ τῶν ἄλλων ἁπάντων ἀνατεθέντων τοὺς
πάντας στρατηγοὺς δεδαπανηκέναι τάλαντα πλείω τῶν
ἑξακισχιλίων, προστιθεμένων δὲ καὶ τῶν χρυσῶν ἀναθημάτων ὑπερβάλλειν τὰ μύρια τάλαντα.

For he coined for money one hundred twenty gold
bricks dedicated by Croesus the king of the Lydians,
each weighing two talents, and three hundred sixty
gold goblets weighing two minae each, and golden
statues of a lion and a woman, weighing in all thirty
talents of gold. The total of gold coined to money,
referred to the standard of silver, is found to be four
thousand talents. The generals had also expended six
thousand talents derived from the silver dedications
of Croesus and all the others, and when the gold
offerings are added to these, the sum exceeded ten
thousand talents.

Diodorus refers to the pillaging of Delphi in the fourth
century B.C.
For the dedications cf. Diodorus 9.10.6.
On the bricks forming the base of the golden lion see
G. W. Elderkin, *Archaeological Papers* II (Springfield,
Mass. 1941) 1–8.

99. Herodotus 1.46ff.　　　5th c. B.C.

μετὰ ὧν τὴν διάνοιαν ταύτην αὐτίκα ἀπεπειρᾶτο τῶν
μαντηίων τῶν τε ἐν Ἕλλησι καὶ τοῦ ἐν Λιβύῃ, διαπέμψας ἄλλους ἄλλῃ, τοὺς μὲν ἐς Δελφοὺς ἰέναι, τοὺς δὲ ἐς
Ἄβας τὰς Φωκέων, τοὺς δὲ ἐς Δωδώνην· οἱ δέ τινες
ἐπέμποντο παρά τε Ἀμφιάρεων καὶ παρὰ Τροφώνιον,
οἱ δὲ τῆς Μιλησίης ἐς Βραγχίδας. ταῦτα μέν νυν τὰ
Ἑλληνικὰ μαντήια ἐς τὰ ἀπέπεμψε μαντευσόμενος Κροῖ-
σος· Λιβύης δὲ παρὰ Ἄμμωνα ἀπέστειλε ἄλλους
χρησομένους. διέπεμπε δὲ πειρώμενος τῶν μαντηίων
ὅ τι φρονέοιεν, ὡς εἰ φρονέοντα τὴν ἀληθείην εὑρεθείη,

ἐπείρηταί σφεα δεύτερα πέμπων εἰ ἐπιχειρέοι ἐπὶ
Πέρσας στρατεύεσθαι.

In accordance with this decision he immediately
tested the oracles in Greece and the one in Libya
sending envoys hither and thither, some to Delphi,
some to Abae in Phocis and some to Dodona.
Others were sent to Amphiaraus and Trophonius
and to the Branchidae at Miletus. These are the
names of the Greek oracles to which Croesus sent
for oracular information; and he sent other messengers to consult Ammon in Libya. He sent to test
the knowledge of the oracles so that if he found they
knew the truth, he could send again to ask if he
should attempt a campaign against the Persians.

*Croesus' instructions to the envoys and the reply of
the Delphic oracle (47). At Sardis Croesus acknowledged the accuracy of Delphi (48). Of the rest only
Amphiaraus proved satisfactory (49). A great sacrifice
was given at Sardis for Apollo and numerous gifts sent
to Delphi: gold bricks, a gold lion, a gold bowl, a gold
statue, a silver bowl, the work of Theodorus of Samos
(50, 51). A gold shield and spear were sent to Amphiaraus (52). Croesus consulted the oracles again (53)
and again rewarded Delphi (54). His third question is
addressed to Delphi (55). Again he misunderstood the
reply and began to seek an alliance with the Greeks
(56).*

By Herodotus' chronology, ca. 551–550 B.C.
On Abae see 8.27, 8.33, 8.134, and cf. Pausanias 10.35.
On Amphiaraus and Trophonius see 8.134. On Apollo at
Didyma see 1.157, 1.158, 2.159, 6.19. Strabo mentions the
Medizing of the Branchidae (14.1.5) and their downfall
(11.11.4). On Zeus Ammon see 2.42.

For another religious holocaust see Lucian, *De dea
Syria* 49. Theodorus was well known (3.41; Pausanias
8.14, 10.38; Pliny *Naturalis historia* 34.83). The Marmor
Parium (*FGrHist* 239 F 41) places Croesus' embassies to
Delphi in the archonship of Euthydemus at Athens. For
gifts from Croesus to Delphi at another occasion see
Plutarch, *De sera numinis vindicta* 556F. For a tripod
dedicated by Croesus at Delphi see Julius Valerius, *Res
gestae Alexandri Macedonis* 1.50.

100. Herodotus 1.92.   5th c. B.C.

Κροίσῳ δὲ ἔστι καὶ ἄλλα ἀναθήματα ἐν τῇ Ἑλλάδι
πολλὰ καὶ οὐ τὰ εἰρημένα μοῦνα, ἐν μὲν γὰρ Θήβῃσι
τῇσι Βοιωτῶν τρίπους χρύσεος, τὸν ἀνέθηκε τῷ Ἀπόλ-
λωνι τῷ Ἰσμηνίῳ, ἐν δὲ Ἐφέσῳ αἵ τε βόες αἱ χρύσεαι
καὶ τῶν κιόνων αἱ πολλαί, ἐν δὲ Προνηίης τῆς ἐν
Δελφοῖσι ἀσπὶς χρυσέη μεγάλη. ταῦτα μὲν καὶ ἔτι ἐς
ἐμὲ ἦν περιεόντα, τὰ δ' ἐξαπόλωλε [τὰ] τῶν ἀναθημάτων. τὰ δ' ἐν Βραγχίδῃσι τῇσι Μιλησίων ἀναθήματα

Κροίσῳ, ὡς ἐγὼ πυνθάνομαι, ἴσα τε σταθμὸν καὶ
ὅμοια τοῖσι ἐν Δελφοῖσι. τὰ μὲν νυν ἔς τε Δελφοὺς
καὶ ἐς τοῦ Ἀμφιάρεω ἀνέθηκε οἰκήιά τε ἐόντα καὶ
τῶν πατρωίων χρημάτων ἀπαρχήν, τὰ δὲ ἄλλα ἀναθήματα ἐξ ἀνδρὸς ἐγένετο οὐσίης ἐχθροῦ, ὅς οἱ πρὶν ἢ
βασιλεῦσαι ἀντιστασιώτης κατεστήκεε συσπεύδων
Πανταλέοντι γενέσθαι τὴν Λυδῶν ἀρχήν. ὁ δὲ Πανταλέων ἦν Ἀλυάττεω μὲν παῖς, Κροίσου δὲ ἀδελφεὸς οὐκ
ὁμομήτριος· Κροῖσος μὲν γὰρ ἐκ Καείρης ἦν γυναικὸς
Ἀλυάττῃ, Πανταλέων δὲ ἐξ Ἰάδος. ἐπείτε δὲ δόντος
τοῦ πατρὸς ἐκράτησε τῆς ἀρχῆς ὁ Κροῖσος, τὸν ἄνθρωπον τὸν ἀντιπρήσσοντα ἐπὶ κνάφου ἕλκων διέφθειρε,
τὴν δὲ οὐσίην αὐτοῦ ἔτι πρότερον κατιρώσας τότε
τρόπῳ τῷ εἰρημένῳ ἀνέθηκε ἐς τὰ εἴρηται.

Croesus made many other dedications in the Greek
world besides those which I have mentioned. For in
Boetian Thebes there is a golden tripod which he
set up to Ismenian Apollo, and at Ephesus the
golden oxen and many of the columns, and a great
gold shield in the temple of Pronoia at Delphi.
These objects survived until my time, but some of
his gifts have been destroyed. It is my understanding
that the dedications of Croesus at Milesian Branchidae were equal in weight and appearance to
those at Delphi. The gifts to Delphi and Amphiaraus
were his own from money inherited from his
family, but the others were paid for out of the estate
of an enemy who opposed him before he became
king and who had exerted his efforts that Pantaleon
should become the monarch. Pantaleon was also
a son of Alyattes and half-brother to Croesus; for
Croesus was Alyattes' son by a Carian, and
Pantaleon by an Ionian. When Croesus became
king by his father's gift, he did away with the man
who had opposed him by putting him on the wheel,
took possession of his estate, and then dedicated it
as I have explained.

On the temple of Ismenian Apollo at Thebes see 8.134,
5.59; Pausanias 9.10.2; and Pindar, *Pythian* 11.6. On
Athena Pronoia see 8.37; Aeschylus, *Eumenides* 21;
Pausanias 10.8.6. On the carding-machine cf. E. L.
Leutsch and F. G. Schneidewin, *Corpus paroemio-
graphorum Graecorum* I (Hildesheim 1958) 410–411.

101. Pindar, *Pythian Odes* 1.93–98.   5th c. B.C.

οὐ φθίνει Κροί-
σου φιλόφρων ἀρετά.
τὸν δὲ ταύρῳ χαλκέῳ καυτῆρα νηλέα νόον
ἐχθρὰ Φάλαριν κατέχει παντᾷ φάτις,
οὐδέ μιν φόρμιγγες ὑπωρόφιαι κοινανίαν
μαλθακὰν παίδων ὀάροισι δέκονται.

The generous excellence of Croesus does not perish, but a grim repute attaches always to Phalaris who pitilessly burnt his enemies in his bronze bull. Lyres sounding in the halls do not welcome him as a gentle topic to be shared with the children's songs.

Croesus continued to get a good press in the Greek world, especially, we may suppose, at Delphi.
Phalaris had been tyrant of Acragas.
For Lydian flutes see *Olympian Odes* 5.19; for Lydian harmony see *Nemean Odes* 4.45; for the Lydian "mode" *Olympian Odes* 14.17; for the Lydian *mitra* see *Nemean Odes* 8.15 and cf. Alcman 1.68 (D. L. Page, *Poetae melici Graeci* [Oxford 1962]); W. Schadewaldt, *Studies Presented to David Moore Robinson on His Seventieth Birthday* (St. Louis 1951) II 48.

102. Schol. Plato, *Republic* 566c.

Κροῖσος υἱὸς 'Αλυάττου, Λυδὸς γένος, βασιλεὺς τῶν ἐντὸς ''Αλυος ποταμοῦ, ὃς περὶ τῆς ἀρχῆς, εἰ πολυχρόνιος ἔσται, χρηστηριαζόμενος, ἀνεῖλεν ὁ 'Απόλλων χρησμὸν τοιοῦτον αὐτῷ·—

ἀλλ' ὅτ' ἂν ἡμίονος βασιλεὺς Μήδοισι γένηται,
καὶ τότε, Λυδὲ πόδαβρε πολυψήφιδα παρ' ''Ερμον
φεύγειν, μὴ δὲ μένειν, μηδ' αἰδεῖσθαι κακὸς εἶναι.

καὶ οὗτος μὲν ὁ ὅλος χρησμός· ἡμίονον δὲ τὸν Κῦρόν φησιν, ἐπείπερ 'Αρυήνης τῆς 'Αλυάττου θυγατρός, Λυδῆς οὔσης αὐτῆς, καὶ 'Αστυάγους τοῦ Μηδῶν βασιλέως Μανδάνη γίγνεται παῖς, ταύτης δὲ καὶ Καμβύσου, Πέρσου τινός, ὁ Κῦρος υἱός, ὁ καθελὼν Κροῖσόν τε καὶ δὴ καὶ αὐτὴν τὴν βασιλείαν Λυδῶν.

Croesus was the son of Alyattes, a Lydian by birth and king of the nations west of the Halys. When he inquired of the oracle whether his rule would be long-lived, Apollo returned the following reply: "Whenever a mule becomes master of the Medes, then, soft-footed Lydian, flee by the stony Hermus, and do not remain nor be ashamed to be a coward." This was the complete response. And they say that the mule was Cyrus. For Mandane, mother of Cyrus, was the daughter of Aryene, a Lydian and daughter of Alyattes, and Astyages king of the Medes. Cyrus was her son by Cambyses the Persian, and it was Cyrus who overthrew Croesus and the Lydian empire.

From Herodotus 1.55 (see *99*); 1.74 (see *60*); 1.91 (see *125*); 107ff.

Croesus and Sparta

(97) Athenaeus, *Deipnosophistae* 6.231e–232a.
2nd–3rd c. A.D.

103. Herodotus 1.69.   5th c. B.C.

πέμψαντες γὰρ οἱ Λακεδαιμόνιοι ἐς Σάρδις χρυσὸν ὠνέοντο, ἐς ἄγαλμα βουλόμενοι χρήσασθαι τοῦτο τὸ νῦν τῆς Λακωνικῆς ἐν Θόρνακι ἵδρυται 'Απόλλωνος, Κροῖσος δέ σφι ὠνεομένοισι ἔδωκε δωτίνην.

For the Spartans sent to Sardis to buy gold, wishing to use it for the statue of Apollo which now stands on Mt. Thornax in Laconia. But though they intended to purchase it, Croesus gave it to them as a gift.

104. Herodotus 1.70.   5th c. B.C.

Τούτων τε ὦν εἵνεκεν οἱ Λακεδαιμόνιοι τὴν συμμαχίην ἐδέξαντο, καὶ ὅτι ἐκ πάντων σφέας προκρίνας 'Ελλήνων αἱρέετο φίλους. καὶ τοῦτο μὲν αὐτοὶ ἦσαν ἕτοιμοι ἐπαγγείλαντι, τοῦτο δὲ ποιησάμενοι κρητῆρα χάλκεον ζῳδίων τε ἔξωθεν πλήσαντες περὶ τὸ χεῖλος καὶ μεγάθεϊ τριηκοσίους ἀμφορέας χωρέοντα ἦγον, δῶρον βουλόμενοι ἀντιδοῦναι Κροίσῳ. οὗτος ὁ κρητὴρ οὐκ ἀπίκετο ἐς Σάρδις δι' αἰτίας διφασίας λεγομένας τάσδε· οἱ μὲν Λακεδαιμόνιοι λέγουσι ὡς ἐπείτε ἀγόμενος ἐς τὰς Σάρδις ὁ κρητὴρ ἐγίνετο κατὰ τὴν Σαμίην, πυθόμενοι Σάμιοι ἀπελοίατο αὐτὸν νηυσὶ μακρῇσι ἐπιπλώσαντες· αὐτοὶ δὲ Σάμιοι λέγουσι ὡς ἐπείτε ὑστέρησαν οἱ ἄγοντες τῶν Λακεδαιμονίων τὸν κρητῆρα, ἐπυνθάνοντο δὲ Σάρδις τε καὶ Κροῖσον ἡλωκέναι, ἀπέδοντο τὸν κρητῆρα ἐν Σάμῳ, ἰδιώτας δὲ ἄνδρας πριαμένους ἀναθεῖναί μιν ἐς τὸ ''Ηραιον.

The Spartans accepted the alliance for these reasons, and because, preferring them above all the Greeks, he had chosen them as his friends. So if he summoned them they were ready. They also made a bronze krater decorated with small figures on the lip and large enough to hold 300 amphorae, and they set off with it wishing to present it to Croesus. This bowl never reached Sardis and the two following reasons are given for this. The Spartans say that when the krater was en route to Sardis and was near Samos, the Samians heard about it, attacked them with warships, and took it off. But the Samians say that when the Spartans who were bringing the krater were late and discovered that Sardis and Croesus were taken, they sold the krater in Samos and the private citizens who purchased it dedicated it in the Heraion.

The treaty with Sparta was struck perhaps ca. 548 B.C.
On this tale see Plutarch, *De Herodoti malignitate* 21 859C and cf. Herodotus 3.47.
A krater similar in size and decoration to this bowl has been recovered in the tomb of a Celtic princess at Vix near Châtillon-sur-Seine: for which see R. Joffroy, *MonPiot* 48 (1954) 1–68.

105. Pausanias 3.10.6.   2nd c. A.D.

Λακεδαιμονίοις γὰρ ἐπιφανέστερά ἐστι τὰ ἐς τὸν
'Αμυκλαῖον, ὥστε καὶ τὸν χρυσόν, ὃν Κροῖσος ὁ Λυδὸς
τῷ 'Απόλλωνι ἔπεμψε τῷ Πυθαεῖ, τούτῳ ἐς κόσμον
τοῦ ἐν 'Αμύκλαις κατεχρήσαντο ἀγάλματος.

For the Spartans the cult of the Amyclean is the
more illustrious, so that they used the gold which
Croesus the Lydian had sent for Apollo Pythaeus,
to decorate the statue in Amyclae.

106. Pausanias 4.5.3.   2nd c. A.D.

Κροίσῳ τε αὐτοῖς δῶρα ἀποστείλαντι γενέσθαι φίλους
βαρβάρῳ πρώτους, ἀφ' οὗ γε τούς τε ἄλλους τοὺς ἐν τῇ
'Ασίᾳ κατεδουλώσατο "Ελληνας καὶ ὅσοι Δωριεῖς ἐν
τῇ Καρικῇ κατοικοῦσιν ἠπείρῳ.

After Croesus had sent them gifts, they were the
first to become friends with the barbarian. This was
when he had enslaved the other Greeks in Asia and
as many Dorians as inhabit the mainland of Caria.

The gifts were gold for the statue of Apollo on Mt.
Thornax. For one of Croesus' dedications at Delphi see
10.8.7. Other references in Pausanias to Croesus include
3.2.3, 8.24.13.

The Campaign to the Halys

107. Aristotle, *Rhetoric* 3.1407a (5.4).   4th c. B.C.

Κροῖσος "Αλυν διαβὰς μεγάλην ἀρχὴν καταλύσει.

When once Croesus has crossed the Halys he will
destroy a great empire.

Aristotle alludes to the oracle: for which cf. Herodotus
1.46 (see 99).
Apparently it was common knowledge that the Halys
formed the frontier between Lydia and Persia in Croesus'
time. At no other period does the river appear to have
been significant politically. Cf. M. Cary, *The Geographic
Background of Greek and Roman History* (Oxford 1949)
7, 151, 159, 161.
On the Halys cf. schol. Apollonius Rhodius 2.948 for
Apollo and Zeus causing the river to wander about.
Cf. also Dio Chrysostom, *Orationes* 10.26.

108. Cicero, *Poetica fragmenta* 90.   1st c. B.C.

Croesus Halyn penetrans magnam pervertet
                 opum vim.

If he crosses the Halys, Croesus will destroy a
great empire.

Another allusion to the oracle reported in Herodotus
1.46 (see 99). See also *De divinatione* 2.115; and cf.
Lucan 3.272 with scholia.

109. Harpocration, s.v. *Eurubaton*.   1st or 2nd c. A.D.

"Εφορος ἐν τῇ ἡ Εὐρύβατόν φησιν ἄνδρα 'Εφέσιον
λαβόντα χρήματα παρὰ Κροίσου ὥστε στρατιὰν συνα-
γαγεῖν εἰς τὸν πόλεμον τὸν εἰς τοὺς Πέρσας, εἶτα
προδότην γενόμενον ἐγχειρίσαι τὰ δοθέντα χρήματα
τῷ Κύρῳ, καὶ ἐντεῦθεν τοὺς πονηροὺς Εὐρυβάτους
καλεῖσθαι.

In his eighth book Ephorus says that Eurybatus,
an Ephesian, took money from Croesus to muster
an army for the war against the Persians. He then
turned traitor and handed over the money he had
been given to Cyrus; and from this event cheats
are called Eurybati.

See Ephorus *FGrHist* 70 F 58; and cf. Suidas, s.v.
Eurybatus.

110. Herodotus 1.71ff.   5th c. B.C.

Κροῖσος δὲ ἁμαρτὼν τοῦ χρησμοῦ ἐποιέετο στρατηίην
ἐς Καππαδοκίην, ἐλπίσας καταιρήσειν Κῦρόν τε καὶ
τὴν Περσέων δύναμιν. παρασκευαζομένου δὲ Κροίσου
στρατεύεσθαι ἐπὶ Πέρσας, τῶν τις Λυδῶν νομιζόμενος
καὶ πρόσθε εἶναι σοφός, ἀπὸ δὲ ταύτης τῆς γνώμης καὶ
τὸ κάρτα οὔνομα ἐν Λυδοῖσι ἔχων, συνεβούλευσε
Κροίσῳ τάδε· οὔνομά οἱ ἦν Σάνδανις.

Croesus misunderstood the oracle and invaded
Cappadocia hoping to overthrow Cyrus and the
might of Persia. But while he was preparing to
campaign against the Persians, one of the Lydians
who had a reputation for wisdom even before this,
and who won great renown among the Lydians as
a result of his counsel at this time, gave the following
advice to Croesus. His name was Sandanis.
*Sandanis to no avail pointed out that Croesus had
more to lose than to gain. The Halys, the frontier
between the Persian and Lydian empires (72). The
reasons for Croesus' campaign (73).*

111. Herodotus 1.76ff.   5th c. B.C.

Κροῖσος δὲ ἐπείτε διαβὰς σὺν τῷ στρατῷ ἀπίκετο τῆς
Καππαδοκίης ἐς τὴν Πτερίην καλεομένην (ἡ δὲ Πτερίη
ἐστὶ τῆς χώρης ταύτης τὸ ἰσχυρότατον κατὰ Σινώπην
πόλιν τὴν ἐν Εὐξείνῳ πόντῳ μάλιστά κῃ κειμένην),
ἐνθαῦτα ἐστρατοπεδεύετο φθείρων τῶν Συρίων τοὺς
κλήρους. καὶ εἷλε μὲν τῶν Πτερίων τὴν πόλιν καὶ ἠνδρα-
ποδίσατο, εἷλε δὲ τὰς περιοικίδας αὐτῆς πάσας,
Συρίους τε οὐδὲν ἐόντας αἰτίους ἀναστάτους ἐποίησε.

Κῦρος δὲ ἀγείρας τὸν ἑωυτοῦ στρατὸν καὶ παραλαβὼν
τοὺς μεταξὺ οἰκέοντας πάντας ἠντιοῦτο Κροίσῳ. πρὶν
δὲ ἐξελαύνειν ὁρμῆσαι τὸν στρατόν, πέμψας κήρυκας
ἐς τοὺς Ἴωνας ἐπειρᾶτό σφεας ἀπὸ Κροίσου ἀπιστάναι.
Ἴωνες μέν νυν οὐκ ἐπείθοντο, Κῦρος δὲ ὡς ἀπίκετο καὶ
ἀντεστρατοπεδεύσατο Κροίσῳ, ἐνθαῦτα ἐν τῇ Πτερίῃ
χώρῃ ἐπειρῶντο κατὰ τὸ ἰσχυρὸν ἀλλήλων. μάχης δὲ
καρτερῆς γενομένης καὶ πεσόντων ἀμφοτέρων πολλῶν
τέλος οὐδέτεροι νικήσαντες διέστησαν νυκτὸς ἐπελ-
θούσης. καὶ τὰ μὲν στρατόπεδα ἀμφότερα οὕτως
ἠγωνίσατο.

When Croesus had crossed with his army he arrived
in the part of Cappadocia called Pteria which is
the strongest area in the country and is situated
close to the city of Sinope on the Euxine. Here he
made his camp and destroyed the settlements of the
Syrians. He captured and enslaved the city of the
Pterians and he took all the places around there,
making the Syrians homeless though they had been
guilty of nothing. Cyrus set his army in motion,
enlisted all who dwelt along his line of march, and
approached Croesus. But before he began the
campaign he sent heralds to the Ionians and asked
them to revolt from Croesus. But the Ionians did
not listen. When Cyrus had arrived and encamped
opposite Croesus, there in the Pterian land they
tested one another's strength. The battle was grim,
many fell on either side, and with no clear victor
they separated at nightfall: such was the outcome
of the two armies' struggle.
*In view of Cyrus' advantage in numbers, Croesus
returned to Sardis and summoned his allies to come
after the winter in the fifth month (77). Snakes
swarmed in Sardis and Croesus sent to consult the
oracle at Telmessus (78). Cyrus took Croesus by
surprise by following him and appearing before
Sardis (79).*

This was the campaigning season of 547 B.C.
Others (Justin 1.7 [see *117*]; Polyaenus 7.6.2 [see *119*])
say that Croesus was defeated on the Halys. Polyaenus
(ibid.) intimates that the Persian pursuit followed fast.
Ephorus (*FGrHist* 70 F 58) reports that one Ionian any-
way, Eurybatus of Ephesus, defected to Cyrus.
On Pteria see K. Bittel, *Hattusha: Capital of the
Hittites* (New York 1970) 11–112.

112. Ctesias of Cnidus, *FGrHist* 688 F 9 (4).

4th c. B.C.

καὶ ὅτι στρατεύει Κῦρος ἐπὶ Κροῖσον καὶ πόλιν Σάρδεις,
συνεργὸν ἔχων Ἀμόργην· ὅπως τε βουλῇ Οἰβάρα
Περσῶν εἴδωλα ξύλινα ἀνὰ τὸ τεῖχος φανέντα εἰς δέος
μὲν κατέστησε τοὺς ἐνοικοῦντας, ἥλω δὲ διὰ ταῦτα.

Cyrus campaigned against Croesus and the city of
Sardis with his ally Amorges. At the suggestion of
Oibares, wooden images of Persians were hoisted
up the wall. When these were seen, they threw the
inhabitants into panic and because of this the city
was taken.

Cf. Polyaenus 7.6.10 (see *119*); Theon, *Progymnasmata*
11.

(117) Justin 1.7.3–4ff.   3rd c. A.D.

The Fall of Sardis

113. Diogenes Laertius 2.3.   3rd c. A.D.

Καὶ γεγένηται μέν, καθά φησιν Ἀπολλόδωρος, περὶ
τὴν Σάρδεων ἅλωσιν, ἐτελεύτησε δὲ τῇ ἑξηκοστῇ τρίτῃ
Ὀλυμπιάδι.

According to what Apollodorus says, he was born
and flourished about the time of the taking of
Sardis, and he died in the sixty-third Olympiad.

Apollodorus (*FGrHist* 244 F 66) describes the life of
Anaximenes. The sixty-third Olympiad fell in 528–525
B.C. Thales also was a contemporary of the events of the
later Mermnad years (Diogenes Laertius 1.38).

114. Favorinus, *De Fortuna* 22.   1st–2nd c. A.D.

τί δὲ μετὰ τοῦ λέοντος Μήλης τὸ τεῖχος περιέρχεται;
κρατήσει γὰρ Μήδων Κῦρος καὶ Βαβυλωνίων Ζώπυρος
καὶ Σάρδεων Μάρδος καὶ Τροίας ὁ ἵππος.

Why does Meles walk around the wall with a lion?
For Cyrus will conquer the Medes, Zopyrus the
Babylonians, a Mardian will overthrow Sardis, and
Troy will fall to the horse.

A favorite of Hadrian, Favorinus was also a friend of
Plutarch and teacher of Herodes Atticus and Gellius. On
him see Philostratus *Vitae sophistarum* 18; Suidas.

115. Herodotus 1.80ff.   5th c. B.C.

ἐς τὸ πεδίον δὲ συνελθόντων τοῦτο τὸ πρὸ τοῦ ἄστεός
ἐστι τοῦ Σαρδιηνοῦ, ἐὸν μέγα τε καὶ ψιλόν (διὰ δὲ
αὐτοῦ ποταμοὶ ῥέοντες καὶ ἄλλοι καὶ Ὕλλος συρ-
ρηγνῦσι ἐς τὸν μέγιστον, καλεόμενον δὲ Ἕρμον, ὃς
ἐξ ὄρεος ἱροῦ μητρὸς Διδυμήνης ῥέων ἐκδιδοῖ ἐς
θάλασσαν κατὰ Φώκαιαν πόλιν).

Then the armies clashed in the plain which is before
the city of Sardis; it is big and broad and the Hyllus
and other rivers course across it and rush together
into the greatest of them all, the Hermus. This

river rises in the mountain holy to the Mother Dindymene and flows into the sea close by the city of Phocaea.

Cyrus employed camels to disturb the horses of the Lydian cavalry, won the victory, and besieged the city. Croesus again summoned his allies (81). The Spartans, in spite of trouble closer to home (82), were ready to help (83).

On the camels see Frontinus, *Strategemata* 2.4.12–13.

116. Herodotus 1.84ff.   5th c. B.C.

Σάρδιες δὲ ἥλωσαν ὧδε· ἐπειδὴ τεσσερεσκαιδεκάτη ἐγένετο ἡμέρη πολιορκεομένῳ Κροίσῳ, Κῦρος τῇ στρατιῇ τῇ ἑωυτοῦ διαπέμψας ἱππέας προεῖπε τῷ πρώτῳ ἐπιβάντι τοῦ τείχεος δῶρα δώσειν. μετὰ δὲ τοῦτο πειρησαμένης τῆς στρατιῆς, ὡς οὐ προεχώρεε, ἐνθαῦτα τῶν ἄλλων πεπαυμένων ἀνὴρ Μάρδος ἐπειρᾶτο προσβαίνων, τῷ οὔνομα ἦν Ὑροιάδης, κατὰ τοῦτο τῆς ἀκροπόλιος τῇ οὐδεὶς ἐτέτακτο φύλακος· οὐ γὰρ ἦν δεινὸν κατὰ τοῦτο μὴ ἁλῷ κοτε. ἀπότομός τε γάρ ἐστι ταύτῃ ἡ ἀκρόπολις καὶ ἄμαχος· τῇ οὐδὲ Μήλης ὁ πρότερον βασιλεὺς Σαρδίων μούνῃ οὐ περιήνεικε τὸν λέοντα τόν οἱ ἡ παλλακὴ ἔτεκε, Τελμησσέων δικασάντων ὡς περιενειχθέντος τοῦ λέοντος τὸ τεῖχος ἔσονται Σάρδιες ἀνάλωτοι. ὁ δὲ Μήλης κατὰ τὸ ἄλλο τεῖχος περιενείκας, τῇ ἦν ἐπίμαχον [τὸ χωρίον] τῆς ἀκροπόλιος, κατηλόγησε τοῦτο ὡς ἐὸν ἄμαχόν τε καὶ ἀπότομον· ἔστι δὲ πρὸς τοῦ Τμώλου τετραμμένον τῆς πόλιος. ὁ ὦν δὴ Ὑροιάδης οὗτος ὁ Μάρδος ἰδὼν τῇ προτεραίῃ τῶν τινα Λυδῶν κατὰ τοῦτο τῆς ἀκροπόλιος καταβάντα ἐπὶ κυνέην ἄνωθεν κατακυλισθεῖσαν καὶ ἀνελόμενον ἐφράσθη καὶ ἐς θυμὸν ἐβάλετο. τότε δὲ δὴ αὐτός τε ἀνεβεβήκεε καὶ κατ' αὐτὸν ἄλλοι Περσέων ἀνέβαινον· προσβάντων δὲ συχνῶν οὕτω δὴ Σάρδιές τε ἡλώκεσαν καὶ πᾶν τὸ ἄστυ ἐπορθέετο.

Sardis was taken in the following way. After he had besieged Croesus for fourteen days, Cyrus sent horsemen about in his army and announced that he would give rewards to the first man who scaled the wall. After this the army attacked but failed to advance. Then when the others had ceased their efforts, a Mardian named Hyroeades tried to climb up the acropolis at the point where there was no guard. There was no fear that the city could ever be taken at this point for the acropolis here was steep and unscalable. This was the only place where Meles the earlier king of Sardis did not carry the lion which his mistress bore him; this was the time when the Telmessians decreed that Sardis should be impregnable when the lion had been carried around the wall. Meles carried the cub around all the rest of the wall where the acropolis could be attacked, but overlooked this place as being unscalable and precipitous. It is on the side of the city towards Tmolus. On the day before, this Mardian, Hyroeades, saw one of the Lydians come down this flank of the acropolis after a helmet that had tumbled down and retrieve it. Hyroeades thought this over. Then he himself climbed up and other Persians after him. And when many had climbed up, Sardis was taken in this way and the whole city was sacked.

Croesus' dumb son was shocked out of his muteness (85).

On 1.84 see G. Bunnens, *Hommages à Marcel Renard*, Collection Latomus 102 (Brussels 1968). On king Meles (a title?) see Nicolas of Damascus *FGrHist* 90 F 16 (see *10*), F 45 (see *31*); cf. Dio Chrysostom, *Orationes* 64.22. For the archaeology of the Mermnad acropolis see G. M. A. Hanfmann, *BASOR* 162 (1961) 34–38, 166 (1962) 35–37, 170 (1963) 31–33.

Some dispute the date of the fall of Sardis. See H. Kaletsch, *Historia* 7 (1958) 39ff; M. Miller, *Klio* 41 (1963) 59ff; H. T. Wade-Gery, *Essays in Greek History* (Oxford 1958) 166, n. 3. The Babylonian archival source is the most laconic; for the Nabonidus-Cyrus Chronicle see S. Smith, *Babylonian Historical Texts* (London 1924) 101, 116 (see *296*); and see also S. Smith, *Isaiah, Chapters XL–LV* (London 1944) 35–36, 135.

On the significance of Croesus and his fate to the Greek mind see M. White, *Phoenix* 23 (1969) 39–48.

117. Justin 1.7.3–4ff.   3rd c. A.D.

Domitis deinde plerisque cum adversus Babylonios bellum gereret, Babyloniis rex Lydorum Croesus, cuius opes divitiaeque insignes ea tempestate erant, in auxilium venit; victusque iam de se sollicitus in regnum refugit. Cyrus quoque post victoriam conpositis in Babylonia rebus bellum transfert in Lydiam.

After subduing several peoples when he was waging war with the Babylonians, the king of the Lydians, Croesus, whose wealth and riches were unparalleled at that time, next came to the help of the Babylonians. He was defeated, and, fearful for his own safety, he fled back to his own kingdom. And when Cyrus had settled matters in Babylon after his victory, he too transferred the war to Lydia.

Croesus was defeated and captured (5), but treated generously (6ff). Help came to Croesus from all sides (9ff) and the Lydians revolted (11), only to be defeated again and turned over to less masculine pursuits (12ff). The story of Gyges and Candaules (14ff).

118. Parthenius, *Love Stories* 22.   1st c. B.C.

Ἔφασαν δέ τινες καὶ τὴν Σαρδίων ἀκρόπολιν ὑπὸ
Κύρου τοῦ Περσῶν βασιλέως ἁλῶναι, προδούσης τῆς
Κροίσου θυγατρὸς Νανίδος. ἐπειδὴ γὰρ ἐπολιόρκει
Σάρδεις Κῦρος καὶ οὐδὲν αὐτῷ εἰς ἅλωσιν τῆς πόλεως
προὔβαινεν, ἐν πολλῷ τε δέει ἦν, μὴ ἀθροισθὲν τὸ
συμμαχικὸν αὖτις τῷ Κροίσῳ διαλύσειεν αὐτῷ τὴν
στρατιάν, τότε τὴν παρθένον ταύτην εἶχε λόγος περὶ
προδοσίας συνθεμένην τῷ Κύρῳ, εἰ κατὰ νόμους
Περσῶν ἕξει γυναῖκα αὐτήν, κατὰ τὴν ἄκραν, μηδενὸς
φυλάσσοντος δι' ὀχυρότητα τοῦ χωρίου, εἰσδέχεσθαι
τοὺς πολεμίους, συνεργῶν αὐτῇ καὶ ἄλλων τινῶν γενο-
μένων· τὸν μέντοι Κῦρον μὴ ἐμπεδῶσαι αὐτῇ τὴν
ὑπόσχεσιν.

Some said that the acropolis of Sardis was captured
by the Persian king Cyrus when Croesus' daughter,
Nanis, betrayed it. For when Cyrus was besieging
Sardis and all his efforts toward taking the city
were fruitless, he was much afraid that Croesus
might muster his allies again and disperse his army.
Then, they said, this girl made an agreement with
Cyrus to betray Sardis on condition that he take
her as his wife in the Persian manner. At the very
top of the citadel where no one was guarding the
place because of its strength, she admitted the
enemy with the help of accomplices. But Cyrus did
not make good his promise.

119. Polyaenus 7.6.2–3ff.   2nd c. A.D.

Κῦρος ἐν ταῖς πρὸς Κροῖσον ἀνοχαῖς ἀπήγαγε τὴν
δύναμιν. ὡς δὲ νὺξ ἐπῆλθε, συντόνως ἀναστρέψας ἐπὶ
τὰς Σάρδεις ἤγαγε καὶ προσπεσὼν τοῖς τείχεσιν ἀφυ-
λάκτοις προσθέμενος κλίμακας κατέσχε τὰς Σάρδεις.

Κῦρος ἐκράτησε Σάρδεων· Κροῖσος κατέσχε τὴν
ἀκρόπολιν ἀναμένων τὴν ἐκ τῆς Ἑλλάδος βοήθειαν.
Κῦρος τοὺς οἰκείους τῶν μετὰ Κροίσου τὴν ἀκρόπολιν
κατεχόντων δήσας ἔδειξε τοῖς πολιορκουμένοις τῷ κή-
ρυκι προστάξας ἀνειπεῖν, ὡς παραδοῦσι μὲν τὴν ἀκρόπολιν ἀποδώσοι τὰ οἰκεῖα σώματα, μὴ βουλομένοις δὲ
παραδοῦναι κρεμάσειε πάντας. οἱ δὲ τὴν ἀκρόπολιν
ἐπὶ σωτηρίᾳ τῶν οἰκείων παρέδωκαν οὐκ ἀναμείναντες
Κροίσου τὰς κενὰς τῶν Ἑλλήνων ἐλπίδας.

During the truce with Croesus Cyrus led his army
away. At nightfall, however, he suddenly reversed
direction, led his troops to Sardis, and fell upon the
unguarded walls; setting ladders against them, he
took the city.

Cyrus took Sardis; but Croesus held the acropolis and waited for help from Greece. Cyrus then
put the relatives of those who held the acropolis
with Croesus in fetters and displayed them to those
who were besieged. At the same time he had instructed a herald to announce that he would surrender their kinfolk alive if they handed over the
acropolis, but if not he would hang them all. Then
they did not wait for Croesus' empty hopes from
the Greeks but gave up the acropolis in return for
the safety of their kin.

*Stern measures against the Lydians when they
revolted (4). Cyrus' tactics against the Lydian
cavalry (6). His method of instilling fear into the
garrison of Sardis and another version of the capture
of the city (10).*

For the Lydian revolt and the treatment of it see
Herodotus 1.154ff (see *142*); Justin 1.7.11–12 (see *117*);
and cf. Plutarch, *Apophthegmata regum et imperatorum:
Xerxes* 2. For the second (7.6.10) version of the capture
of the city see Frontinus, *Strategemata* 3.8.3; Ctesias,
FGrHist 688 F 9 (4) (see *112*).

120. Thucydides 1.16.   5th c. B.C.

ἐπεγένετο δὲ ἄλλοις τε ἄλλοθι κωλύματα μὴ αὐξηθῆναι,
καὶ Ἴωσι προχωρησάντων ἐπὶ μέγα τῶν πραγμάτων
Κῦρος καὶ ἡ Περσικὴ βασιλεία Κροῖσον καθελοῦσα
καὶ ὅσα ἐντὸς Ἅλυος ποταμοῦ πρὸς θάλασσαν, ἐπεσ-
τράτευσε καὶ τὰς ἐν τῇ ἠπείρῳ πόλεις ἐδούλωσε,
Δαρεῖός τε ὕστερον τῷ Φοινίκων ναυτικῷ κρατῶν καὶ
τὰς νήσους.

Hindrances to their growth came to some Hellenic
peoples in some places and to others in others. For
when the Ionians' affairs had greatly prospered,
Cyrus and the Persian empire first overthrew
Croesus and all the communities west of the Halys
and then campaigned against them and enslaved
the mainland cities. Subsequently Darius conquered
the islands with the help of the Phoenician fleet.

For a contrasting view of the power of the Greek
cities in Asia Minor after the fall of Sardis see Herodotus
1.143. See also A.W. Gomme, *A Historical Commentary
on Thucydides* I (Oxford 1945) 127.

121. Xenophon, *Cyropaedia* 6.2.11ff.   5th–4th c. B.C.

συλλέγεσθαι δὲ τὸ στράτευμα ἀμφὶ τὸν Πακτωλὸν
ποταμόν, προϊέναι δὲ μέλλειν αὐτοὺς εἰς Θύμβραρα,
ἔνθα καὶ νῦν ὁ σύλλογος τῶν ὑπὸ βασιλέα βαρβάρων
τῶν κάτω [Συρίας], καὶ ἀγορὰν πᾶσι παρηγγέλθαι
ἐνταῦθα κομίζειν.

The army, they said, was being mustered along the
banks of the Pactolus, but it planned to advance to
Thymbrara. This is the place where nowadays, too,
the king gathers the barbarians from the hinter-

land. And instructions had been given to all to bring goods for market to that place.

Cyrus' scouts sighted the Lydian army (6.3.5) and took prisoners (6.3.9). Croesus marshaled his forces (6.3.11) and sent out cavalry to reconnoiter (6.3.12). Araspas, a spy of Cyrus, returned with information on Croesus' order of battle (6.3.13ff). Cyrus described his battle plan (6.3.21ff) and drew up his forces (6.4.1). Abradatas and Panthea (6.4.2ff). Cyrus addressed his troops (6.4.12ff) and the armies advanced and joined battle (7.1.1ff). Abradatas died in battle (7.1.29ff) and the Persians charged Croesus' Egyptians (7.1.32ff). The Egyptians were won over by Cyrus and settled subsequently by him (7.1.41ff). Cyrus' victory owed primarily to his cavalry; the camel a proletarian animal (7.1.46ff).

For general reference to Cyrus' conquest of Lydia see *Cyropaedia* 1.1.4; for Assyrian alliance with Croesus, see *Cyropaedia* 1.5.3.

122. Xenophon, *Cyropaedia* 7.2.1–4ff. 5th–4th c. B.C.

Καὶ οἱ μὲν ἀμφὶ τὸν Κῦρον δειπνοποιησάμενοι καὶ φυλακὰς καταστήσαντες, ὥσπερ ἔδει, ἐκοιμήθησαν. Κροῖσος μέντοι εὐθὺς ἐπὶ Σάρδεων ἔφευγε σὺν τῷ στρατεύματι· τὰ δ' ἄλλα φῦλα ὅποι ἐδύνατο προσωτάτω ἐν τῇ νυκτὶ τῆς ἐπ' οἶκον ὁδοῦ ἕκαστος ἀπεχώρει. ἐπειδὴ δὲ ἡμέρα ἐγένετο, εὐθὺς ἐπὶ Σάρδεις ἦγε Κῦρος. ὡς δ' ἐγένετο πρὸς τῷ τείχει τῷ ἐν Σάρδεσι, τάς τε μηχανὰς ἀνίστη ὡς προσβαλῶν πρὸς τὸ τεῖχος καὶ κλίμακας παρεσκευάζετο. ταῦτα δὲ ποιῶν κατὰ τὰ ἀποτομώτατα δοκοῦντα εἶναι τοῦ Σαρδιανῶν ἐρύματος τῆς ἐπιούσης νυκτὸς ἀναβιβάζει Χαλδαίους τε καὶ Πέρσας. ἡγήσατο δ' αὐτοῖς ἀνὴρ Πέρσης δοῦλος γεγενημένος τῶν ἐν τῇ ἀκροπόλει τινὸς φρουρῶν καὶ καταμεμαθηκὼς κατάβασιν εἰς τὸν ποταμὸν καὶ ἀνάβασιν τὴν αὐτήν. ὡς δ' ἐγένετο τοῦτο δῆλον ὅτι εἴχετο τὰ ἄκρα, πάντες δὴ ἔφευγον οἱ Λυδοὶ ἀπὸ τῶν τειχῶν ὅποι ἐδύνατο ἕκαστος τῆς πόλεως. Κῦρος δὲ ἅμα τῇ ἡμέρᾳ εἰσῄει εἰς τὴν πόλιν καὶ παρήγγειλεν ἐκ τῆς τάξεως μηδένα κινεῖσθαι.

Those around Cyrus had their supper, posted sentries as was appropriate, and retired for the night. Croesus, however, fled directly toward Sardis with his army; and the other troops made their way as far as they could at night, each on the way to his home. At daybreak Cyrus made straight for Sardis, and when he reached the city walls, he set up his engines and prepared ladders as if he were about to attack the wall. While he was doing this, he sent some Chaldeans and Persians after nightfall up what seemed to be the steepest part of the acropolis of Sardis. A Persian who had been the slave of one of the guards on the acropolis and who had learnt a way down to the river and the same ascent led them. And when it became clear that the acropolis was held, all the Lydians fled from the walls wherever they could in the city. At daybreak Cyrus entered the city and issued orders that no one should move from his position.

Croesus shut himself up in the palace (7.2.5) and later came face to face with Cyrus (7.2.9). The exchange between Cyrus and Croesus (7.2.10ff). Cyrus asked Croesus about the Delphic oracle (7.2.15ff) and gave him back his household (7.2.26ff).

(276) Xenophon, *Cyropaedia* 7.3.4–5ff. 5th–4th c. B.C.

(277) Xenophon, *Cyropaedia* 7.3.15. 5th–4th c. B.C.

123. Zonaras, *Epitome historiarum* 3.23B.

καὶ οἱ ἀμφὶ τὸν Κῦρον δειπνήσαντες ἐκοιμήθησαν, Κροῖσος μέντοι εὐθὺς ἐπὶ Σάρδεις σὺν τῷ στρατεύματι ἔφευγε, τὰ δ' ἄλλα φῦλα ἐν τῇ νυκτὶ ὅπῃ ἠδύναντο ἀπεχώρουν. ἕωθεν δὲ ἐπὶ Σάρδεις καὶ ὁ Κῦρος ἦγε, καὶ πρὸς τῇ πόλει γενόμενος τάς τε μηχανὰς ἀνίστη καὶ ἡτοίμαζε κλίμακας. τῆς δ' ἐπιούσης νυκτὸς ἀναβιβάζει Χαλδαίους τε καὶ Πέρσας κατὰ τὰ ἀποτομώτατα δοκοῦντα εἶναι τοῦ Σαρδιανῶν ἐρύματος. ἡγήσατο δὲ τῆς ὁδοῦ τούτοις Πέρσης ἀνήρ, δοῦλος τῶν ἐν τῇ ἀκροπόλει φρουρῶν ἑνός. ὡς δὲ τὰ ἄκρα εἴχετο, ἔφευγον οἱ Λυδοὶ ἀπὸ τῶν τειχῶν.

Those with Cyrus ate their supper and went to bed, but Croesus immediately fled to Sardis with his army, and the other companies withdrew during the night wherever they could. At dawn Cyrus also came to Sardis and, after arriving at the city, set up his artillery and prepared scaling ladders. As it was dropping dark he sent the Chaldeans and Persians up what appeared to be the steepest part of the fortification of Sardis. A Persian who had been a slave of one of the members of the garrison showed them the way; and when the heights were secured the Lydians fled from the walls.

Cyrus and Croesus conversed and Croesus surrendered the city.

Croesus on the Pyre

124. Bacchylides, *Epinicia* 3.23–62. 5th c. B.C.

ἐπεί ποτε καὶ δαμασίππου
Λυδίας ἀρχαγέταν,

εὖτε τὰν πεπ[ρωμέναν
  Ζηνὸς τελέ[σσαντος κρί]σιν
Σάρδιες Περσᾶ[ν ἁλίσκοντο στρ]ατῶι,
Κροῖσον ὁ χρυσά[ορος
φύλαξ' Ἀπόλλων. [ὁ δ' ἐς] ἄελπτον ἆμαρ
μ[ο]λὼν πολυδ[άκρυο]ν οὐκ ἔμελλε
μίμνειν ἔτι δ[ουλοσύ]ναν, πυ[ρ]ὰν δὲ
  χαλκ[ο]τειχέος π[ροπάροι]θεν αὐ[λᾶς
ναήσατ', ἔνθα σὺν ἀλόχωι τε κεδ[νᾶι
σὺν εὐπλοκάμοι[ς τ'] ἐπέβαιν' ἄλα[στον
θ]υ[γ]ατράσι δυρομέναις· χέρας δ' [ἐς
  αἰ]πὺν αἰθέρα σφετέρας ἀείρας
γέγω]νεν· "ὑπέρ[βι]ε δαῖμον,
πο]ῦ θεῶν ἐστιν χάρις;
πο]ῦ δὲ Λατοίδας ἄναξ;
  ἔρρουσ]ιν Ἀλυά[τ]τα δόμοι
  _∪_×_∪_×] μυρίων
  _∪_×_∪_]ν.
×_∪∪∪×∪∪∪_∪] ἄστυ,
ἐρεύθεται αἵματι χρυσο]δίνας
Πακτωλός, ἀεικελίως γυναῖκες
ἐξ ἐϋκτίτων μεγάρων ἄγονται·
  τὰ πρόσθεν [ἐχ]θρὰ φίλα· θανεῖν γλύκιστον."
τόσ' εἶπε, καὶ ἁβ[ρο]βάταν κ[έλε]υσεν
ἅπτειν ξύλινον δόμον. ἔκ[λα]γον δὲ
  παρθένοι, φίλας τ' ἀνὰ ματρὶ χεῖρας
ἔβαλλον· ὁ γὰρ προφανὴς θνα-
  τοῖσιν ἔχθιστος φόνων·
ἀλλ' ἐπεὶ δεινοῦ πυρὸς
  λαμπρὸν διάϊσσεν μένος,
Ζεὺς ἐπιστάσας [μελαγκευ]θὲς νέφος
σβέννυεν ξανθὰ[ν φλόγα.
ἄπιστον οὐδέν, ὅ τι θ[εῶν μέ]ριμνα
τεύχει· τότε Δαλογενὴ[ς Ἀπό]λλων
φέρων ἐς Ὑπερβορέο[υς γ]έροντα
  σὺν τανισφύροις κατ[έν]ασσε κούραις
δι' εὐσέβειαν, ὅτι μέ[γιστα] θνατῶν
ἐς ἀγαθέαν ⟨ἀν⟩έπεμψε Π[υθ]ώ.

For when, in accordance with the fated will of Zeus the Accomplisher, Sardis was taken by the Persian army, Apollo of the sword of gold protected Croesus, lord of the horse-taming Lydians. For he who had come to a day he could not have expected did not intend to be mindful ever of tearful slavery, but rather piled up a pyre in front of his bronze-walled court and climbed up there with his dear wife and his fair-tressed daughters weeping inconsolably. Holding out his hands to high heaven he cried, "O wanton godhead, where is the gratitude of deities? Where is the king, the son of Leto? Alyattes' house races doomward, the Pactolus that swirls with gold is red with blood, our women are

dragged indecently from their well-built halls. What formerly was vile is sweet; to die is the very best now." So much he said and ordered the eunuch to kindle the pyre. His daughters cried out and threw their arms around their mother. For death close by is most terrifying to mortals. But when the might of the terrible flame shone bright, Zeus caused a deep black cloud to stand over them and put out the yellow flames. Nothing touched by the gods' concern is incredible. Delian-born Apollo carried off the old man and his slim-ankled daughters to the land of the Hyperboreans and settled him there; and this for his piety, because he of all mortals had sent the greatest gifts to holy Delphi.

By the first quarter of the fifth century B.C. the pyre incident was firmly established in the biography of Croesus; cf. the amphora by Myson in the Louvre depicting the scene, J. D. Beazley, *Attic Red-Figure Vase-Painters* (Oxford 1963) 238.

A stratum of oak ashes was found atop the chamber within the mound known as the Tomb of Alyattes; H. Spiegelthal in von Olfers, *AbhBerlAkad* 1858 (1859) 539–556, and G. M. A. Hanfmann, *BASOR* 170 (1963) 55. Perhaps the kings of Sardis were cremated, as were the Hittites; cf. E. Akurgal, *Die Kunst der Hethiter* (Munich 1961) 73ff.

For Croesus as survivor see also Ctesias, *FGrHist* 688 F 9 (5); Xenophon, *Cyropaedia* 7.2.1; as a wise man, Plato, *Epistle* 2.311a.

125. Herodotus 1.86ff.   5th c. B.C.

Οἱ δὲ Πέρσαι τάς τε δὴ Σάρδις ἔσχον καὶ αὐτὸν Κροῖσον ἐζώγρησαν, ἄρξαντα ἔτεα τεσσερεσκαίδεκα καὶ τεσσερεσκαίδεκα ἡμέρας πολιορκηθέντα, κατὰ τὸ χρηστήριόν τε καταπαύσαντα τὴν ἑωυτοῦ μεγάλην ἀρχήν. λαβόντες δὲ αὐτὸν οἱ Πέρσαι ἤγαγον παρὰ Κῦρον. ὁ δὲ συννήσας πυρὴν μεγάλην ἀνεβίβασε ἐπ' αὐτὴν τὸν Κροῖσόν τε ἐν πέδῃσι δεδεμένον καὶ δὶς ἑπτὰ Λυδῶν παρ' αὐτὸν παῖδας, ἐν νόῳ ἔχων εἴτε δὴ ἀκροθίνια ταῦτα καταγιεῖν θεῶν ὅτεῳ δή, εἴτε καὶ εὐχὴν ἐπιτελέσαι θέλων, εἴτε καὶ πυθόμενος τὸν Κροῖσον εἶναι θεοσεβέα τοῦδε εἵνεκεν ἀνεβίβασε ἐπὶ τὴν πυρήν, βουλόμενος εἰδέναι εἴ τίς μιν δαιμόνων ῥύσεται τοῦ μὴ ζῶντα κατακαυθῆναι.

The Persians then took Sardis and captured Croesus alive after he had reigned for fourteen years and been besieged for fourteen days, and, just as the oracle had foretold, they ended his great empire. When they had captured him, they took him to Cyrus. Cyrus heaped up a great pyre and set Croesus, bound in chains, upon it accompanied by fourteen Lydian youths. Either he had in mind to sacrifice these first-fruits to one of the gods or he wanted to fulfill a vow or, understanding that Croesus was a reverent man, he put him on the pyre for this very reason, wanting to know if any of the gods would prevent his being burnt alive. *Croesus remembered Solon and groaned his name aloud; Cyrus sent interpreters and Croesus told the whole tale of his encounter with Solon with all its implications. Cyrus repented of his action but his servants could not quench the fire. Croesus is saved by the intervention of Apollo (87). Cyrus, advised by Croesus (88, 89) granted his requests (90). The Delphic apologia (91).*

126. Nicolas of Damascus, *FGrHist* 90 F 68.

Ist c. B.C.–Ist c. A.D.

καὶ οἱ Πέρσαι μεγάλην ἔνησαν πυρὰν Κροίσῳ ὑπό τινα ὑψηλὸν τόπον, ἀφ' οὗ ἔμελλον θεάσασθαι τὰ γινόμενα. καὶ μετὰ ταῦτα Κῦρος ἐξήλαυνεν ἐκ τῶν βασιλείων, καὶ ἡ δύναμις παρῆν ἅπασα πολύς τε ὅμιλος καὶ ἀστῶν καὶ ξένων. ὀλίγον δ' ὕστερον θεράποντες ἦγον Κροῖσον δεσμώτην καὶ Λυδῶν δὶς ἑπτά. ὡς δὲ ἐθεάσοντο Λυδοί, πάντες οἰμωγῇ καὶ στόνῳ ἀνέκλαυσαν καὶ ἔπληξαν τὰς κεφαλάς. τοσοῦτος δ' ἐκ τοῦ ὁμίλου κωκυτὸς ἀνδρῶν ὁμοῦ καὶ γυναικῶν μετὰ δακρύων καὶ βοῆς ἐξερράγη, ὁπόσος οὐδὲ ἁλισκομένης τῆς πόλεως. τότε δή τις ἂν καὶ τὴν τύχην ᾤκτειρεν καὶ Κροῖσον ἐθαύμασε τῆς πρὸς τῶν ἀρχομένων φιλίας. ὥσπερ γὰρ πατέρα ἑωρακότες οἱ μὲν τὰς ἐσθῆτας κατερρήγνυντο, οἱ δὲ τὰς κόμας ἔτιλλον· γυναικῶν δὲ ἡγεῖτο πληθὺς μυρία μετὰ κόμμου καὶ ὀλολυγῆς. αὐτὸς δὲ ἄδακρυς προσήιει καὶ σκυθρωπός.

The Persians heaped a great pyre for Croesus beneath a high spot from which they intended to watch the events. Then Cyrus drove out from the palace and all his army and a great crowd of citizens and strangers was there. A little later servants brought out the captive Croesus with fourteen Lydians. When the Lydians saw this, they all cried out with wailing and groaning and struck their heads; and a louder uproar of men and women alike broke out with tears and shouting than when the city was being taken. At that moment anybody would have pitied Croesus and his lot and been astonished at the devotion of his subjects. For they regarded him as a father, and some tore at their garments, others their hair, and a countless crowd of women led the way with weeping and wailing. Croesus, however, came forward tearless but sadly. *Croesus begged Cyrus to bring his son to him (4). The son asked to be burnt with his father, as much an enemy of the Persians as he (5). The conversation*

between father and son (6). Croesus approached the pyre while his son appealed to the gods (7). The appearance of the Sibyl and her pronunciamento (8). Croesus on the pyre called out to Solon three times (9). Cyrus ordered the flames to be put out too late. Croesus appealed to Apollo and a sudden squall extinguished the fire (10). The onlookers were terrified and appealed for divine favor (11). Thales and Zoroaster are introduced into the narrative (12). Cyrus took Croesus to the palace and told him to ask for whatever he wanted. Croesus' message to Delphi (13). Cyrus became friendly toward Croesus, gave him wives and children when he left Sardis, and kept him by his side (14).

On the Sibyl see Nicolas of Damascus, *FGrHist* 90 F 67. On Zoroaster see Diogenes Laertius 1.2, quoting Xanthus.

The Palace of Croesus

(290) Pliny, *Naturalis historia* 35.172. Ist c. A.D.

(291) Vitruvius 2.8.9–10. Ist c. B.C.–Ist c. A.D.

SARDIAKA

127. Alcman 16 (24 B, 13 D). 7th c. B.C.

οὐκ ἦς ἀνὴρ ἀγρεῖος οὐ-
δὲ σκαιὸς οὐδὲ †παρὰ σοφοῖ-
σιν† οὐδὲ Θεσσαλὸς γένος,
Ἐρυσιχαῖος οὐδὲ ποιμήν,
ἀλλὰ Σαρδίων ἀπ' ἀκρᾶν.

You are no simpleton nor clumsy fellow, nor a Thessalian nor an Erysichean shepherd; but you are a man of lofty Sardis.

Cf. Strabo 10.2.22; Schol. Apollonius Rhodius 4.972; Aelian, *Epistulae* 20.15.

Sardian Customs

128. Athenaeus, *Deipnosophistae* 2.48b, quoting Plato, the comic poet. 2nd–3rd c. A.D.

ὁ δ' ὁμώνυμος αὐτῷ ποιητής φησι·

"κᾆτ' ἐν κλίναις ἐλεφαντόποσιν καὶ στρώμασι
    πορφυροβάπτοις
κἂν φοινικίσι Σαρδιακαῖσιν κοσμησάμενοι κατά-
    κεινται."

But the poet with the same name says, "Then they recline in finery on couches with ivory feet, with purple-dyed coverlets and red Sardis blankets."

Reference has just been made to Plato the philosopher. Plato the comic poet lived in the 5th c. B.C.

Quoting Heracleides of Cumae, Athenaeus (*Deipnosophistae* 12.514c) asserts the quality of Sardian textiles and their popularity among the Persians.

129. Athenaeus, *Deipnosophistae* 2.53f. 2nd–3rd c. A.D.

Φυλότιμος δὲ ἐν τοῖς περὶ τροφῆς φησι· "τὸ πλατὺ καὶ τὸ καλούμενον Σαρδιανὸν δυσκατέργαστά ἐστιν ὠμὰ πάντα καὶ δυσδιάλυτα, κατεχόμενα ὑπὸ τοῦ φλέγματος ἐν τῇ κοιλίᾳ, καὶ στρυφνότητα ἔχοντα."

Phylotimos in his book on food says that the flat chestnut and the one called Sardian are all indigestible when uncooked since they are kept in the stomach by the phlegm and are very sour.

For the other aspects of the Sardian dinner table cf. Athenaeus 2.54c, 68a (more on chestnuts); 3.76b (on Lydian figs); 3.112c (on Lydian bread); 4.132f, 4.172b, and 12.516d (on Lydian *kandaulos* for which cf. Herodotus 1.7 [see 26]; Photius, *kandutos*); 4.160a and 12.516c (on Lydian *karyke* for which cf. Zenobius 5.3); 10.418d (on Lydian appetites); 2.38f (on Lydian nectar).

130. Athenaeus, *Deipnosophistae* 12.515d–f.

2nd–3rd c. A.D.

Λυδοὶ δὲ εἰς τοσοῦτον ἦλθον τρυφῆς ὡς καὶ πρῶτοι γυναῖκας εὐνουχίσαι, ὡς ἱστορεῖ Ξάνθος ὁ Λυδὸς ἢ ὁ τὰς εἰς αὐτὸν ἀναφερομένας ἱστορίας συγγεγραφώς— Διονύσιος δ' ὁ Σκυτοβραχίων, ὡς Ἀρτέμων φησὶν ὁ Κασανδρεὺς ἐν τῷ περὶ Συναγωγῆς Βιβλίων, ἀγνοῶν ὅτι Ἔφορος ὁ συγγραφεὺς μνημονεύει αὐτοῦ ὡς παλαιοτέρου ὄντος καὶ Ἡροδότῳ τὰς ἀφορμὰς δεδωκότος— ὁ δ' οὖν Ξάνθος ἐν τῇ δευτέρᾳ τῶν Λυδιακῶν Ἀδραμύτην φησὶ τὸν Λυδῶν βασιλέα πρῶτον γυναῖκας εὐνουχίσαντα χρῆσθαι αὐταῖς ἀντὶ ἀνδρῶν εὐνούχων. Κλέαρχος δ' ἐν τῇ τετάρτῃ περὶ Βίων "Λυδοί," φησί, "διὰ τρυφὴν παραδείσους κατασκευασάμενοι καὶ κηπαίους αὐτοὺς ποιήσαντες ἐσκιατροφοῦντο, τρυφερώτερον ἡγησάμενοι τὸ μηδ' ὅλως αὐτοῖς ἐπιπίπτειν τὰς τοῦ ἡλίου αὐγάς. καὶ πόρρω προάγοντες ὕβρεως τὰς τῶν ἄλλων γυναῖκας καὶ παρθένους εἰς τὸν τόπον τὸν διὰ τὴν πρᾶξιν Ἁγνεῶνα κληθέντα συνάγοντες ὕβριζον. καὶ τέλος τὰς ψυχὰς ἀποθηλυνθέντες ἠλλάξαντο τὸν τῶν γυναικῶν βίον, διόπερ καὶ γυναῖκα τύραννον ὁ βίος εὕρετο αὐτοῖς μίαν τῶν ὑβρισθεισῶν Ὀμφάλην."

The Lydians came to such a pitch of wantonness that they were the first to sterilize women as Xanthus the Lydian records or whoever it was that wrote the histories attributed to him—Dionysios Skytobrachion, as Artemon of Cassandreia says in his publication *On the Collecting of Books*, ignoring the fact that the historian Ephorus said that he was older and had given sources to Herodotus. In the second book of the Lydiaka Xanthus says that Adramytes, the king of Lydia, was the first to sterilize women and use them instead of male eunuchs. Clearchus, in the fourth book of his *Lives*, says that on account of their luxuriousness the Lydians planned parks and made them like gardens and so kept in the shade. For they thought it more dainty not to have the sun's rays touch them at all. They went so much further in their arrogance that they collected the wives and daughters of other men into the place which, because of their behavior, they called in irony the Place of Purity and had intercourse with them. Finally they became so spiritually unmanned that they took on the women's way of life; and this way of living found for them a woman tyrant named Omphale, one of those that had been outraged.

This passage gives some idea of the depths to which some of their neighbors thought the Sardians sank. For the influence of Sardis on Colophon cf. Athenaeus 12.526a–b, where Athenaeus draws on Xenophanes, and 13.598b (the love story of Antimachus and Lyde). For Sardian influence on Polycrates and the Samians, see 12.540f where Clearchus is the source. On Lydian depravity cf. Athenaeus 14.638e–f.

For analogous luxurious living, Athenaeus (12.526f–527) quotes Theopompus who cites the Umbrians; and for power leading to indulgence (12.545c–d) he names the kings of Persia, Media, and Assyria as well as the rulers in Sardis.

Dionysios Skytobrachion lived in Alexandria in the 2nd–1st c. B.C. Artemon of Cassandreia was a contemporary of his. Clearchus of Soli (in Cyprus) lived in the 3rd c. B.C., a polymath given to sensationalism. Ephorus lived in the 4th c. B.C.

131. Athenaeus, *Deipnosophistae* 15.690b–d.

2nd–3rd c. A.D.

Ἴων Ὀμφάλῃ·

βάκκαρις δὲ καὶ μύρα
καὶ Σαρδιανὸν κόσμον εἰδέναι χροὸς
ἄμεινον ἢ τὸν Πέλοπος ἐν νήσῳ τρόπον.

ἐν τούτοις Σαρδιανὸν κόσμον εἴρηκε τὸ μύρον, ἐπεὶ διαβόητοι ἐπὶ ἡδυπαθείᾳ οἱ Λυδοί· καὶ τὸ παρὰ Ἀνακρέοντι "Λυδοπαθὴς" ἀκούουσιν ἀντὶ τοῦ ἡδυπαθής. μνημονεύει τῆς βακκάριδος καὶ Σοφοκλῆς. Μάγνης δ' ἐν Λυδοῖς·

λούσαντα χρὴ καὶ βακκάριδι κεχριμένον . . .

καὶ μήποτε οὔκ ἐστι μύρον ἡ βάκκαρις. Αἰσχύλος γὰρ
ἐν ’Ἀμυμώνῃ ἀντιδιαστέλλων φησίν·

κἄγωγε τὰς σὰς βακκάρεις τε καὶ μύρα.

καὶ Σιμωνίδης·

κηλειφόμην μύροισι καὶ θυώμασι
καὶ βακκάρι.

’Ἀριστοφάνης δ’ ἐν Θεσμοφοριαζούσαις·

ὦ Ζεῦ πολυτίμηθ’, οἷον ἐνέπνευσ’ ὁ μιαρὸς
φάσκωλος εὐθὺς λυόμενός μοι τοῦ μύρου
καὶ βακκάριδος.

Ion in *Omphale*: "Knowing baccaris and perfumes and the skin ointments of Sardis is better
than being familiar with the way of life in the
Peloponnese."

Here Sardian ointments means perfume since the
Lydians were famous for their soft living. The word
"Lydian-living" in Anacreon is taken to be the
same as "soft-living."

Sophocles mentions baccaris as does Magnes in
The Lydians: "After bathing and being anointed
with baccaris he should . . ."

It is possible that baccaris is not a perfume, for
in *Amymone* Aeschylus makes a distinction when
he says: "Your baccaris and your perfumes are not
for me."

And Simonides too: "I anointed myself with
perfumes and scents and baccaris."

Aristophanes, too, in *Thesmophoriazusae*:
"Much-honored Zeus, what a stench that vile bag
breathed on me the minute it was opened of perfume
and baccaris."

Athenaeus is listing the mentions of baccaris in the
comic poets: for ointments and perfumes cf. 15.691c–d
(quoting the comic poet Alexis on the Sardians' fondness
for perfume); 15.688c (on the origin of perfumes).

For the high quality of the baccaris which Croesus had
at his disposal in Daskyleion see Hipponax F 104.21ff
(Masson); on baccaris generally, Schol. Aeschylus
Persae 42.

132. Herodotus 1.94.   5th c. B.C.

Λυδοὶ δὲ νόμοισι μὲν παραπλησίοισι χρέωνται καὶ
Ἕλληνες, χωρὶς ἢ ὅτι τὰ θήλεα τέκνα καταπορνεύουσι.
πρῶτοι δὲ ἀνθρώπων τῶν ἡμεῖς ἴδμεν νόμισμα χρυσοῦ
καὶ ἀργύρου κοψάμενοι ἐχρήσαντο, πρῶτοι δὲ καὶ
κάπηλοι ἐγένοντο. φασὶ δὲ αὐτοὶ Λυδοὶ καὶ τὰς παι-
γνίας τὰς νῦν σφίσι τε καὶ Ἕλλησι κατεστεώσας
ἑωυτῶν ἐξεύρημα γενέσθαι.

The Lydians have customs which are close to those
of the Greeks except that their girls practice prostitution. As far as I know, they were the first people
to mint currency in gold and silver and put it into
circulation, and they were the first people to become
traders. The Lydians themselves say that the games
which are now common practice among them and
among the Greeks were their invention.

On the origins of coinage see Pollux 9.83, P. Jacobsthal,
JHS 71 (1951) 85–95, and E. S. G. Robinson, *JHS* 71
(1951) 156–167, and *NumChron* (1956) 1–8.

On the archaeology of the market place at Sardis see
G. F. Swift, Jr., in G. M. A. Hanfmann, *BASOR* 182
(1966) 11–15, Swift in Hanfmann, *BASOR* 186 (1967)
31–37.

On prostitution in Sardis see Strabo 11.14.16, 12.3.36,
13.4.7 (see *279*); Athenaeus 12.515d–f (see *130*); for
similar attitudes elsewhere cf. B.-F. Leguevel de La-
combe, *Voyage à Madagascar et aux îles Comores*, I
(Paris 1840) 145.

Manufactures in Sardis

(128) Athenaeus, *Deipnosophistae* 2.48b.

2nd–3rd c. A.D.

(131) Athenaeus, *Deipnosophistae* 15.690b–d.

2nd–3rd c. A.D.

133. Pliny, *Naturalis historia* 7.196.   1st c. A.D.

Aegyptii textilia, inficere lanas Sardibus Lydi,
fusos in lanificio Closter filius Arachnae.

The Egyptians introduced textiles and the Lydians
at Sardis the dyeing of wool, while Closter, the son
of Arachne, invented spindles for spinning and
weaving.

On Sardian dyes see Aristophanes, *Acharnians* 112;
Pax 1174; Clement of Alexandria, *Paedagogus* 2.10.108.
On Sardian woolens and textiles see also Varro quoted
in Nonius 542.13; Pollux 7.77.

Another version of the myth states that Arachne was
daughter of a dyer from Colophon (Ovid, *Metamorphoses* 6.5ff).

134. Vitruvius 2.3.3.   1st c. B.C.–1st c. A.D.

Fiunt autem laterum genera tria: unum, quod
graece Lydium appellatur, id est quo nostri utun-
tur, longum sesquipede, latum pede. Ceteris duobus
Graecorum aedificia struuntur.

There are three kinds of bricks: one which in
Greek is called Lydian, which our builders use, a

foot and a half in length, and a foot wide. Greek structures are built with the other two.

On bricks in Sardis see G. F. Swift, Jr., in G. M. A. Hanfmann, *BASOR* 182 (1966) 12, with reference to R. Naumann, *Architektur Kleinasiens von ihren Anfängen bis zum Ende der hethitischen Zeit* (Tübingen 1955) 46–48. More recent discoveries substantiate the notion of two standard brick sizes in Sardis; this may have chronological implications.

Naturalia

(**247**) Philostratus, *Life of Apollonius* 6.37.

2nd–3rd c. A.D.

135. Pliny, *Naturalis historia* 12.57.　　Ist c. A.D.

cortice lauri esse constat, quidam et folium simile dixere; talis certe fuit arbor Sardibus, nam et Asiae reges serendi curam habuerunt.

Naturalists agree that the bark is that of the laurel tree, and some have claimed that the leaf also is similar. Certainly the tree at Sardis was like that, for the kings of Asia, too, took care to plant it.

Pliny describes the frankincense tree. On nuts from Sardis see *Naturalis historia* 15.93 with which cf. Athenaeus 2.53f (see *129*), 54c, 68a. On onions from Sardis and their quality see *Naturalis historia* 19.104.

136. Pliny, *Naturalis historia* 33.160.　　Ist c. A.D.

Sile pingere instituere primi Polygnotus et Micon, Attico dumtaxat. secuta aetas hoc ad lumina usa est, ad umbras autem Scyrico et Lydio. Lydium Sardibus emebatur, quod nunc obmutuit.

Polygnotus and Micon were the first to use yellow ochre in painting, albeit they used only Attic. The subsequent period used this for light effects, but ochre from Scyros and Lydia for shade. Lydian ochre used to be sold at Sardis, but now is not available.

137. Pliny, *Naturalis historia* 37.105.　　Ist c. A.D.

E diverso ad haec sarda utilissima, quae nomen cum sardonyche communicavit. ipsa volgaris et primum Sardibus reperta, sed laudatissima circa Babylona.

On the other hand, the sard, which has come to share its name with the sardonyx, is most useful in these respects. The stone itself is common enough and was first found at Sardis, but the most wanted specimens are found around Babylon.

For sards see also *Naturalis historia* 37.86, 37.90, 37.116, etc.

Sappho on Sardis

138. Sappho F 218 (96) 1–9.　　6th c. B.C.

]σαρδ.[ ]
πόλ]λακι τυίδε [ν]ῶν ἔχοισα
ὡς π.[...].ώομεν, .[...]..χ[..]-
σε θέᾳ σ’ ἰκέλαν ἀρι-
γνώται, σᾷ δὲ μάλιστ’ ἔχαιρε μόλπᾳ·
νῦν δὲ Λύδαισιν ἐμπρέπεται γυναί-
κεσσιν ὥς ποτ’ ἀελίω
δύντος ἀ βροδοδάκτυλος †μήνα†
πάντα περρέχοισ’ ἄστρα.

[She is] in Sardis, often turning her mind to us here, [remembering] you as a glorious goddess and that she delighted especially in your song. But now she is preeminent among the ladies of Lydia as the rosy-fingered [moon] outshining every star when the sun is set.

For Anactoria in Sardis see Sappho F 195 (16); see also E. Lobel and D. L. Page, *Poetarum Lesbiorum fragmenta* (Oxford 1955) 14–15, 78–79; D. L. Page, *Sappho and Alcaeus* (Oxford 1955) 52–57, 87–96.

139. Sappho F 219 (98), (a) 10–12, (b) 1–3.　　6th c. B.C.

μ]ιτράναν δ’ ἀρτίως κλ[
ποικίλαν ἀπὺ Σαρδίω[ν
]. αονιασπολεις

(b)

· · · ·
σοὶ δ’ ἔγω Κλέι ποικίλαν
οὐκ ἔχω πόθεν ἔσσεται
μιτράν⟨αν⟩· ἀλλὰ τῷ Μυτιληνάῳ
· · · · ·

But recently, Kleis . . . [to have] a colorful headband from Sardis . . .

But, Kleis, I do not have a colorful headband nor do I know where you shall have one from; but . . . the Mytilenaean . . .

See A. Vogliano, *Philologus* 93 (1939) 277ff; A. Vogliano, *Sappho: Una nuova ode della poetessa* (Milan 1941); E. Lobel and D. L. Page, *Poetarum Lesbiorum fragmenta* (Oxford 1955) 80–81; W. Schadewaldt, *Studies Presented to David Moore Robinson on His Seventieth Birthday* (St. Louis 1951) II 499–506; D. L. Page, *Sappho and Alcaeus* (Oxford 1955) 97–103.

On Kleis see Sappho F 239 (132). On the Lydian mitra see also Pindar, *Nemean Odes* 8.15; on other Lydian garments Sappho F 201 (39).

III. From the Persian Conquest to the End of the Seleucid Era

Source materials for the historical events involving Sardis during the period from ca. 547 B.C. until the establishment of the Roman province of Asia are gathered together in this chapter. They range from authors who deal with Cyrus' behavior after the fall of Sardis, through those who focus on Persian and Greek interrelations and those who concentrate on Alexander, down to those who are concerned with the Roman presence in Asia after the battle of Magnesia. Methodologically the material is handled in the same way as before.

THE PERSIAN PERIOD

Cyrus the Great

140. Diodorus Siculus 9.33.4.   1st c. B.C.

Ὅτι μετὰ τὸ γενέσθαι αἰχμάλωτον τὸν Κροῖσον καὶ τὴν πυρὰν σβεσθῆναι, ἰδὼν τὴν πόλιν διαρπαζομένην καὶ πρὸς τοῖς ἄλλοις πολὺν ἄργυρόν τε καὶ χρυσὸν διαφορούμενον, ἐπηρώτησε τὸν Κῦρον, τί ποιοῦσιν οἱ στρατιῶται. τοῦ δὲ μετὰ γέλωτος ἀποκριθέντος, Τὰ σὰ χρήματα διαρπάζουσι, Μὰ Δία μὲν οὖν, εἶπεν, ἀλλὰ τὰ σά· Κροίσου γὰρ ἴδιον οὐκέτι οὐθὲν ὑπάρχει. ὁ δὲ Κῦρος θαυμάσας τὸν λόγον εὐθὺς μετενόησε καὶ τοὺς στρατιώτας ἀνείρξας τῆς διαρπαγῆς εἰς τὸ βασιλικὸν ἀνέλαβε τὰς τῶν Σαρδιανῶν κτήσεις.

When Croesus had been taken prisoner and the pyre had been put out, and he saw that the city was being ravaged and much silver and gold as well as other things were being removed, he asked Cyrus what the soldiers were doing. With a laugh he replied that they were plundering Croesus' wealth. "By Zeus, no," said Croesus, "it is yours they pillage; for Croesus no longer possesses a thing."

Cyrus was impressed by this argument and immediately changed his plans, checking the plundering of his soldiers and taking the belongings of the Sardians for the Imperial Treasury.

Cf. Herodotus 1.88 (see *125*).

141. Herodotus 1.141.   5th c. B.C.

Ἴωνες δὲ καὶ Αἰολέες, ὡς οἱ Λυδοὶ τάχιστα κατεστράφατο ὑπὸ Περσέων, ἔπεμπον ἀγγέλους ἐς Σάρδις παρὰ Κῦρον, ἐθέλοντες ἐπὶ τοῖσι αὐτοῖσι εἶναι τοῖσι καὶ Κροίσῳ ἦσαν κατήκοοι.

Directly the Lydians had been overthrown by the Persians the Ionians and the Aeolians sent messengers to Sardis to Cyrus to declare their readiness to be subject to him on the same terms that had existed between them and Croesus.
Cyrus replied angrily and the Ionians fortified themselves and appealed to Sparta.

Miletus was the single Greek city with which Cyrus came to terms.

142. Herodotus 1.152ff.   5th c. B.C.

οἱ μὲν δὴ ἀπαλλάσσοντο, Λακεδαιμόνιοι δὲ ἀπωσάμενοι τῶν Ἰώνων τοὺς ἀγγέλους ὅμως ἀπέστειλαν πεντηκοντέρῳ ἄνδρας, ὡς μὲν ἐμοὶ δοκέει, κατασκόπους τῶν τε Κύρου πρηγμάτων καὶ Ἰωνίης. ἀπικόμενοι δὲ οὗτοι ἐς Φώκαιαν ἔπεμπον ἐς Σάρδις σφέων αὐτῶν τὸν δοκιμώτατον, τῷ οὔνομα ἦν Λακρίνης, ἀπερέοντα Κύρῳ Λακεδαιμονίων ῥῆσιν, γῆς τῆς Ἑλλάδος μηδεμίαν πόλιν σιναμωρέειν ὡς αὐτῶν οὐ περιοψομένων.

Then they left; but though the Lacedaimonians had dismissed the Ionian messengers, they nevertheless dispatched some men in a warship to spy out, it seems to me, Cyrus' situation and that of

Ionia. When these had arrived in Phocaea they sent the most illustrious of their number, whose name was Lacrines, to Sardis to disclose to Cyrus a statement of the Lacedaimonians to the effect that they would not overlook his damaging any city on Greek land.

Cyrus mocked the Spartans' declaration, turned Sardis over to Tabalus and Croesus' treasure to Pactyes, and left for Ecbatana (153). Pactyes led a Lydian revolt and besieged Tabalus in the citadel at Sardis (154). Croesus advised Cyrus to deprive the Lydians of their arms (155) and convinced Cyrus (156), Pactyes fled to Cyme, and Mazares in Sardis obliged the Lydians to change their way of life (157).

For the surviving Croesus see Ctesias, *FGrHist* 688 F 9 (5); Nicolas of Damascus, *FGrHist* 90 F 68 (see *126*); Xenophon, *Cyropaedia* 7.2.15ff (see *122*).

On the enfeeblement of the Lydians see Choricius, *Oratio in Justiniani Brumalia* 14.

143. Theophanes, *Chronographia* I 474B.　　8th c. A.D.

οἱ δὲ καταφυγόντες πρὸς αὐτὸν Πέρσαι ἔλεγον, ὅτι φυγὼν ὁ Χοσρόης πυρὶ ἀνήλωσε πάντα τὰ λήϊα ἐν ἐκείνοις τοῖς τόποις ἐλθὼν εἰς Θηβαρμαῒς τὴν πόλιν ἐν τῇ ἀνατολῇ, ἐν ᾗ ὑπῆρχεν ὁ ναὸς τοῦ Πυρὸς καὶ τὰ χρήματα Κροίσου, τοῦ Λυδῶν βασιλέως, καὶ ἡ πλάνη τῶν ἀνθράκων.

The Persians fleeing to him said that Chosroes in his flight had destroyed all the crops in those places as he made his way to the city of Thybarmais in the east. At this place there was a fire temple and the treasure of Croesus, king of the Lydians.

Thybarmais was in Persia.

144. Xenophon, *Cyropaedia* 7.4.12.　　5th–4th c. B.C.

Κῦρος δὲ ὡρμᾶτο ἐκ Σάρδεων, φρουρὰν μὲν πεζὴν καταλιπὼν πολλὴν ἐν Σάρδεσι, Κροῖσον δὲ ἔχων, ἄγων δὲ πολλὰς ἁμάξας πολλῶν καὶ παντοδαπῶν χρημάτων. ἧκε δὲ καὶ ὁ Κροῖσος γεγραμμένα ἔχων ἀκριβῶς ὅσα ἐν ἑκάστῃ ἦν τῇ ἁμάξῃ· καὶ διδοὺς τῷ Κύρῳ τὰ γράμματα εἶπε· "Ταῦτ'," ἔφη, "ἔχων, ὦ Κῦρε, εἴσῃ τόν τέ σοι ὀρθῶς ἀποδιδόντα ἃ ἄγει καὶ τὸν μή."

Cyrus, however, left behind a large garrison of infantry in Sardis and set out from there with Croesus and many wagons full of every kind of treasure. And Croesus had come along with an accurately written list of the number of things in each wagon. When he gave the inventories to Cyrus he said, "With these things, Cyrus, you shall recognize the man who gives you rightly what he has and he who does not."

On the removal of the Lydian treasure, see *Cyropaedia* 7.3.1, 7.5.57, 8.4.29ff, with which cf. Herodotus 1.154 (see *142*) and Theophanes, *Chronographia* (ed. De Boor Teubner 1883) I 474B (see *143*).

Darius and Oroetes

145. Herodotus 3.126ff.　　5th c. B.C.

Χρόνῳ δὲ οὐ πολλῷ ὕστερον καὶ Ὀροίτεα Πολυκράτεος τίσιες μετῆλθον. μετὰ γὰρ τὸν Καμβύσεω θάνατον καὶ τῶν μάγων τὴν βασιληίην μένων ἐν τῇσι Σάρδισι ὁ Ὀροίτης ὠφέλεε μὲν οὐδὲν Πέρσας ὑπὸ Μήδων ἀπαραιρημένους τὴν ἀρχήν.

A little later the furies that were to avenge Polycrates caught up with Oroetes. For after the death of Cambyses and the assumption of the kingship by the Magians, Oroetes remained in Sardis and did nothing to help the Persians to take back the power of which they had been deprived by the Medes.

Darius determined to punish Oroetes (127) and succeeded in persuading Bagaeus to work the cunning overthrow of Oroetes (128).

Polycrates had been murdered in Magnesia at Oroetes' instigation (*125*).

On Oroetes see 3.120ff (where the satrapy is referred to as "Sardis," not "Lydia"). On the size of Persian Sardis see 3.5.

146. Herodotus 5.11ff.　　5th c. B.C.

Δαρεῖος δὲ ὡς διαβὰς τάχιστα τὸν Ἑλλήσποντον ἀπίκετο ἐς Σάρδις, ἐμνήσθη τῆς ἐξ Ἱστιαίου τε τοῦ Μιλησίου εὐεργεσίης καὶ τῆς παραινέσιος τοῦ Μυτιληναίου Κώεω, μεταπεμψάμενος δέ σφεας ἐς Σάρδις ἐδίδου αὐτοῖσι αἵρεσιν.

Directly Darius had crossed the Hellespont and had come to Sardis, he remembered the good offices of Histiaeus of Miletus on his behalf and the advice of Coes of Mytilene. Accordingly he sent for them to come to Sardis and gave them the choice of whatever they wanted.

Pigres and Mantyes, Paeonians, came to Sardis (12) and convinced Darius through the industry of their sister (13) to transport the Paeonians to Lydia (14). Megabazus brought the Paeonians to the Hellespont and in Sardis urged Darius to beware of Histiaeus (23). Darius summoned Histiaeus from Thrace to Sardis (24) and took him with him when he left for

Susa (25). With Naxos on his mind Aristagoras came to Artaphrenes in Sardis.

Ca. 512 B.C.
Darius' campaign in Europe is described in Herodotus book 4. On the forced movement of peoples see 3.93. For the incident of the Paeonians and their sister cf. a similar tale involving Alyattes and a Mysian and his wife (Nicolas of Damascus, *FGrHist* 90 F 71). This is evidently an old Lydian folk motif. On Lydians and Mysians see Strabo 12.8.3.

147. Herodotus 5.73.   5th c. B.C.

οὗτοι μέν νυν δεδεμένοι ἐτελεύτησαν, Ἀθηναῖοι δὲ μετὰ ταῦτα Κλεισθένεα καὶ τὰ ἑπτακόσια ἐπίστια τὰ διωχθέντα ὑπὸ Κλεομένεος μεταπεμψάμενοι πέμπουσι ἀγγέλους ἐς Σάρδις, συμμαχίην βουλόμενοι ποιήσασθαι πρὸς Πέρσας· ἠπιστέατο γὰρ σφίσι [πρὸς] Λακεδαιμονίους τε καὶ Κλεομένεα ἐκπεπολεμῶσθαι.

These then were bound and put to death, and afterwards the Athenians sent for Cleisthenes and the seven hundred families that had been sent into exile by Cleomenes. They also sent envoys to Sardis since they were anxious to make an alliance with the Persians. For they knew very well that they had made themselves hostile to the Spartans and Cleomenes.
The envoys agreed to give earth and water to Darius.

Ca. 507 B.C. The executed prisoners were the partisans of Isagoras. Cf. Aristotle, *Athenaion Politeia* 20.1 and H. T. Wade-Gery, *Essays in Greek History* (Oxford 1958) 138.
For Athenian envoys in Sardis later and for a different purpose see 5.96.

The Ionian Revolt and Attack on Sardis

148. Aristotle, *Analytica Posteriora* 94a, b.   4th c. B.C.

Ἀθηναῖοι δ' εἴκοσι τριήρησιν ἔπλευσαν ἐπικουρήσαντες τοῖς Ἴωσι· καὶ εἰς Σάρδεις ἐστρατεύσαντο καὶ εἷλον τὰ περὶ Σάρδεις ἅπαντα χωρὶς τοῦ τείχους τοῦ βασιληίου· ταῦτα δὲ ποιήσαντες ἐπαναχωροῦσιν εἰς Μίλητον.

With twenty ships the Athenians sailed to help the Ionians. They marched to Sardis and took all the area around Sardis outside the wall of the royal palace. When they had done this they withdrew to Miletus.

Aristotle discusses types of causes. The raid of the Athenians and Eretrians is used as an example of an *efficient* cause.

149. Charon of Lampsacus, *FGrHist* 262 F 10.

    4th c. B.C.

Τὸ δὲ διὰ τί ὁ Μηδικὸς πόλεμος ἐγένετο Ἀθηναίοις; τίς αἰτία τοῦ πολεμεῖσθαι Ἀθηναίους; ὅτι εἰς Σάρδεις μετ' Ἐρετριέων ἐνέβαλον· τοῦτο γὰρ ἐκίνησε πρῶτον.

Why did the Persian war come upon the Athenians? What was the cause of the Athenians going to war? It was because the Athenians with the Eretrians attacked Sardis; this first started the war.

Recorded also at *FGrHist* 687b F 5.

150. Herodotus 5.99ff.   5th c. B.C.

Ἀρισταγόρης δέ, ἐπειδὴ οἵ τε Ἀθηναῖοι ἀπίκοντο εἴκοσι νηυσί, ἅμα ἀγόμενοι Ἐρετριέων πέντε τριήρεας, οἳ οὐ τὴν Ἀθηναίων χάριν ἐστρατεύοντο ἀλλὰ τὴν αὐτῶν Μιλησίων, ὀφειλόμενά σφι ἀποδιδόντες (οἱ γὰρ δὴ Μιλήσιοι πρότερον τοῖσι Ἐρετριεῦσι τὸν πρὸς Χαλκιδέας πόλεμον συνδιήνεικαν, ὅτε περ καὶ Χαλκιδεῦσι ἀντία Ἐρετριέων καὶ Μιλησίων Σάμιοι ἐβοήθεον), οὗτοι ὦν ἐπείτε σφι ἀπίκοντο καὶ οἱ ἄλλοι σύμμαχοι παρῆσαν, ἐποιέετο στρατηίην ὁ Ἀρισταγόρης ἐς Σάρδις.

When the Athenians arrived with their twenty ships, they brought also five Eretrian triremes. These were campaigning not to favor the Athenians but the Milesians, since this way they paid back what they owed. For formerly the Milesians had helped the Eretrians in the war against Chalcis when the Samians aided the Chalcidians against the Eretrians and Milesians. When these and the other allies had arrived, Aristagoras formulated a campaign against Sardis.
The Ionians marched up the valley of the Caicus, over Tmolus, fell upon Sardis, and took the city (100).

Ca. 499 B.C.
On the Lelantine War see Thucydides 1.15; Archilochus F 3 (Diehl); Strabo 10.1.11; Aristotle, *Politics* 1289b 36ff; Plutarch, *Amatorius* 17 (760F); and cf. A. Blakeway, *Greek Poetry and Life* (Oxford 1936) 34–55; W. G. Forrest, *Historia* 6 (1957) 160ff.

(282) Herodotus 5.101.   5th c. B.C.

(272) Herodotus 5.102ff.   5th c. B.C.

151. Herodotus 6.1ff.   5th c. B.C.

Ἀρισταγόρης μέν νυν Ἰωνίην ἀποστήσας οὕτω τελευτᾷ, Ἱστιαῖος δὲ ὁ Μιλήτου τύραννος μεμετιμένος ὑπὸ Δαρείου παρῆν ἐς Σάρδις. ἀπιγμένον δὲ αὐτὸν ἐκ τῶν Σούσων εἴρετο Ἀρταφρένης ὁ Σαρδίων ὕπαρχος κατὰ κοῖόν τι δοκέοι Ἴωνας ἀπεστάναι· ὁ δὲ οὔτε εἰδέναι ἔφη ἐθώμαζέ τε τὸ γεγονὸς ὡς οὐδὲν δῆθεν τῶν παρεόντων πρηγμάτων ἐπιστάμενος.

After causing Ionia to revolt, Aristagoras then perished in that way, but Histiaeus the tyrant of Miletus, being released by Darius, came to Sardis. And when he had arrived from Susa, Artaphrenes the governor of Sardis asked him why in his opinion the Ionians had revolted. But he said that he did not know and that he was surprised at what had taken place, claiming complete ignorance of the current events.

Histiaeus fled from Sardis to Chios (2) where he was interrogated by the Ionians (3) and whence he sent messages to conspirators in Sardis. The plot was detected (4) and uproar overtook Sardis (5). After Lade and the fall of Miletus, Histiaeus was captured in Mysia and executed in Sardis (30).

The battle of Lade took place ca. 495 B.C., and Histiaeus was captured ca. 493 B.C. On the Ionian revolt see A. R. Burn, *Persia and the Greeks* (London 1962) 193–220.

On Histiaeus see S. Heinlein, *Klio* 9 (1909) 341–351.

152. Himerius, *Orationes* 6.15.   4th c. A.D.

μόνοι δὲ Ἑλλήνων οἱ τῇδε κείμενοι καὶ τὴν φύσιν ἐγνώρισαν, καὶ τὴν ἱκετηρίαν ἐδέξαντο, καὶ πῦρ ἐπὶ Σάρδεις κομίζοντες ἔδειξαν τότε τοῖς Πέρσαις, ὅτι τινὲς ἀνθρώπων εἰσὶν ὑπὲρ ἐλευθερίας ἔτι μαχόμενοι.

Alone of the Greeks settled here, they acknowledged this relationship, they received the supplication, and, carrying fire to Sardis, they showed the Persians then that there were still men ready to fight for freedom.

See also Himerius 42.2 (on Croesus).

153. Plato, *Menexenus* 240A.   4th c. B.C.

αἰτιασάμενος δὲ Δαρεῖος ἡμᾶς τε καὶ Ἐρετριᾶς, Σάρδεσιν ἐπιβουλεῦσαι προφασιζόμενος, πέμψας μυριάδας μὲν πεντήκοντα ἔν τε πλοίοις καὶ ναυσίν, ναῦς δὲ τριακοσίας, Δᾶτιν δὲ ἄρχοντα, εἶπεν ἥκειν ἄγοντα Ἐρετριᾶς καὶ Ἀθηναίους, εἰ βούλοιτο τὴν ἑαυτοῦ κεφαλὴν ἔχειν.

Darius accused us and the Eretrians of having plotted against Sardis and sent five hundred thousand men in boats and ships and three hundred warships under the command of Datis. He told him to come bringing Eretrians and Athenians with him if he wished to keep his head.

154. Plutarch, *De Herodoti malignitate* 24 (861B, C).

1st–2nd c. A.D.

εἶτ' ἀναστρέψαντες ὀπίσω καὶ τὰς ναῦς ἐν Ἐφέσῳ καταλιπόντες ἐπέθεντο Σάρδεσι καὶ Ἀρταφέρνην ἐπολιόρκουν εἰς τὴν ἀκρόπολιν καταφυγόντα, βουλόμενοι τὴν Μιλήτου λῦσαι πολιορκίαν· καὶ τοῦτο μὲν ἔπραξαν καὶ τοὺς πολεμίους ἀνέστησαν ἐκεῖθεν, ἐν φόβῳ θαυμαστῷ γενομένους· πλήθους δ' ἐπιχυθέντος αὐτοῖς, ἀπεχώρησαν.

Then turning back they left their ships at Ephesus and attacked Sardis. They besieged Artaphernes who had fled onto the acropolis, because they wished to raise the siege of Miletus. They accomplished this and made the enemy retreat from there, thrown into an astonishing state of dismay. And when a large company attacked them, then they withdrew.

155. Plutarch, *De Herodoti malignitate* 24 (861C, D).

1st–2nd c. A.D.

ὁ δὲ καὶ κρατηθέντας αὐτοὺς ὑπὸ τῶν βαρβάρων φησὶν εἰς τὰς ναῦς καταδιωχθῆναι, μηδὲν τοιοῦτο τοῦ Λαμψακηνοῦ Χάρωνος ἱστοροῦντος, ἀλλὰ ταυτὶ γράφοντος κατὰ λέξιν· "Ἀθηναῖοι δ' εἴκοσι τριήρεσιν ἔπλευσαν ἐπικουρήσοντες τοῖς Ἴωσι, καὶ εἰς Σάρδεις ἐστρατεύσαντο καὶ εἷλον τὰ περὶ Σάρδεις ἅπαντα χωρὶς τοῦ τείχους τοῦ βασιληίου· ταῦτα δὲ ποιήσαντες ἐπαναχωροῦσιν εἰς Μίλητον."

But he says that they were conquered by the barbarians and pursued all the way to their ships. Charon of Lampsacus records no such thing, but what he says follows, and I quote, "With twenty ships the Athenians sailed to help the Ionians. They marched to Sardis and took possession of everything around the city with the exception of the royal fortress. And when they had done this they retreated to Miletus."

Charon of Lampsacus (*FGrHist* 262 F 10) lived around 400 B.C. For Eretrian involvement see also Lysanias of Mallus (*FGrHist* 426 F 1). Archaeological evidence for the Ionian destruction has been isolated (G. M. A. Hanfmann, *BASOR* 166 [1962] 5–9).

Xerxes

156. Diodorus 11.2.3ff.   1st c. B.C.

ὡς δ' ἧκεν εἰς Σάρδεις, κήρυκας ἐξέπεμψεν εἰς τὴν Ἑλλάδα, προστάξας εἰς πάσας τὰς πόλεις ἰέναι καὶ τοὺς Ἕλληνας αἰτεῖν ὕδωρ καὶ γῆν.

When he had arrived in Sardis he sent envoys to Greece with instructions to go to every city and to demand earth and water of the Greeks.
Xerxes set out from Sardis (11.3.6). The Persians at Mycale sent to Sardis for help (11.34.3), by which time Xerxes had returned there (11.36.3). After Mycale the Persian troops withdrew to Sardis (11.36.6) and Xerxes left for home (11.36.7). At a later date Samian aristocrats came to Sardis to ask for Persian help (12.27.3).

Cf. Aeschylus *Persae* 41ff. Datis had already accused the Greeks of the destruction of Sardis (10.27.2).

157. Herodotus 7.32ff.   5th c. B.C.

ἀπικόμενος δὲ ἐς Σάρδις πρῶτα μὲν ἀπέπεμπε κήρυκας ἐς τὴν Ἑλλάδα αἰτήσοντας γῆν τε καὶ ὕδωρ καὶ προερέοντας δεῖπνα βασιλέϊ παρασκευάζειν· πλὴν οὔτε ἐς Ἀθήνας οὔτε ἐς Λακεδαίμονα ἀπέπεμπε ἐπὶ γῆς αἴτησιν, τῇ δὲ ἄλλῃ πάντῃ.

On arrival in Sardis he first sent heralds into Greece to ask for earth and water and to demand that preparations be made for dinners for the king; except that he did not send a command for earth either to Athens or to Sparta, but to every other place.
Xerxes watched his departing army at Sardis (37) and followed them himself (41). Portents at the Hellespont and previously in Sardis did not deter him (57). The Lydian contingent (74) and a cavalry commander left behind in Sardis (88). The Greeks heard that Xerxes was in the Lydian capital (145).

Herodotus describes events in the spring, 480 B.C.
For Xerxes en route to Sardis see 7.26, 7.31. On the reasons for Xerxes not sending to Athens and Sparta see 7.133.

158. Herodotus 8.117.   5th c. B.C.

καὶ οὗτοι μὲν τοῦτον τὸν μισθὸν ἔλαβον· οἱ δὲ Πέρσαι ὡς ἐκ τῆς Θρηίκης πορευόμενοι ἀπίκοντο ἐπὶ τὸν πόρον, ἐπειγόμενοι τὸν Ἑλλήσποντον τῇσι νηυσὶ διέβησαν ἐς Ἄβυδον· τὰς γὰρ σχεδίας οὐκ εὗρον ἔτι ἐντεταμένας ἀλλ᾽ ὑπὸ χειμῶνος διαλελυμένας. ἐνθαῦτα δὲ κατεχόμενοι σιτία [τε] πλέω ἢ κατ᾽ ὁδὸν ἐλάγχανον οὐδένα τε κόσμον ἐμπιπλάμενοι καὶ ὕδατα μεταβάλλοντες ἀπέθνησκον τοῦ στρατοῦ τοῦ περιεόντος πολλοί. οἱ δὲ λοιποὶ ἅμα Ξέρξῃ ἀπικνέονται ἐς Σάρδις.

These took this reward; but the Persians marching from Thrace came to the narrows and hastily crossed the Hellespont in ships to Abydus. For they did not find the bridges still intact but loosened by a storm. At Abydus they halted and obtained more food than they had had on their way; accordingly they filled themselves without restraint. And for this reason and because they changed their drinking water, many of the army that still survived perished. The remainder with Xerxes himself came to Sardis.

Winter, 480–479 B.C.
On the bridge see 7.34, 9.106, 9.114. Aeschylus (*Persae* 725) has Xerxes use the bridge. On drinking water see Hippocrates, *Aer.* 7. On Xerxes in Sardis see 9.3, 9.108. Fugitives from Mycale made their way to the Lydian capital (9.107).

159. Himerius, *Orationes* 6.23.   4th c. A.D.

μᾶλλον δὲ τὸ μῖσος πλέον τότε κατ᾽ Ἀθηναίων Ξέρξῃ, ἢ πάλαι παρὰ Δαρείῳ πρότερον. τὸν μὲν γὰρ Σάρδεις ἐλύπουν· τὸν δὲ καὶ Μαραθὼν πρὸς Σάρδεσι.

At that time Xerxes' hatred for the Athenians was greater than Darius' had been before. For the fate of Sardis had grieved Darius, but Xerxes was vexed by events at Marathon as well as those at Sardis.

160. Seneca, *De Beneficiis* 6.31.12.

1st c. B.C.–1st c. A.D.

Itaque Xerxes pudore quam damno miserior Demarato gratias egit, quod solus sibi verum dixisset, et permisit petere, quod vellet. Petit ille, ut Sardis, maximam Asiae civitatem, curru vectus intraret rectam capite tiaram gerens; id solis datum regibus.

Therefore Xerxes, more wretched because of his shame than his loss, thanked Demaratus because he alone had told him the truth and permitted him to ask whatever he should wish. He asked to enter Sardis, the largest city of Asia, riding a chariot and with a tiara upright on his head, a privilege given to kings alone.

Seneca describes a conversation between Xerxes and Demaratus following the Persian defeat in Greece.

Alcibiades in Sardis

161. Plutarch, *Alcibiades* 27, 28.   1st–2nd c. A.D.

Οὕτω δὲ λαμπρᾷ χρησάμενος εὐτυχίᾳ, καὶ φιλοτιμούμενος εὐθὺς ἐγκαλλωπίσασθαι τῷ Τισσαφέρνῃ, ξένια καὶ δῶρα παρασκευασάμενος καὶ θεραπείαν ἔχων ἡγεμονικὴν ἐπορεύετο πρὸς αὐτόν. οὐ μὴν ἔτυχεν ὧν προσεδόκησεν, ἀλλὰ πάλαι κακῶς ἀκούων ὁ Τισσαφέρνης ὑπὸ τῶν Λακεδαιμονίων, καὶ φοβούμενος αἰτίαν λαβεῖν ἐκ βασιλέως, ἔδοξεν ἐν καιρῷ τὸν Ἀλκι-

βιάδην ἀφῖχθαι, καὶ συλλαβὼν αὐτὸν εἶρξεν ἐν Σάρδεσιν, ὡς λύσιν ἐκείνης τῆς διαβολῆς τὴν ἀδικίαν
ταύτην ἐσομένην.

Τριάκοντα δ' ἡμερῶν διαγενομένων ὁ 'Αλκιβιάδης
ἵππου ποθὲν εὐπορήσας καὶ ἀποδρὰς τοὺς φύλακας, εἰς
Κλαζομενὰς διέφυγε.

Alcibiades used so glorious a stroke of fortune,
being ambitious to boast of it to Tissaphernes forth-
with. He accordingly prepared gifts of all kinds and
with a princely retinue made his way to him. He
did not, however, encounter what he had expected;
but Tissaphernes, who had for a long time been
reviled by the Lacedaimonians and who was afraid
that he might be the recipient of accusations from
the king, thought that Alcibiades had arrived just
in time. He took him and locked him up in Sardis
in the expectation that this injustice would free
him from Spartan slander. But after thirty days had
passed Alcibiades got hold of a horse somewhere
or other, outran his guards, and escaped to Clazomenae.

These events followed a naval victory over the Pelo-
ponnesians in the Hellespont, the winter of 411/410 B.C.
On Alcibiades in Asia Minor see Thucydides 8.45ff.

162. Xenophon, *Hellenica* 1.1.9–10.   5th–4th c. B.C.

μετὰ δὲ ταῦτα Τισσαφέρνης ἦλθεν εἰς 'Ελλήσποντον·
ἀφικόμενον δὲ παρ' αὐτὸν μιᾷ τριήρει 'Αλκιβιάδην
ξένιά τε καὶ δῶρα ἄγοντα συλλαβὼν εἶρξεν ἐν Σάρδεσι,
φάσκων κελεύειν βασιλέα πολεμεῖν 'Αθηναίοις. ἡμέραις
δὲ τριάκοντα ὕστερον 'Αλκιβιάδης ἐκ Σάρδεων μετὰ
Μαντιθέου τοῦ ἁλόντος ἐν Καρίᾳ ἵππων εὐπορήσαντες
νυκτὸς ἀπέδρασαν εἰς Κλαζομενάς.

After this Tissaphernes came to the Hellespont.
And when Alcibiades who was bringing him gifts
and tokens of friendship came to him in a single
trireme, he took hold of him and put him in prison
in Sardis. He said that the king had instructed him
to make war on the Athenians. Thirty days later,
however, Alcibiades and Mantitheos, who had
been captured in Caria, got hold of some horses
and escaped from Sardis by night to Clazomenae.

On Tissaphernes and his policies cf. Thucydides 8.109.
For Mantitheos see *Hellenica* 1.3.13.

Cyrus and Lysander

(287) Cicero, *De senectute* 59.   1st c. B.C.

163. Diodorus 13.70.3.   1st c. B.C.

ἀκούσας δὲ Κῦρον τὸν Δαρείου τοῦ βασιλέως υἱὸν ὑπὸ
τοῦ πατρὸς ἀπεσταλμένον συμπολεμεῖν τοῖς Λακεδαιμονίοις, ἧκεν εἰς Σάρδεις πρὸς αὐτόν, καὶ παροξύνας
τὸν νεανίσκον εἰς τὸν κατὰ τῶν 'Αθηναίων πόλεμον
μυρίους μὲν δαρεικοὺς παραχρῆμα ἔλαβεν εἰς τὸν τῶν
στρατιωτῶν μισθόν, καὶ [εἰς] τὸ λοιπὸν δὲ ὁ Κῦρος
ἐκέλευσεν αἰτεῖν μηδὲν ὑποστελλόμενον· ἐντολὰς γὰρ
ἔχειν παρὰ τοῦ πατρός, ὅπως ὅσα ἂν προαιρῶνται
Λακεδαιμόνιοι χορηγῆσαι αὐτοῖς.

When he heard that Cyrus, the son of Darius the
king, had been dispatched by his father to assist
the Spartans in the war, he came to Sardis to him
and aroused the young man's zest for the war
against the Athenians. He was immediately given
ten thousand darics toward his soldiers' pay, and
for the future Cyrus told him that no restrictions
whatever were placed on his requests. For he said
that he had instructions from his father to give the
Spartans whatever they wanted.

Diodorus describes Lysander's political maneuvers in
Asia Minor ca. 408 B.C.
Cyrus was seventeen years old when he was made
governor of Asia Minor: cf. Xenophon, *Hellenica* 1.4.3;
on his subsequent conduct see of course *inter alia*
Xenophon's *Anabasis* (see *169, 271, 170*).

164. Plutarch, *Lysander* 9.   1st–2nd c. A.D.

'Ο δ' οὖν Κῦρος εἰς Σάρδεις μεταπεμψάμενος τὸν
Λύσανδρον, τὰ μὲν ἔδωκε τὰ δ' ὑπέσχετο, νεανιευ-
σάμενος εἰς τὴν ἐκείνου χάριν, καὶ εἰ μηδὲν ὁ πατὴρ
διδῷη, καταχορηγήσειν τὰ οἰκεῖα.

Cyrus then sent for Lysander to come to Sardis and
gave him some things and promised him others. He
even promised wildly that, to please him, he would
spend his own money lavishly in the event that his
father would give him nothing.

See also *Lysander 4, 6.*

165. Xenophon, *Hellenica* 1.5.1.   5th–4th c. B.C.

Οἱ δὲ Λακεδαιμόνιοι πρότερον τούτων οὐ πολλῷ χρόνῳ
Κρατησιππίδα τῆς ναυαρχίας παρεληλυθυίας Λύσανδρον ἐξέπεμψαν ναύαρχον. ὁ δὲ ἀφικόμενος εἰς 'Ρόδον
καὶ ναῦς ἐκεῖθεν λαβών, εἰς Κῶ καὶ Μίλητον ἔπλευσεν,
ἐκεῖθεν δ' εἰς Ἔφεσον, καὶ ἐκεῖ ἔμεινε ναῦς ἔχων
ἑβδομήκοντα μέχρι οὗ Κῦρος εἰς Σάρδεις ἀφίκετο. ἐπεὶ
δ' ἧκεν, ἀνέβη πρὸς αὐτὸν σὺν τοῖς ἐκ Λακεδαίμονος
πρέσβεσιν.

A short while before, when Cratesippidas handed over the office of admiral, the Spartans sent out Lysander as the commander of the fleet. When he came to Rhodes and had taken some ships from there, he sailed to Cos and Miletus and thence to Ephesus. There he stopped with seventy ships until Cyrus arrived in Sardis. And when Cyrus had come to Sardis, he went up to him with the envoys from Sparta.

Xenophon describes events not long before Alcibiades' departure from Athens, perhaps October, 407 B.C. Cyrus arrived from Gordium (1.4.3). On Cyrus' providing Lysander with money see *Hellenica* 2.1.11, 14; Pausanias 5.6.5 (see *168*), 9.32.7; Diodorus 13.104.3.

(289) Xenophon, *Oeconomicus* 4.20.

5th–4th c. B.C.

Cyrus and the Anabasis

166. Diodorus 14.19.6.   1st c. B.C.

Κῦρος δὲ τούς τε ἀπὸ τῆς Ἀσίας στρατολογηθέντας καὶ μισθοφόρους μυρίους τρισχιλίους ἀθροίσας εἰς Σάρδεις, Λυδίας μὲν καὶ Φρυγίας κατέστησεν ἐπιμελητὰς Πέρσας ἑαυτοῦ συγγενεῖς, Ἰωνίας δὲ καὶ τῆς Αἰολίδος, ἔτι δὲ τῶν σύνεγγυς τόπων Ταμώ, φίλον μὲν ὄντα πιστόν, τὸ δὲ γένος ὑπάρχοντα Μεμφίτην· αὐτὸς δὲ μετὰ τῆς δυνάμεως προῆγεν ὡς ἐπὶ τῆς Κιλικίας καὶ Πισιδίας, διαδιδοὺς λόγον ὅτι τινὲς τῶν ἐκεῖ κατοικούντων ἀφεστήκασιν.

When Cyrus had mustered his enlisted Asian troops and thirteen thousand mercenaries in Sardis, he set Persian relatives of his in command of Lydia and Phrygia. And after making his trusted friend Tamos, whose family came from Memphis, governor of Ionia, Aeolis, and the neighboring areas, he himself set out with his army toward Cilicia and Pisidia, putting about the report that some of the peoples there were in revolt.

The march to Cunaxa began in Sardis, 401 B.C.

167. Diogenes Laertius 2.49.   3rd c. A.D.

Κύρῳ δὲ φίλος ἐγένετο τοῦτον τὸν τρόπον. ἦν αὐτῷ συνήθης Πρόξενος ὄνομα, γένος Βοιώτιος, μαθητὴς μὲν Γοργίου τοῦ Λεοντίνου, φίλος δὲ Κύρῳ. οὗτος ἐν Σάρδεσι διατρίβων παρὰ τῷ Κύρῳ ἔπεμψεν εἰς Ἀθήνας ἐπιστολὴν Ξενοφῶντι, καλῶν αὐτὸν ἵνα γένηται Κύρῳ φίλος.

He became a friend of Cyrus in the following way. He had a close friend called Proxenus, a Boeotian student of Gorgias of Leontini, and a friend of Cyrus. While Proxenus was staying in Sardis with Cyrus, he sent a letter to Athens to Xenophon summoning him so that he might become a friend to Cyrus.

Diogenes describes how Xenophon became acquainted with Cyrus.

168. Pausanias 5.6.5.   2nd c. A.D.

ἐδιώχθη δὲ ὁ Ξενοφῶν ὑπὸ Ἀθηναίων ὡς ἐπὶ βασιλέα τῶν Περσῶν σφισιν εὔνουν ὄντα στρατείας μετασχὼν Κύρῳ πολεμιωτάτῳ τοῦ δήμου· καθήμενος γὰρ ἐν Σάρδεσιν ὁ Κῦρος Λυσάνδρῳ τῷ Ἀριστοκρίτου καὶ Λακεδαιμονίοις χρήματα ἀνήλισκεν ἐς τὰς ναῦς.

Xenophon was banished by the Athenians because he had participated in a campaign against their friend, the king of the Persians, with Cyrus, the greatest opponent of the democracy. For Cyrus from his vantage point in Sardis had dispensed money for ships to Lysander, son of Aristocritus, and the Spartans.

169. Xenophon, *Anabasis* 1.2.2–3ff.   5th–4th c. B.C.

ἐκάλεσε δὲ καὶ τοὺς Μίλητον πολιορκοῦντας, καὶ τοὺς φυγάδας ἐκέλευσε σὺν αὐτῷ στρατεύεσθαι, ὑποσχόμενος αὐτοῖς, εἰ καλῶς καταπράξειεν ἐφ' ἃ ἐστρατεύετο, μὴ πρόσθεν παύσεσθαι πρὶν αὐτοὺς καταγάγοι οἴκαδε. οἱ δὲ ἡδέως ἐπείθοντο· ἐπίστευον γὰρ αὐτῷ· καὶ λαβόντες τὰ ὅπλα παρῆσαν εἰς Σάρδεις. Ξενίας μὲν δὴ τοὺς ἐκ τῶν πόλεων λαβὼν παρεγένετο εἰς Σάρδεις ὁπλίτας εἰς τετρακισχιλίους, Πρόξενος δὲ παρῆν ἔχων ὁπλίτας μὲν εἰς πεντακοσίους καὶ χιλίους, γυμνῆτας δὲ πεντακοσίους, Σοφαίνετος δὲ ὁ Στυμφάλιος ὁπλίτας ἔχων χιλίους, Σωκράτης δὲ ὁ Ἀχαιὸς ὁπλίτας ἔχων ὡς πεντακοσίους, Πασίων δὲ ὁ Μεγαρεὺς τριακοσίους μὲν ὁπλίτας, τριακοσίους δὲ πελταστὰς ἔχων παρεγένετο· ἦν δὲ καὶ οὗτος καὶ ὁ Σωκράτης τῶν ἀμφὶ Μίλητον στρατευομένων. οὗτοι μὲν εἰς Σάρδεις αὐτῷ ἀφίκοντο.

He sent for those who were besieging Miletus and urged the exiles to campaign with him, promising them that if he achieved his objectives, he would not rest until he had restored them to their homes. They gladly consented, for they trusted him, and they took up their weapons and came to Sardis. Xenias also mustered troops from the cities, to the tune of 4000 hoplites, and came to Sardis. Proxenus too arrived with up to 1500 hoplites and 500 light-armed men, Sophaenetus of Stymphalus with 1000 and Socrates of Achaea with 500 hoplites, and

Pasion of Megara with 300 hoplites and 300 targeteers. This fellow and Socrates had been among those fighting before Miletus. These joined him at Sardis.

Tissaphernes hastened to warn the king, who took appropriate measures (4). Cyrus began the march from Sardis (5).

Cyrus collects his army.

170. Xenophon, *Anabasis* 3.1.8ff.   5th–4th c. B.C.

ὁ μὲν δὴ Ξενοφῶν οὕτω θυσάμενος οἷς ἀνεῖλεν ὁ θεὸς ἐξέπλει, καὶ καταλαμβάνει ἐν Σάρδεσι Πρόξενον καὶ Κῦρον μέλλοντας ἤδη ὁρμᾶν τὴν ἄνω ὁδόν, καὶ συνεστάθη Κύρῳ.

Then Xenophon sacrificed to the gods appointed by the [Delphic] oracle and sailed away. He caught up with Proxenus and Cyrus in Sardis as they were just about to embark on the march upcountry, and he was introduced to Cyrus.

Cyrus urged him to go with them, and it was said the expedition was against the Pisidians (9). Xenophon joined the project unaware of the real objective (10).

At 3.1.31 we learn of a Lydian, Apollonides by (assumed) name, masquerading as a Boeotian and being detected because of his pierced ears: for Lydians wearing earrings see G. M. A. Hanfmann, *BASOR* 162 (1961) 29; Hanfmann, *BASOR* 174 (1964) 10; and cf. J. G. Pedley, *Sardis in the Age of Croesus* (Norman, Oklahoma 1968) 102, 112.

(271) Xenophon, *Anabasis* 1.6.6–7.

5th–4th c. B.C.

Agesilaus near Sardis

171. Dio Chrysostom, *Orationes* 56.7.   1st c. A.D.

ὕστερον δὲ Ἀγησίλαον πολεμοῦντα βασιλεῖ τῷ μεγάλῳ καὶ περὶ Σάρδεις νενικηκότα μάχῃ καὶ κρατήσαντα πάσης τῆς κάτω Ἀσίας ὑπηρέτην πέμψαντες ἐκάλουν παρ' αὐτούς· καὶ ὃς οὐδεμίαν ἡμέραν ἀνεβάλετο, τοσούτων μὲν Ἑλλήνων, τοσούτων δὲ βαρβάρων γεγονὼς κύριος.

Later, Agesilaus made war on the great king and won a victory in battle near Sardis and conquered all of lower Asia. Whereupon the ephors dispatched a servant and summoned him to their presence. And he did not delay one day though he had become the master of so many Greeks and so many barbarians.

For the recall of Agesilaus see Xenophon, *Hellenica* 4.2.1–3.

(288) Diodorus 14.80.2.   1st c. B.C.

172. *Hellenica Oxyrhynchia* 12.1.   4th c. B.C.

Γενομένης δὲ τ[ῆς] μάχης τοιαύ[τ]ης οἱ μὲ[ν βά]ρβαροι καταπλαγέντες [τοὺς] Ἕλληνας ἀπεχώρησ[αν σὺν] τῷ Τισσαφέρνει πρὸς τὰς Σάρδεις· Ἀγησίλαος δὲ περ-[ιμε]ίνας αὐτοῦ τρεῖς ἡμέρας, ἐν αἷς τοὺς νεκροὺς ὑποσπ[όν]δους ἀπέδωκεν τοῖς π[ο]λεμίοις καὶ τροπαῖον ἔστη[σε] καὶ τὴν γῆν ἅπασαν ἐ[πόρθ]ησεν, προῆγεν τὸ στρ[άτε]υμα εἰς Φρυγίαν πάλιν [τὴν] μεγάλην.

After the battle the Persians in amazement at the Greeks withdrew with Tissaphernes toward Sardis. Agesilaus remained there three days during which time he returned the dead under truce to the enemy, set up a trophy, and ravaged all the countryside around. Thereafter he set his army in motion again toward Phrygia.

Cf. *Hellenica Oxyrhynchia* 13.1. For Tithraustes in Sardis see *Hellenica Oxyrhynchia* 19.3.

173. Nepos, *Agesilaus* 3.4–5.   1st c. B.C.

Huic cum tempus esset visum copias extrahere ex hibernaculis, vidit, si, quo esset iter facturus, palam pronuntiasset, hostis non credituros aliasque regiones praesidiis occupaturos neque dubitaturos aliud eum facturum, ac pronuntiasset. Itaque cum ille Sardis iturum se dixisset, Tissaphernes eandem Cariam defendendam putavit. In quo cum eum opinio fefellisset victumque se vidisset consilio, sero suis praesidio profectus est. Nam cum illo venisset, iam Agesilaus multis locis expugnatis magna erat praeda potitus.

When the time seemed right to him to bring his troops from their winter quarters, he saw that if he declared openly where he intended to campaign, the enemy distrusting him would secure other areas with garrison forces and would not doubt that he would do other than he had announced. Accordingly, after he had said that he would go to Sardis, Tissaphernes thought that Caria was his real objective. And when his thinking in this had proved wrong and he realized that in planning he had been defeated, he set out to protect his men too late. For when he arrived there, Agesilaus had already stormed many places and taken hold of much booty.

Cf. Frontinus, *Strategemata* 1.8.12.

174. Pausanias 3.9.5ff.   2nd c. A.D.

Ἀγησίλαον δὲ ἐλύπει μὲν ἡ θυσία μὴ τελεσθεῖσα, διέβαινε δὲ ὅμως ἐς τὴν Ἀσίαν καὶ ἤλαυνεν ἐπὶ τὰς Σάρδεις· ἦν γὰρ δὴ τῆς Ἀσίας τῆς κάτω μέγιστον μέρος τηνικαῦτα ἡ Λυδία, καὶ αἱ Σάρδεις πλούτῳ καὶ παρασκευῇ προεῖχον, τῷ τε σατραπεύοντι ἐπὶ θαλάσσῃ τοῦτο οἰκητήριον ἀπεδέδεικτο καθάπερ γε αὐτῷ βασιλεῖ τὰ Σοῦσα.

That the sacrifice was incomplete troubled Agesilaus, but he crossed nevertheless to Asia and made for Sardis. For at this time Lydia was the largest part of lower Asia and Sardis excelled in riches and resources; the city had been designated as the seat of the satrap of the coastal zone, just as Susa had been assigned to the king himself.
In view of Agesilaus' success, Tissaphernes was executed and Tithraustes sent to Sardis in his stead (3.9.7f).

For Tissaphernes lured from Sardis by Artaxerxes see Polyaenus 7.16.1; cf. Diodorus 14.80.8.

175. Plutarch, *Agesilaus* 10.   1st–2nd c. A.D.

ἀλλ' ἐκεῖνος ἑαυτὸν ἐξηπάτησε, διὰ τὴν ἔμπροσθεν ἀπάτην ἀπιστῶν τῷ Ἀγησιλάῳ, καὶ νῦν γοῦν αὐτὸν ἅψεσθαι τῆς Καρίας νομίζων, οὔσης δυσίππου, πολὺ τῷ ἱππικῷ λειπόμενον. ἐπεὶ δ' ὥσπερ προεῖπεν ὁ Ἀγησίλαος ἧκεν εἰς τὸ περὶ Σάρδεις πεδίον, ἠναγκάζετο κατὰ σπουδὴν ἐκεῖθεν αὖ βοηθεῖν ὁ Τισσαφέρνης· καὶ τῇ ἵππῳ διεξελαύνων διέφθειρε πολλοὺς τῶν ἀτάκτως τὸ πεδίον πορθούντων.

But the satrap deceived himself, distrusting Agesilaus because of his earlier trickery and believing that now at any rate he would make for Caria, since it was territory difficult for horses and it was cavalry which he most lacked. But when, just exactly as he had said, Agesilaus had come to the plain around Sardis, then Tissaphernes was obliged to hurry back from Caria to help the city. And, galloping through the plain with his cavalry, he killed many Greeks in disorder there busily plundering.

176. Polyaenus 2.1.9.   2nd c. A.D.

Ἀγησίλαος ἐπὶ Σάρδεις ἐλαύνων καθῆκε λογοποιούς, ὡς ἐξαπατῶν Τισαφέρνην στέλλεται μὲν φανερῶς ἐπὶ Λυδίας, τρέπεται δὲ ἀφανῶς ἐπὶ Καρίας. ἠγγέλη ταῦτα Τισαφέρνῃ. ὁ μὲν Πέρσης ὥρμησε Καρίαν φυλάττειν, ὁ δὲ Λάκων κατέδραμε Λυδίαν καὶ λείαν πολλὴν κατέσυρεν.

Agesilaus made for Sardis and sent out reports deceiving Tissaphernes, to the effect that he was ostensibly aiming for Lydia but secretly was turning against Caria. This was reported to Tissaphernes. Accordingly the Persian set out to defend Caria while the Spartan overran Lydia and plundered much booty.

177. Xenophon, *Agesilaus* 1.33.   5th–4th c. B.C.

ὡς δ' ἤκουσε τοὺς πολεμίους ταράττεσθαι διὰ τὸ αἰτιᾶσθαι ἀλλήλους τοῦ γεγενημένου, εὐθὺς ἦγεν ἐπὶ Σάρδεις. κἀκεῖ ἅμα μὲν ἔκαιε καὶ ἐπόρθει τὰ περὶ τὸ ἄστυ, ἅμα δὲ καὶ κηρύγματι ἐδήλου τοὺς μὲν ἐλευθερίας δεομένους ὡς πρὸς σύμμαχον αὐτὸν παρεῖναι· εἰ δέ τινες τὴν Ἀσίαν ἑαυτῶν ποιοῦνται, πρὸς τοὺς ἐλευθεροῦντας διακρινουμένους ἐν ὅπλοις παρεῖναι.

When he heard that the enemy were in disarray because they were blaming one another for what had happened, he immediately marched on Sardis. Once there he burnt and pillaged the outlying areas of the city and proclaimed that any who desired freedom should come to him as to an ally. And if any claimed Asia for themselves, they should present themselves to the liberators for the outcome to be decided by arms.
With no opposition Agesilaus plundered the country so completely that in two years he was able to dedicate more than two hundred talents to Apollo at Delphi (34).

Ca. 395–394 B.C.
For Agesilaus in Asia Minor see Xenophon, *Hellenica* 3.4.5ff, 4.1.1ff; Xenophon, *Agesilaus* 1ff; Plutarch, *Agesilaus* 7–16 (see *175*); Pausanias 3.9.5 (see *174*); Diodorus 14.80.2 (see *288*); Nepos, *Agesilaus* 3.4–6 (see *173*).

178. Xenophon, *Hellenica* 3.4.21ff.   5th–4th c. B.C.

ὁ δ' Ἀγησίλαος οὐκ ἐψεύσατο, ἀλλ' ὥσπερ προεῖπεν εὐθὺς εἰς τὸν Σαρδιανὸν τόπον ἐνέβαλε. καὶ τρεῖς μὲν ἡμέρας δι' ἐρημίας πολεμίων πορευόμενος πολλὰ τὰ ἐπιτήδεια τῇ στρατιᾷ εἶχε, τῇ δὲ τετάρτῃ ἧκον οἱ τῶν πολεμίων ἱππεῖς.

But Agesilaus had not lied. Rather, just as he had declared, he made straight for the area around Sardis. For three days he advanced through territory left unoccupied by the enemy and had plenty of provisions for his army; but on the fourth day the enemy's cavalry made contact with him.
The Greek forces were ordered to camp across the Pactolus, some were killed, and lines of battle were drawn up (22). The Greek plan of attack (23). The

Persians without their infantry were defeated and their camp captured (24).

Ca. 395–394 B.C.
The journey from Ephesus to Sardis took three days (Xenophon, *Hellenica* 3.2.11; Herodotus 5.54 [see *191*]). Tissaphernes had remained at Sardis (3.4.25) (though cf. Plutarch, *Agesilaus* 10 [see *175*]) and for this reason the Persians thought he had betrayed them. Cf. Xenophon, *Agesilaus* 1.35.

Other Greeks and Sardis

179. Diogenes Laertius 4.29.   3rd c. A.D.

ἤκουσε δὴ κατ’ ἀρχὰς μὲν Αὐτολύκου τοῦ μαθηματικοῦ πολίτου τυγχάνοντος, πρὶν ἀπαίρειν εἰς ’Αθήνας, μεθ’ οὗ καὶ εἰς Σάρδεις ἀπεδήμησεν· ἔπειτα Ξάνθου τοῦ ’Αθηναίου μουσικοῦ· μεθ’ ὃν Θεοφράστου διήκουσεν. ἔπειτα μετῆλθεν εἰς ’Ακαδήμειαν πρὸς Κράντορα.

At first, before he left for Athens, he studied with a fellow countryman, the mathematician Autolycus, with whom he visited Sardis. Next he studied with Xanthus of Athens, the musician; and then with Theophrastus. Finally he went across to the Academy and to Crantor.

Diogenes describes the career of Arcesilaus of Aeolian Pitane. He lived from ca. 318–ca. 242 B.C.

180. Nepos, *Conon* 5.3–4.   1st c. B.C.

Id cum minus diligenter esset celatum, Tiribazus, qui Sardibus praeerat, Cononem evocavit, simulans ad regem eum se mittere velle magna de re. Hujus nuntio parens cum venisset, in vincla coniectus est; in quibus aliquamdiu fuit. Inde nonnulli eum ad regem abductum ibique [eum] perisse scriptum reliquerunt: contra ea Dinon historicus, cui nos plurimum de Persicis rebus credimus, effugisse scripsit; illud addubitat, utrum Tiribazo sciente an imprudente sit factum.

Since this plan had not been hidden carefully enough, Tiribazus, who was the satrap at Sardis, summoned Conon pretending that he wished to send him to the king on an important matter. When in obedience to the message Conon had arrived, he was thrown into prison and remained there for some time. Some have recorded that from there he was led away to the king and died there; on the other hand, the historian Dinon, whom I trust most in Persian matters, said that he escaped, but

it is doubtful whether this happened with the collusion of Tiribazus or without.

Ca. 392 B.C.
Cf. Xenophon, *Hellenica* 4.8.12ff. For Conon’s death see Lysias 19.39ff. Dinon (*FGrHist* 690) flourished in the middle of the fourth century.

181. Thucydides 1.115.4.   5th c. B.C.

τῶν δὲ Σαμίων ἦσαν γάρ τινες οἳ οὐχ ὑπέμειναν, ἀλλ’ ἔφυγον ἐς τὴν ἤπειρον, ξυνθέμενοι τῶν ἐν τῇ πόλει τοῖς δυνατωτάτοις καὶ Πισσούθνῃ τῷ ῾Υστάσπου ξυμμαχίαν, ὃς εἶχε Σάρδεις τότε, ἐπικούρους τε ξυλλέξαντες ἐς ἑπτακοσίους διέβησαν ὑπὸ νύκτα ἐς τὴν Σάμον.

There were some of the Samians who did not remain but fled to the mainland after aligning themselves with the leading oligarchs who remained in the city, and with Pissuthnes, son of Hystaspes, who was at that time satrap of Sardis. When they had collected up to seven hundred mercenaries, they crossed under cover of darkness to Samos.

The establishment of the democracy in Samos has just taken place: 440 B.C.
On Pissuthnes see also 3.31.1, 8.5.5; Plutarch, *Pericles* 25; Ctesias *FGrHist* 688 F 15 (53).

182. Xenophon, *Hellenica* 4.1.27.   5th–4th c. B.C.

ἐκεῖνοι μέντοι ταῦτα παθόντες οὐκ ἤνεγκαν, ἀλλ’ ὡς ἀδικηθέντες καὶ ἀτιμασθέντες νυκτὸς συσκευασάμενοι ᾤχοντο ἀπιόντες εἰς Σάρδεις πρὸς ’Αριαῖον, πιστεύσαντες, ὅτι καὶ ὁ ’Αριαῖος ἀποστὰς βασιλέως ἐπολέμησεν αὐτῷ.

When they were treated in this manner they did not tolerate it, but thinking they had been done an injustice and had been dishonored, they packed up and went off by night to Sardis to Ariaeus. For they trusted him since he too had revolted from the king and made war on him.

Perhaps 395–394 B.C. Spithridates and the Paphlagonians.
Ariaeus had been an aide to Cyrus (*Anabasis* 1.8.5, 2.4.2ff) and on the left wing at Cunaxa (*Oeconomicus* 4.19; *Anabasis* 1.9.31).

183. Xenophon, *Hellenica* 4.8.21.   5th–4th c. B.C.

ὁ μὲν δὴ Διφρίδας ταῦτ’ ἐποίει, καὶ τά τ’ ἄλλα ἐπετύγχανε καὶ Τιγράνην τὸν τὴν Στρούθα ἔχοντα θυγατέρα πορευόμενον εἰς Σάρδεις λαμβάνει σὺν αὐτῇ τῇ γυναικί, καὶ χρημάτων πολλῶν ἀπέλυσεν· ὥστ’ εὐθὺς ἐντεῦθεν εἶχε μισθοδοτεῖν.

Diphridas was busy with these matters. He met with good fortune in many of his projects but especially in capturing Tigranes, son-in-law to Struthas, and his wife as they were on their way to Sardis. He received a large ransom for them with which he was immediately able to hire mercenaries.

Ca. 390 B.C.
Diphridas was the Spartan general dispatched to Asia Minor after the death of Thibron. Struthas was taking the Athenian side (4.8.17).

Sardis in the Greek Poets

184. Aelian, *De natura animalium* 12.9.

2nd–3rd c. A.D.

καὶ Αὐτοκράτης ἐν Τυμπανισταῖς
οἷα παίζουσιν φίλαι
παρθένοι Λυδῶν κόραι
κοῦφα πηδῶσαι κόμαν,
κἀνακρούουσαι χεροῖν,
Ἐφεσίαν παρ' Ἄρτεμιν
καλλίσταν, καὶ τοῖν ἰσχίοιν
τὸ μὲν κάτω τὸ δ' αὖ
εἰς ἄνω ἐξαίρουσα,
οἷα κίγκλος ἄλλεται.

And Autocrates in the *Tympanistae* writes, "As dear maidens, Lydian girls, play lightly, jumping this way and that, clapping their hands by the temple of Artemis the Beautiful at Ephesus. At one moment they sink down onto their haunches and at the next leap up just as the wagtail bobs about."

Autocrates wrote in the 4th c. B.C.
For Lydians living close by the sanctuary of Artemis at Ephesus see Pausanias 7.2.8, and for close relation between Artemis of Ephesus and Artemis of Sardis see F. Eichler, *AnzWien* 99 (1962) 50ff; D. Knibbe, *JOAI* 46 (1961–1963) 175–182.
For Lydian attention to (worship of) Artemis elsewhere see Athenaeus, *Deipnosophistae* 14.636a quoting Diogenes the tragic poet. Cf. Aristophanes, *Lysistrata* 1310ff, *Clouds* 595 (see *186*).
For Lydian rhythm and music see Athenaeus, *Deipnosophistae* 12.517a (martial; cf. Herodotus 1.17 [see *62*]); 14.625e, f (modes); 14.634c, f (instruments); 14.635d (Terpander and the *barbitos*). See also Plutarch, *Praecepta gerendae reipublicae* 30 (822C); *De musica* 8 (1134B), 11 (1135B), 15–17 (1136B–1137A).

185. Aeschylus, *Persae* 41–47.

5th c. B.C.

ἁβροδιαίτων δ' ἕπεται Λυδῶν
ὄχλος, οἵτ' ἐπίπαν ἠπειρογενὲς

κατέχουσιν ἔθνος, τοὺς Μητρογαθὴς
Ἀρκτεύς τ' ἀγαθός, βασιλῆς δίοποι,
χαὶ πολύχρυσοι Σάρδεις ἐπόχους
πολλοῖς ἅρμασιν ἐξορμῶσιν,
δίρρυμά τε καὶ τρίρρυμα τέλη,
φοβερὰν ὄψιν προσιδέσθαι.

Then came the host of graceful-living Lydians who control all the mainland race. Princely commanders, Metrogathes and noble Arcteus, and Sardis rich in gold set these in motion mounted up with numerous chariots. In varied squadrons, with three-, four-, or six-horse chariots, they are a dreadful sight to behold.

The Lydians are no longer warlike (Herodotus 1.155–157 [see *142*]); on this cf. Schol. Sophocles, *Oedipus Coloneus* 337. For chariot types cf. Xenophon, *Cyropaedia* 6.1.51. See also *Persae* 321.

186. Aristophanes, *Clouds* 595–600.   5th c. B.C.

ἀμφί μοι αὖτε Φοῖβ' ἄναξ
Δήλιε Κυνθίαν ἔχων
ὑψικέρατα πέτραν,
ἤ τ' Ἐφέσου μάκαιρα πάγχρυσον ἔχεις
οἶκον ἐν ᾧ κόραι σε Λυδῶν μεγάλως σέβουσιν . . .

Delian lord Apollo, be with me still, you who rule the high cliff of Cynthus. And you blessed lady Artemis who hold the golden temple of Ephesus in which Lydian maidens honor you greatly . . .

On Cynthus see Strabo 10.5.2; Ovid, *Metamorphoses* 2.221.
On the temple at Ephesus see Aelian, *Varia historia* 3.26 (see *69*); Herodotus 1.26 (see *71*), 1.92 (see *100*), 2.148; Pliny, *Naturalis historia* 36.95; Polyaenus 6.50 (see *72*).
On Lydian girls dancing in honor of Artemis see Aelian, *De natura animalium* 12.9 quoting Autocrates (see *184*); and cf. A. Greifenhagen, *Antike Kunst* 8:1 (1965) 13–19.

187. Aristophanes, *Wasps* 1135–1140.   5th c. B.C.

Βδ. ἔχ' ἀναβαλοῦ τηνδὶ λαβὼν καὶ μὴ λάλει.
Φι. τουτὶ τὸ κακὸν τί ἐστι πρὸς πάντων θεῶν;
Βδ. οἱ μὲν καλοῦσι Περσίδ' οἱ δὲ καυνάκην.
Φι. ἐγὼ δὲ σισύραν ᾠόμην Θυμαιτίδα.
Βδ. κοὐ θαυμά γ'. ἐς Σάρδεις γὰρ οὐκ ἐλήλυθας.
ἔγνως γὰρ ἄν· νῦν δ' οὐχὶ γιγνώσκεις.

B. Come on, take it and put it on and stop chatting away.
P. Good god, what is this thing?
B. Some call it Persian, others a Caunacian.

P. I thought it was a Thymaetian eiderdown.

B. Small wonder. Since you've never been to Sardis. Otherwise you'd have known. But you don't.

> For the *caunaces* see Pollux 6.11, 7.59, and cf. Thucydides 1.130. See also *Acharnians* 112, *Pax* 1174.

188. Callimachus, *Hymns* 3.242–247.   3rd c. B.C.

ὑπήεισαν δὲ λίγειαι
λεπταλέον σύριγγες, ἵνα ῥήσσωσιν ὁμαρτῇ
(οὐ γάρ πω νέβρεια δι' ὀστέα τετρήναντο,
ἔργον 'Αθηναίης ἐλάφῳ κακόν). ἔδραμε δ' ἠχώ
Σάρδιας ἔς τε νομὸν Βερεκύνθιον. αἱ δὲ πόδεσσιν
οὖλα κατεκροτάλιζον, ἐπεψόφεον δὲ φαρέτραι.

The shrill pipes sounded loud that they might dance together (they did not yet pierce the bones of the fawn; that was an accomplishment of Athena's and an act of evil for the deer). And the echo rang to Sardis and the Berecynthian pasture, as they drummed loudly with their feet and their quivers rattled.

> The Amazons are honoring Artemis in Ephesus.
> According to Pindar (*Pythian Odes* 12.22) Athena invented the flute, which, according to Pollux (4.71), was sometimes made from the bones of fawns.
> Berecynthia was between Lydia and Phrygia: so the scholiast.

(257) Euripides, *Bacchae* 461–464.   5th c. B.C.

189. Sophocles, *Antigone* 1037–1039.   5th c. B.C.

κερδαίνετ', ἐμπολᾶτε τἀπὸ Σάρδεων
ἤλεκτρον, εἰ βούλεσθε, καὶ τὸν 'Ινδικὸν
χρυσόν.

Make money, then, trade if you wish in the electrum from Sardis and Indian gold.

> Creon charges Teiresias.
> On electrum see Pliny, *Naturalis historia* 33.80, Pausanias 5.12.7 with which cf. Herodotus 3.115, *Odyssey* 15.460.
> On refined and unrefined gold see Herodotus 1.50 (see 99); and on Indian gold see Herodotus 3.94.

190. Timotheus, *Persae* 116–118 (Page, 791).
5th–4th c. B.C.

οὐ γὰρ ἂ[ν Τμῶ]λον οὐδ'
ἄστυ Λύδιον [λι]πὼν Σάρδεων
ἦλθον ["Ε]λλαν' ἀπέρξων "Αρ[η.

For I would not have left Tmolus or the Lydian city of Sardis to ward off Greek Ares.

> Xerxes seems just to have expressed the wish that he had never built the bridges across the Hellespont. Cf. Timotheus, *Persae* 158.

The Royal Road

191. Herodotus 5.52ff.   5th c. B.C.

καταγωγαὶ μὲν νυν σταθμῶν τοσαῦταί εἰσι ἐκ Σαρδίων ἐς Σοῦσα ἀναβαίνοντι· εἰ δὲ ὀρθῶς μεμέτρηται ἡ ὁδὸς ἡ βασιληίη τοῖσι παρασάγγῃσι καὶ ὁ παρασάγγης δύναται τριήκοντα στάδια, ὥσπερ οὗτός γε δύναται ταῦτα, ἐκ Σαρδίων στάδιά ἐστι ἐς τὰ βασιλήια τὰ Μεμνόνεια καλεόμενα πεντακόσια καὶ τρισχίλια καὶ μύρια παρασαγγέων ἐόντων πεντήκοντα καὶ τετρακοσίων. πεντήκοντα δὲ καὶ ἑκατὸν στάδια ἐπ' ἡμέρῃ ἑκάστῃ διεξιοῦσι ἀναισιμοῦνται ἡμέραι ἀπαρτὶ ἐνενήκοντα.

That then is the number of way-stations which the traveler encounters going down from Sardis to Susa. If the royal road has been accurately measured in parasangs and the parasang is the equivalent of thirty stades, as it is, then from Sardis to the royal palace known as the Memnonian is a distance of thirteen thousand five hundred stades, that is to say, four hundred and fifty parasangs. For those who travel one hundred and fifty stades each day, exactly ninety days are spent.
The distance between Sardis and Ephesus is five hundred forty stades (54).

> Strabo (11.11.5) admits differences of opinion on the length of the parasang in terms of stades.
> On Memnon see W. W. How and J. Wells, *A Commentary on Herodotus* (Oxford 1968) *ad* 2.106.
> Herodotus (5.54) allows only three days for the journey from Ephesus to Sardis: cf. Xenophon, *Hellenica* 3.2.11. On the archaeological evidence for the royal road in Sardis see G. M. A. Hanfmann, *BASOR* 166 (1962) 40.

ALEXANDER AND THE SELEUCIDS

Alexander

(235) Arrian, *Anabasis* 1.17.3–6.   2nd c. A.D.

192. Diodorus 17.21.7.   1st c. B.C.

Αὐτὸς δ' ἀναλαβὼν τὴν δύναμιν προῆγε διὰ τῆς Λυδίας, καὶ τὴν μὲν τῶν Σαρδιανῶν πόλιν καὶ τὰς ἀκροπόλεις, ἔτι δὲ τοὺς ἐν αὐταῖς θησαυροὺς παρέλαβε Μιθρίνους τοῦ σατράπου παραδόντος ἑκουσίως.

When he had recovered his forces Alexander led them through Lydia and took possession of the city of the Sardians and the citadels and the treasure still there, since Mithrines the satrap handed them over willingly.

Ca. 334 B.C.
For Mithrines' reward see Diodorus 17.64.6; Arrian, *Anabasis* 3.16.5.

193. Himerius, *Orationes* 2.15.   4th c. A.D.

οὕτω Σάρδεις εἷλεν, οὕτω Καρίαν ἐπόρθησεν, οὕτω Λυκίαν παρέσυρεν, οὕτω Παμφυλίαν ἐπέδραμεν.

It was by this means that he took Sardis, by this means that he sacked Caria, by this means that he swept Lycia away, and by this means that he overran Pamphylia.

Himerius describes Alexander's tactics.

194. Orosius 3.16.5.   5th c. A.D.

magna igitur caedes Persarum fuit. in exercitu Alexandri CXX equites et novem tantum pedites defuere. deinde Gordien Phrygiae civitatem, quae nunc Sardis vocitatur, obsessam oppugnatamque cepit ac diriptioni dedit.

A great slaughter of Persians ensued, though in Alexander's army only one hundred twenty cavalry and nine infantrymen were missing. Next he besieged, attacked, and captured Gordien, a Phrygian city which is now called Sardis, and gave it over to plunder.

A confused account of Alexander's progress through Asia Minor.

195. Plutarch, *Alexander* 17.   1st–2nd c. A.D.

Οὗτος ὁ ἀγὼν μεγάλην εὐθὺς ἐποίησε τῶν πραγμάτων μεταβολὴν πρὸς Ἀλέξανδρον, ὥστε καὶ Σάρδεις, τὸ πρόσχημα τῆς ἐπὶ θαλάσσῃ τῶν βαρβάρων ἡγεμονίας, παραλαβεῖν καὶ τἆλλα προστίθεσθαι.

This battle made an immediate change in the political situation in Alexander's favor so that he took Sardis, the focal point of the barbarians' control on the sea coast, and added other states.

196. Pompeius Trogus, *Historiae Philippicae* 11 F 74.
1st c. B.C.

Mox regem Indorum et omnes Asiae gentes sub potestate sua redegit et nobilissimas urbes Asiae cepit Sardes Bactra Susa Babyloniam.

Soon he conquered and brought under his sway the king of the Indi and all the nations of Asia; and he took possession of the noblest cities of Asia— Sardis, Bactra, Susa, and Babylonia.

Pompeius describes Alexander's career. Cf. Ampelius 16.2; Pompeius Trogus *Historiae Philippicae* 12 F 101d.

197. Pompeius Trogus, *Historiae Philippicae* 11 F 80.
1st c. B.C.

Hoc mulierum errore conperto Alexander fortunae Darei et pietati earum inlacrimasse fertur. Ac primo Mithrenem, qui Sardis tradiderat, peritum linguae Persicae, ire ad consolandas eas iusserat.

When the women's error was known, Alexander is said to have wept for the fortune of Darius and the devotion of his womenfolk. And first he instructed Mithrenes, who had surrendered Sardis and who knew Persian, to go and console them.

Darius' women believed he was dead.

Cleopatra and Sardis

198. Diodorus 20.37.3ff.   1st c. B.C.

Ἅμα δὲ τούτοις πραττομένοις Κλεοπάτρα τῷ μὲν Ἀντιγόνῳ προσκόπτουσα, τῇ δ᾽ αἱρέσει πρὸς τὸν Πτολεμαῖον ἀποκλίνουσα προῆγεν ἐκ Σάρδεων, ὡς διακομισθησομένη πρὸς ἐκεῖνον. ἦν δὲ ἀδελφὴ μὲν Ἀλεξάνδρου τοῦ Πέρσας καταπολεμήσαντος, θυγάτηρ δὲ Φιλίππου τοῦ Ἀμύντου, γυνὴ δὲ γεγενημένη τοῦ εἰς Ἰταλίαν στρατεύσαντος Ἀλεξάνδρου.

While these things were happening Cleopatra argued with Antigonus, and, leaning in her choice toward Ptolemy, she set out from Sardis with the intention of crossing to him. She was the sister of Alexander who conquered the Persians and daughter of Philip, son of Amyntas; and she had been wife to the Alexander who made an expedition into Italy.
All Alexander's generals were seeking her hand after his death (4). On Antigonus' orders, Cleopatra was murdered in Sardis before she could depart (5).

For Cleopatra's predilection for Sardis see Arrian, *FGrHist* 156 F 9 (26). For Cleopatra's marriage to Alexander see 16.91ff; and for her subsequent marriage to Leonnatus see Plutarch, *Eumenes* 3.5. For Lysimachus' winning control of Sardis see 20.107.4.

199. Justin 14.1.7.   3rd c. A.D.

Inde Sardis profectus est ad Cleopatram, sororem Alexandri Magni, ut eius voce centuriones principesque confirmarentur, existimaturos ibi maiestatem regiam verti, unde soror Alexandri staret.

From there he set out for Sardis to Cleopatra, sister of Alexander the Great, so that by her voice the centurions and officers might be emboldened to believe that royal authority was being dispensed from the point where Alexander's sister stood.

Eumenes' activities after the death of Perdiccas.

The Third Century B.C.

200. Plutarch, *Demetrius* 46.   1st–2nd c. A.D.

καὶ μετὰ τὸν γάμον εὐθὺς ἐπὶ τὰς πόλεις τρέπεται, πολλῶν μὲν ἑκουσίως προστιθεμένων, πολλὰς δὲ καὶ βιαζόμενος. ἔλαβε δὲ καὶ Σάρδεις· καί τινες τῶν Λυσιμάχου στρατηγῶν ἀπεχώρησαν πρὸς αὐτόν, χρήματα καὶ στρατιὰν κομίζοντες.

After the marriage he turned directly against the cities, of which many joined him willingly and many he compelled. He took Sardis also: and some of Lysimachus' generals came to his side with money and soldiery.

The marriage was with Ptolemais, a daughter of Ptolemy. For the betrothal cf. *Demetrius* 32.

On the date of Demetrius' campaign into Asia Minor see W. S. Ferguson, *CP* 24 (1929) 28f.

(237) Polyaenus 4.9.4.   2nd c. A.D.

201. Strabo 13.4.2.   1st c. B.C.–1st c. A.D.

ἐκ μὲν οὖν τοῦ Εὐμένους ἐγένετο ὁμώνυμος τῷ πατρὶ Εὐμένης, ὅσπερ καὶ διεδέξατο τὸ Πέργαμον, καὶ ἦν ἤδη δυνάστης τῶν κύκλῳ χωρίων, ὥστε καὶ περὶ Σάρδεις ἐνίκησε μάχῃ συμβαλὼν Ἀντίοχον τὸν Σέλευκον· δύο δὲ καὶ εἴκοσιν ἄρξας ἔτη τελευτᾷ τὸν βίον.

Eumenes had a son to whom he gave his own name, Eumenes, and he succeeded to the throne in Pergamum and had already made himself master of the surrounding municipalities. He even joined battle with Antiochus son of Seleucus near Sardis and defeated him. He died after a reign of twenty-two years.

The battle took place ca. 262 B.C.
263–241 B.C. are the years of Eumenes' reign. On his victory near Sardis over Antiochus see D. Magie, *Roman Rule in Asia Minor* (Princeton 1950) 6, 733.

Achaeus and the Siege of Sardis

202. Polybius 5.77.1.   2nd c. B.C.

Ἀχαιὸς δὲ ποιησάμενος ὑφ' ἑαυτὸν τὴν Μιλυάδα καὶ τὰ πλεῖστα μέρη τῆς Παμφυλίας ἀνέζευξε, καὶ παραγενόμενος εἰς Σάρδεις ἐπολέμει μὲν Ἀττάλῳ συνεχῶς, ἀνετείνετο δὲ Προυσίᾳ, πᾶσι δ' ἦν φοβερὸς καὶ βαρὺς τοῖς ἐπὶ τάδε τοῦ Ταύρου κατοικοῦσι.

Achaeus made Milyas and most areas of Pamphylia subject to him, and when he reached Sardis he made war on Attalus continually and threatened Prusias. To all who lived this side of the Taurus he became a symbol of terror and oppression.

On Achaeus, and on Attalus' campaign of 218 B.C., see F. W. Walbank, *A Historical Commentary on Polybius* I (Oxford 1957) 501–502, 601.

203. Polybius 7.15.1ff.   2nd c. B.C.

Περὶ δὲ τὰς Σάρδεις ἄπαυστοι καὶ συνεχεῖς ἀκροβολισμοὶ συνίσταντο καὶ κίνδυνοι καὶ νύκτωρ καὶ μεθ' ἡμέραν, πᾶν γένος ἐνέδρας, ἀντενέδρας, ἐπιθέσεως ἐξευρισκόντων τῶν στρατιωτῶν καὶ ἀλλήλων· περὶ ὧν γράφειν τὰ κατὰ μέρος οὐ μόνον ἀνωφελὲς ἀλλὰ καὶ μακρὸν ἂν εἴη τελέως.

Around Sardis there were ceaseless and continual engagements and skirmishes both by night and day, the soldiers contriving against each other every kind of ambush, counterambush, and assault. To write about these one by one would not only be pointless, but also extremely lengthy.
After a year's siege Lagoras the Cretan took things into his own hands (2), remarking that strong cities are often captured at their points of strength (3). Due to the strength of Sardis all believed the city would be taken only by famine (4), but Lagoras sought an opportunity (5).

215–214 B.C.
Lagoras was a deserter from Ptolemy IV (Polybius 5.61.9): cf. H. van Effenterre, *La Crète et le monde grec de Platon à Polybe* (Paris 1948) 295.

For the chronology of the siege and capture see F. W. Walbank, *A Historical Commentary on Polybius* II (Oxford 1967) 3.

(283) Polybius 7.15.6–7.   2nd c. B.C.

(284) Polybius 7.16.6.   2nd c. B.C.

(285) Polybius 7.17.6.   2nd c. B.C.

(286) Polybius 8.20.5–6.   2nd c. B.C.

204. Pompeius Trogus, *Historiae Philippicae* 30 proleg.

1st c. B.C.

Transitus deinde ad res Antiochi, qui post regnum acceptum persecutus defectores in Mediam Molonem, in Asiam Achaeum, quem obsedit Sardibus, pacata superiore Asia Bactris tenus in bella Romana descendit.

Next there is a transition to the affairs of Antiochus. After he had taken over the empire he pursued the rebels, Molon into Media and Achaeus, whom he besieged in Sardis, into Asia. When upper Asia had been pacified as far as the Bactri, he came down for the wars with Rome.

Antiochus the Great

205. Livy 37.18.6ff.

1st c. B.C.–1st c. A.D.

eodem ferme tempore et Antiochus ab Apamea profectus Sardibus primum, deinde haud procul Seleuci castris ad caput Caici amnis stativa habuit cum magno exercitu mixto variis ex gentibus.

At about the same time Antiochus also set out from Apamea and established quarters, first at Sardis, and subsequently not far from the camp of Seleucus at the mouth of the river Caicus, with a large army comprising men of many nationalities. *After an expedition to the north he returned to Sardis (37.21.5). His departure from Sardis obliged the Romans to continue their guard on Ionia and Aeolis (37.25.2). His journey to Ephesus to inspect the fleet (37.26.1). He abandoned the siege of Colophon and retreated to Sardis (37.31.3).*

Ca. 190 B.C.
For Antiochus' sons in Sardis see 33.19.10.

The Aftermath of Magnesia

206. Appian, *The Syrian Wars* 36.

2nd c. A.D.

ὡς δὲ κατεῖδε τὴν ἧτταν καὶ τὸ πεδίον ἄπαν νεκρῶν ἰδίων πλῆρες, ἀνδρῶν τε καὶ ἵππων καὶ ἐλεφάντων, τό τε στρατόπεδον εἰλημμένον ἤδη κατὰ κράτος, τότε δὴ καὶ ὁ Ἀντίοχος ἔφευγεν ἀμεταστρεπτὶ καὶ μέχρι μέσων νυκτῶν ἐς Σάρδεις παρῆλθε. παρῆλθε δὲ καὶ ἀπὸ Σάρδεων ἐς Κελαινάς, ἣν Ἀπάμειαν καλοῦσιν, οἳ τὸν υἱὸν ἐπυνθάνετο συμφεύγειν. τῆς δ' ἐπιούσης ἐς Συρίαν ἐκ Κελαινῶν ἀνεζεύγνυ, τοὺς στρατηγοὺς ἐν Κελαιναῖς καταλιπὼν ὑποδέχεσθαί τε καὶ ἀθροίζειν

τοὺς διαφυγόντας. περί τε καταλύσεως τοῦ πολέμου πρέσβεις ἔπεμπε πρὸς τὸν ὕπατον.

But when he saw his defeat and all the plain full of the bodies of his men and horses and elephants, and his camp already taken by force, then Antiochus took to headlong flight and came to Sardis about midnight. From Sardis he went to the town of Celaenae, called Apamea by some, whither he understood his son was fleeing. The next day he withdrew from Celaenae into Syria, leaving his generals in Celaenae to receive and gather the stragglers of his army. And he sent envoys to the consul to discuss a cessation of hostilities.

207. Livy 37.44.5ff.

1st c. B.C.–1st c. A.D.

Antiochus cum paucis fugiens, in ipso itinere pluribus congregantibus se, modica manu armatorum media ferme nocte Sardis concessit. inde, cum audisset Seleucum filium et quosdam amicorum Apameam progressos, et ipse quarta vigilia cum coniuge ac filia petit Apameam, Xenoni tradita custodia urbis, Timone Lydiae praeposito; quibus spretis consensu oppidanorum et militum, qui in arce erant, legati ad consulem missi sunt.

Antiochus fled with a few aides. More joined him in his flight, so that he reached Sardis close to midnight with a fair-sized company of soldiers. When he heard that his son Seleucus and some friends had gone to Apamea, at about the fourth watch he, too, with his wife and daughter made for Apamea. The protection of Sardis was handed over to Xeno, and Timo was made prefect of Lydia. These two were completely ignored, and by agreement between the townsfolk and the soldiers who were on the acropolis, envoys were sent to the consul. *The states of Asia submitted to Rome and the consul who was then in Sardis (37.45.3).*

Romans in Sardis

208. Livy 45.34.11.

1st c. B.C.–1st c. A.D.

ver primum ex domo Gallos exciverat; iamque Synnada pervenerant, cum Eumenes ad Sardis undique exercitum contraxerat. ibi Romani cum et Solovettium ducem Gallorum Synnadis * * adlocuturi. et Attalus cum eis profectus; sed castra Gallorum intrare eum non placuit, ne animi ex disceptatione inritarentur.

First spring roused the Gauls from their homes and they had already reached Synnada; Eumenes had brought together an army from all sides to Sardis. In Sardis when the Romans had discovered that Solovettius, the leader of the Gauls, was at Synnada, [they determined to go there] to talk to him; Attalus went along with them, but they decided that he should not go into the Gauls' camp lest feathers be ruffled in some dispute.

Ca. 167 B.C.

209. Polybius 21.16.1–2.   2nd c. B.C.

*"Ότι μετὰ τὴν νίκην οἱ 'Ρωμαῖοι τὴν αὐτῶν πρὸς 'Αντίοχον παρειληφότες καὶ τὰς Σάρδεις καὶ τὰς ἀκροπόλεις ἄρτι * * * ἧκε Μουσαῖος ἐπικηρυκευόμενος παρ' 'Αντιόχου. τῶν δὲ περὶ τὸν Πόπλιον φιλανθρώπως προσδεξαμένων αὐτόν, ἔφη βούλεσθαι τὸν 'Αντίοχον ἐξαποσταλῆναι πρεσβευτὰς τοὺς διαλεχθησομένους ὑπὲρ τῶν ὅλων.*

After their victory over Antiochus the Romans took Sardis and its acropolis . . . . and Musaeus came from Antiochus under conditions of truce. When those around Scipio received him generously, he said that Antiochus wished to send envoys to discuss the whole state of affairs.

From Sardis Antiochus had invited Prusias to be his ally (21.11.1); cf. Livy 37.25.4.

After his naval defeat near Teos, Antiochus had remained listlessly in Sardis (21.13.1); cf. Livy 37.30.1–31.4.

210. Polybius 31.6.   2nd c. B.C.

"Ότι Γάιος ὁ Γάλλος, χωρὶς τῶν ἄρτι ῥηθέντων ἀλογημάτων, παραγενόμενος εἰς τὴν 'Ασίαν ἐκθέματα κατὰ τὰς πόλεις ἐξέθηκε τὰς ἐπιφανεστάτας, κελεύων, εἴ τις βούλεται κατηγορεῖν Εὐμένους τοῦ βασιλέως, ἀπαντᾶν εἰς Σάρδεις ἐπί τινα χρόνον ὡρισμένον. μετὰ δὲ ταῦτα παραγενηθεὶς αὐτὸς εἰς τὰς Σάρδεις, ἀποκαθίσας ἐν τῷ γυμνασίῳ περὶ δέχ' ἡμέρας διήκουε τῶν κατηγορούντων, πᾶσαν ἐπιδεχόμενος αἰσχρολογίαν καὶ λοιδορίαν κατὰ τοῦ βασιλέως καὶ καθόλου πᾶν ἕλκων πρᾶγμα καὶ κατηγορίαν, ἅτε παρεστηκὼς ἄνθρωπος τῇ διανοίᾳ καὶ φιλοδοξῶν ἐν τῇ πρὸς Εὐμένην διαφορᾷ.

When Gaius Gallus arrived in Asia, as well as the follies already mentioned, he posted notices in the leading cities instructing anyone who wished to make a charge against King Eumenes to meet him in Sardis by an appointed time. After this, when he himself had reached Sardis, he sat in the gymnasium for about ten days and heard those who brought charges. He allowed vile language and slander against the king, dragged in the least thing and every accusation, for he was a man afflicted in his mind who sought credit in his quarrel with Eumenes.

Ca. 164–163 B.C.
Gaius Sulpicius was an appointee of the senate (31.1.6ff); cf. Diodorus 31.7.2. It is possible that Eumenes did not have the best relations with the Greek cities (M. Holleaux, *BCH* 48 [1924] 53) though cf. D. Magie, *Roman Rule in Asia Minor* (Princeton 1950) 768; and also G. Daux, *Mélanges Gustave Glotz* (Paris 1932) I 289ff, 296, for two decrees recording the establishment by the Sardians of a festival of the Panathenaia and Eumeneia; with which cf. *Sardis* VII: 1 (1932) 50 no. 27.13.

For the Hellenistic gymnasium in which Gaius presided see *Sardis* I (1922) 31; and cf. *Sardis* VII: 1 (1932) 46 no. 21.9, 50 no. 27.18.

IV. From the Establishment of the Roman Province of Asia to A.D. 284

Much of the written evidence for Roman Sardis is contained in the inscriptions, and the following notices should be read in conjunction with L. Robert's forthcoming volume on the Sardis inscriptions in this series. In that volume Robert will both publish the new material and present a critique of the publication of the epigraphic material recovered by the Princeton expedition (*Sardis* VII: 1 [1932]). The sources carry us from the incursions of Mithridates in the first century B.C. through the devastating earthquake that rocked Asia Minor in A.D. 17, to the emergence of Christianity in the same century, and to the civil discord in the second century, of which Plutarch informs us.

The First Century B.C.

211. Cicero, *Ad familiares* 13.57.2. 1st c. B.C.

Illud quod tecum et coram et per litteras diligentissime egi, id et nunc etiam atque etiam rogo curae tibi sit, ut suum negotium, quod habet cum populo Sardiano, pro causae veritate et pro sua dignitate conficiat.

That which I most urgently begged of you before, both in person and in correspondence, I now request again and again that you see to: namely, that he may complete the business that he has with the people of Sardis in accordance with the justness of his case and his honor.

Written from Laodicea, 50 B.C.
Cicero wrote to the propraetor, Q. Minucius Thermus, on behalf of a legatus of his, M. Anneius, who was engaged in a dispute with the Sardians. Cf. *Ad familiares* 13.55.1. Elsewhere (*Ad Quintum fratrem* 1.2.14) Cicero mentions a citizen of Sardis, Plato, who used to spend a good deal of time in Athens.

(275) Josephus, *Antiquitates Judaicae* 14.235.

1st c. A.D.

212. Josephus, *Antiquitates Judaicae* 16.171. 1st c. A.D.

Γάιος Νωρβανὸς Φλάκκος ἀνθύπατος Σαρδιανῶν ἄρχουσι καὶ βουλῇ χαίρειν. Καῖσάρ μοι ἔγραψε κελεύων
μὴ κωλύεσθαι τοὺς Ἰουδαίους ὅσα ἂν ὦσι κατὰ τὸ
πάτριον αὐτοῖς ἔθος συναγαγόντας χρήματα ἀναπέμπειν
εἰς Ἱεροσόλυμα. ἔγραψα οὖν ὑμῖν, ἵν᾿ εἰδῆτε ὅτι
Καῖσαρ κἀγὼ οὕτως θέλομεν γίνεσθαι.

Gaius Norbanus Flaccus, proconsul, to the magistrates and council of Sardis, greetings. Caesar has written me instructions that the Jews are not to be prevented from collecting money in accordance with the customs of their ancestors, however much it may be, and sending it to Jerusalem. Accordingly I have written you so that you may know that Caesar and I are anxious for this to be done.

For the date of Norbanus' proconsulship see Philo Judaeus, *Legatio ad Gaium*, ed. E. M. Smallwood (Leiden 1961) 309–310. See also Josephus, *Antiquitates* 14.235 (see *275*) with notes.

213. Orosius 6.2.8. 5th c. A.D.

porro autem Mithridates in Asia nobilissimarum urbium principes occidere bonaque eorum publicare animo intenderat. cumque jam mille sescentos ita interfecisset, Ephesii exemplum verentes excluso praesidio eius portas obiecerunt; similiter Smyrnaei Sardi Colophonii Trallianique fecerunt.

Moreover Mithridates had planned to kill the leaders of the noblest cities in Asia and to make their possessions public. And when he had already in this way slaughtered sixteen hundred, the

Ephesians, fearing the example he had set, locked out his garrison and barred their gates; and the citizens of Smyrna, Sardis, Colophon, and Tralles did likewise.

Events in the fall of 86 B.C., for which see D. Magie, *Roman Rule in Asia Minor* (Princeton 1950) 225. Orosius' source is presumably Livy.

214. Plutarch, *Brutus* 34.1ff.　　　　1st–2nd c. A.D.

Κάσσιον δὲ Βροῦτος εἰς Σάρδεις ἐκάλει, καὶ προσιόντι μετὰ τῶν φίλων ἀπήντησε· καὶ πᾶς ὁ στρατὸς ὡπλισμένος αὐτοκράτορας ἀμφοτέρους προσηγόρευσεν.

Brutus then summoned Cassius to Sardis, and as he approached he met him with his friends. And all the army, in full panoply, hailed them both as Imperators.
Mutual recriminations (2) gave way, thanks to the intervention of Favonius (3), to restored friendship (4). Brutus and Cassius differed on the subject of a just punishment for Lucius Pella (35) and Brutus confronted his evil genius (36).

42 B.C.
These events took place directly before the army crossed to march to Philippi; cf. Shakespeare, *Julius Caesar* IV.ii, V.iii.

215. Plutarch, *Pompey* 37.2.　　　　1st–2nd c. A.D.

ὑπομνήματα γὰρ ἦν, ἐξ ὧν ἐφωράθη φαρμάκοις ἄλλους τε πολλοὺς καὶ τὸν υἱὸν Ἀριαράθην ἀνῃρηκὼς καὶ τὸν Σαρδιανὸν Ἀλκαῖον, ὅτι παρευδοκίμησεν αὐτὸν ἵππους ἀγωνιστὰς ἐλαύνων.

For there were memoranda from which it became evident that among many others he had removed his own son, Ariarathes, by poison, and Alcaeus of Sardis because he had outdone him in driving racehorses.

Mithridates' documents were discovered by Pompey in Caenum.
On Alcaeus see L. Robert, *REA* 62 (1960) 342–346.

216. Strabo 13.4.9.　　　　1st c. B.C.–1st c. A.D.

Ἄνδρες δ' ἀξιόλογοι γεγόνασι τοῦ αὐτοῦ γένους Διόδωροι δύο οἱ ῥήτορες, ὧν ὁ πρεσβύτερος ἐκαλεῖτο Ζωνᾶς, ἀνὴρ πολλοὺς ἀγῶνας ἠγωνισμένος ὑπὲρ τῆς Ἀσίας, κατὰ δὲ τὴν Μιθριδάτου τοῦ βασιλέως ἔφοδον αἰτίαν ἐσχηκώς, ὡς ἀφιστὰς παρ' αὐτοῦ τὰς πόλεις, ἀπελύσατο τὰς διαβολὰς ἀπολογησάμενος· τοῦ δὲ νεωτέρου φίλου ἡμῖν γενομένου καὶ ἱστορικὰ συγγράμματά ἐστι καὶ μέλη καὶ ἄλλα ποιήματα, τὴν

ἀρχαίαν γραφὴν ἐπιφαίνοντα ἱκανῶς. Ξάνθος δὲ ὁ παλαιὸς συγγραφεὺς Λυδὸς μὲν λέγεται, εἰ δὲ ἐκ Σάρδεων, οὐκ ἴσμεν.

The two Diodoruses, the orators, noteworthy men, were born at Sardis into the same family. Of these the elder was called Zonas and had pleaded many cases on behalf of Asia. When King Mithridates invaded the province, he stood accused of urging the cities to revolt from him, but by his defense he dismissed these slanders. The younger Diodorus, who became a friend of mine, was responsible for some historical writings and some melic and other poems, which are characterized plainly enough by the ancient style. Xanthus, the ancient historian, is called a Lydian, but I do not know whether he came from Sardis.

The First Century A.D.

217. Philostratus, *Letters of Apollonius of Tyana* 75.
　　　　2nd–3rd c. A.D.

τοῖς ἐν Σάρδεσιν. Ὁ παῖς Ἀλυάττεω σῶσαι τὴν ἑαυτοῦ πόλιν ἀδύνατος ἐγένετο καὶ ἀμήχανος καίπερ ὢν βασιλεύς τε καὶ Κροῖσος, ὑμεῖς δὲ ποίῳ πεποιθότες ἄρα λέοντι πόλεμον ἄσπονδον ἤρασθε παῖδες νέοι πάντες ἄνδρες γέροντες, ἀλλὰ καὶ παρθένοι καὶ γυναῖκες; Ἐρινύων νομίσαι ἄν τις τὴν πόλιν εἶναι, καὶ οὐχὶ Δήμητρος. ἡ δὲ θεὰ φιλάνθρωπος· ὑμῖν δὲ τίς οὗτος ὁ χόλος;

To the people of Sardis: The son of Alyattes was powerless to save his city and without any resource, though he was a king and Croesus. But you, trusting in what lion, have you, all of you, children, youths, adults, old men, and even girls and women, fallen in love with truceless war? Anyone would think that your city belonged to the Erinyes and not to Demeter. But the goddess is friendly to man; what on earth is this anger of yours?

Apollonius lived in the first century A.D.
On *stasis* and (other) unappealing habits in Sardis see also *Letters* 38, 39, 40, 41, 56, 76.

218. Plutarch, *De exilio* 6 (601 B).　　　　1st–2nd c. A.D.

Τὸ δέ σε μὴ κατοικεῖν Σάρδεις οὐδέν ἐστιν· οὐδὲ γὰρ Ἀθηναῖοι πάντες κατοικοῦσι Κολλυτὸν οὐδὲ Κορίνθιοι Κράνειον οὐδὲ Πιτάνην Λάκωνες.

That you do not live in Sardis is nothing; for all Athenians do not live in Collytus, nor all Corinthians in Craneion, nor all Laconians in Pitane.

The exiled Sardian to whom Plutarch addressed the *De exilio* (after A.D. 96) is probably the Menemachus to whom Plutarch also addressed the *Praecepta gerendae reipublicae* (between A.D. 96 and 114): so C. P. Jones, *JRS* 56 (1966) 72.

For Sardis and Sardians see also *De exilio* 3 (600 A), 17 (607 E).

219. Strabo 12.8.18. 1st c. B.C.–1st c. A.D.

καὶ τὰ περὶ Σίπυλον δὲ καὶ τὴν ἀνατροπὴν αὐτοῦ μῦθον οὐ δεῖ τίθεσθαι· καὶ γὰρ νῦν τὴν Μαγνησίαν τὴν ὑπ’ αὐτῷ κατέβαλον σεισμοί, ἡνίκα καὶ Σάρδεις καὶ τῶν ἄλλων τὰς ἐπιφανεστάτας κατὰ πολλὰ μέρη διελυμήναντο.

And it is wrong to attribute the tale about Mt. Sipylus and its overthrow to myth. For in my own day earthquake devastated Magnesia, which is situated at its foot, at the time when the seismic activity severely harmed Sardis and the most renowned of the other cities in many areas.

The earthquake of A.D. 17. The city was restored by Tiberius.

See also Strabo 13.4.8.

220. Tacitus, *Annales* 2.47. 1st–2nd c. A.D.

Eodem anno duodecim celebres Asiae urbes conlapsae nocturno motu terrae, quo improvisior graviorque pestis fuit. neque solitum in tali casu effugium subveniebat in aperta prorumpendi, quia diductis terris hauriebantur. sedisse immensos montes, visa in arduo quae plana fuerint, effulsisse inter ruinam ignes memorant. asperrima in Sardianos lues plurimum in eosdem misericordiae traxit: nam centies sestertium pollicitus Caesar, et quantum aerario aut fisco pendebant, in quinquennium remisit.

The same year twelve important cities of Asia collapsed in an earthquake during the night, so that the devastation was all the more unexpected and crushing. The customary escape in such a calamity, that of rushing out into the open fields, was not possible because people were being consumed by the gaping earth. They say that huge mountains were flattened, what had been level ground seemed to be carried aloft, and conflagrations blazed among the destruction. The disaster was harshest to the citizens of Sardis and brought them the largest share of pity; for Tiberius promised ten million sesterces and remitted for five years whatever they used to pay to the public exchequer or his privy purse.

On the earthquake of A.D. 17 cf. Pliny, *Naturalis historia* 2.86.200; Suetonius, *Tiberius* 48.2; Seneca, *Naturales quaestiones* 6.1.13; Dio 57.17.7. See also D. Magie, *Roman Rule in Asia Minor* (Princeton 1950) 499f, 1358f n. 23; E. Koestermann, *Cornelius Tacitus: Annales* (Heidelberg 1963) 341.

On the fiscus see P. A. Brunt, *JRS* 56 (1966) 75–91.

221. Tacitus, *Annales* 4.55. 1st–2nd c. A.D.

Sardiani decretum Etruriae recitavere ut consanguinei: nam Tyrrhenum Lydumque Atye rege genitos ob multitudinem divi⟨sis⟩se gentem; Lydum patriis in terris resedisse, Thyrrheno datum novas ut conderet sedes; et ducum e nominibus indita vocabula illis per Asiam, his in Italia; auctamque adhuc Lydorum opulentiam missis in Graeciam populis, cui mox a Pelope nomen.

As kinsmen, the Sardians read a decree of Etruria. For they said that in the reign of Atys, his sons Tyrrhenus and Lydus divided the nation because of its size. Lydus remained in their homeland and it fell to Tyrrhenus to found a new settlement. From the names of their leaders names were given to the two branches of the family, Asian and Italian. The influence of the Lydians was further increased by people sent to Greece, to a part of which Pelops soon lent his name.

Tacitus describes deliberation in the senate, centering on Sardis and Smyrna, as to which city of Asia should build a temple to Tiberius. Smyrna prevailed.

Early Christianity in Sardis

222. Eusebius, *Historiae ecclesiasticae* 4.13.8.

3rd–4th c. A.D.

τούτοις οὕτω χωρήσασιν ἐπιμαρτυρῶν Μελίτων τῆς ἐν Σάρδεσιν ἐκκλησίας ἐπίσκοπος, κατ’ αὐτὸ γνωριζόμενος τοῦ χρόνου, δῆλός ἐστιν ἐκ τῶν εἰρημένων αὐτῷ ἐν ᾗ πεποίηται πρὸς αὐτοκράτορα Οὐῆρον ὑπὲρ τοῦ καθ’ ἡμᾶς δόγματος ἀπολογία.

Melito, the well-known bishop of the church in Sardis at that time, bears witness to these events. This is clear from what was said by him in the apologia on behalf of our faith which he made to the emperor Verus.

Melito substantiates accounts of the persecution of Christians recorded in a letter from Antoninus Pius to the Council of Asia (Eusebius, *Historiae ecclesiasticae* 4.13.1–7) dated to A.D. 161.

Bishop of Sardis, Melito was the author of many

books and treatises (Eusebius, *Historiae ecclesiasticae* 4.26.1–2) on the style of which see Jerome, *De viris illustribus* 24. He may have died ca. A.D. 185, because Polycrates, bishop of Ephesus, writing to Victor and the church in Rome ca. A.D. 190 (Eusebius, *Historiae ecclesiasticae* 5.24.5), mentions him as dead.

On Melito see C. Bonner, *The Homily on the Passion by Melito, Bishop of Sardis* (London 1940); B. Lohse, *Die Passa-Homilie des Bischofs Meliton von Sardes* (Leiden 1958); M. Testuz, *Meliton de Sardes: Homilie sur la Pâque* (Cologny-Genève 1960) Papyrus Bodmer 13; F. V. Filson, *BiblArch* 25 (1962) 50–57; A. T. Kraabel in Fogg Art Museum, Harvard University, Monographs in Art and Archaeology II, *Studies Presented to George M. A. Hanfmann* (Cambridge, Massachusetts and Mainz 1971) 76–85.

223. Revelation of St. John the Divine 1.11.

1st c. A.D.

Ὃ βλέπεις γράψον εἰς βιβλίον καὶ πέμψον ταῖς ἑπτὰ ἐκκλησίαις, εἰς Ἔφεσον καὶ εἰς Σμύρναν καὶ εἰς Πέργαμον καὶ εἰς Θυάτειρα καὶ εἰς Σάρδεις καὶ εἰς Φιλαδελφίαν καὶ εἰς Λαοδικίαν.

Write what you see in a book and send it to the seven churches—to Ephesus, and to Smyrna and to Pergamon, and to Thyatira and to Sardis, and to Philadelphia and to Laodicia.

224. Revelation of St. John the Divine 3.1–6.

1st c. A.D.

Καὶ τῷ ἀγγέλῳ ⌈τῆς⌉ ἐν Σάρδεσιν ἐκκλησίας γράψον:
Τάδε λέγει ὁ ἔχων τὰ ἑπτὰ πνεύματα τοῦ θεοῦ καὶ τοὺς ἑπτὰ ἀστέρας: Οἶδά σου τὰ ἔργα, ὅτι ὄνομα ἔχεις ὅτι ζῇς, καὶ νεκρὸς εἶ. γίνου γρηγορῶν, καὶ στήρισον τὰ λοιπὰ ἃ ἔμελλον ἀποθανεῖν, οὐ γὰρ εὕρηκά σου ἔργα πεπληρωμένα ἐνώπιον τοῦ θεοῦ μου· μνημόνευε οὖν πῶς εἴληφας καὶ ἤκουσας καὶ τήρει, καὶ μετανόησον· ἐὰν οὖν μὴ γρηγορήσῃς, ἥξω ὡς κλέπτης, καὶ οὐ μὴ ⌈γνῷς⌉ ποίαν ὥραν ἥξω ἐπὶ σέ· ἀλλὰ ἔχεις ὀλίγα ὀνόματα ἐν Σάρδεσιν ἃ οὐκ ἐμόλυναν τὰ ἱμάτια αὐτῶν, καὶ περιπατήσουσιν μετ' ἐμοῦ ἐν λευκοῖς, ὅτι ἄξιοί εἰσιν. Ὁ νικῶν οὕτως περιβαλεῖται ἐν ἱματίοις λευκοῖς, καὶ οὐ μὴ ἐξαλείψω τὸ ὄνομα αὐτοῦ ἐκ τῆς βίβλου τῆς ζωῆς καὶ ὁμολογήσω τὸ ὄνομα αὐτοῦ ἐνώπιον τοῦ πατρός μου καὶ ἐνώπιον τῶν ἀγγέλων αὐτοῦ. Ὁ ἔχων οὖς ἀκουσάτω τί τὸ πνεῦμα λέγει ταῖς ἐκκλησίαις.

And write to the angel of the church in Sardis:
He who holds the seven spirits of God and the seven stars speaks as follows: I know your deeds, that you have a name that you live, and you are dead. Be awake, and secure what is left that is about to die. For I have not found any of your works completed in the face of my God. Remember then how you took and heard, and keep it and repent. If you shall not be wakeful, I shall come as a thief and you will not know at what hour I shall be upon you. But you have a few names in Sardis which have not shamed their garments; and they shall walk with me in white because they are worthy. The victor shall thus be clothed in white and I shall not eradicate his name from the book of life, and I will declare his name before my father and his angels. Let him who has an ear hear what the spirit says to the churches.

Early Christianity in Sardis will be treated by Clive Foss in a forthcoming monograph in this series.

The Second Century A.D.

225. Straton in *Anthologia Palatina* 12.202.

Πτηνὸς Ἔρως ἄγαγέν με δι' ἠέρος, ἡνίκα, Δᾶμι,
γράμμα σὸν εἶδον, ὅ μοι δεῦρο μολεῖν σ' ἔλεγεν·
ῥίμφα δ' ἀπὸ Σμύρνης ἐπὶ Σάρδιας ...

Winged passion drew me through the air, Damis, when I saw your letter telling me you were coming here. Come soon from Smyrna to Sardis ...

Straton lived in Sardis in the second century A.D. For other composition in similar vein see *Anthologia Palatina* 11: 19, 21, 22, 117, 225; and 12: 1–11, 13, 15, 16, 21, 175–229, 231, 234–255, 258.

(236) Lucian, *De mercede conductis* 13.   2nd c. A.D.

226. Philostratus, *Lives of the Sophists* I 524.

2nd–3rd c. A.D.

ἐγήρασκε μὲν ὁ Διονύσιος ἐν δόξῃ λαμπρᾷ, παρῄει δ' ἐς ἀκμὴν ὁ Πολέμων οὔπω γιγνωσκόμενος τῷ Διονυσίῳ καὶ ἐπεδήμει ταῖς Σάρδεσι ἀγορεύων δίκην ἐν τοῖς ἑκατὸν ἀνδράσιν, ὑφ' ὧν ἐδικαιοῦτο ἡ Λυδία. ἑσπέρας οὖν ἐς τὰς Σάρδεις ἥκων ὁ Διονύσιος ἤρετο Δωρίωνα τὸν κριτικὸν ξένον ἑαυτοῦ· "εἰπέ μοι," ἔφη "ὦ Δωρίων, τί Πολέμων ἐνταῦθα;"

Dionysius was growing old with a brilliant reputation, and Polemo, though not yet known to Dionysius, was nearing the height of his career when he visited Sardis to argue a case before the Centumviri by whom Lydia was regulated. In the evening Dionysius came to Sardis and asked Dorion, the critic who was his host, "Tell me, Dorion," he said, "why is Polemo here?"

Polemo of Laodicia (ca. A.D. 90–145) won a reputation as a Sophist in Smyrna.

227. Plutarch, *Praecepta gerendae reipublicae* 32 (825 D).
1st–2nd c. A.D.

ἔχεις δὲ δήπου καὶ αὐτὸς οἰκεῖα παραδείγματα, τὴν
Παρδαλᾶ πρὸς Τυρρηνὸν ἔχθραν, ὡς ὀλίγον ἐδέησεν
ἀνελεῖν τὰς Σάρδεις, ἐξ αἰτιῶν μικρῶν καὶ ἰδίων εἰς
ἀπόστασιν καὶ πόλεμον ἐμβαλοῦσα.

And indeed you have examples at home, the
hostility between Pardalas and Tyrrhenus that nar-
rowly missed overwhelming Sardis, throwing the
city into revolt and war for the pettiest personal
reasons.

Addressed to Menemachus after A.D. 96 and before
A.D. 114. So C. P. Jones, *JRS* 56 (1966) 72.
On Sardis and Pardalas see also *Praecepta* 17 (813
E, F); *Sardis* VII: 1 (1932) 116, no. 127.
For civil strife in Sardis cf. Philostratus, *Letters of
Apollonius of Tyana* 56, 65, 66, 75 (see *217*).

228. Plutarch, *Praecepta gerendae reipublicae* 17 (813
D, E). 1st–2nd c. A.D.

ἀλλὰ κἀκεῖνο λέγειν πρὸς ἑαυτόν "ἀρχόμενος ἄρχεις,
ὑποτεταγμένης πόλεως ἀνθυπάτοις, ἐπιτρόποις Καίσ-
αρος· 'οὐ ταῦτα λόγχη πεδιάς, οὐδ' αἱ παλαιαὶ Σάρδεις
οὐδ' ἡ Λυδῶν ἐκείνη δύναμις.'"

But you ought to say this too to yourself: "Since
you rule a city controlled by proconculs, Caesar's
governors, you rule as a subject. 'These are not the
hoplites of the plain,' nor is this ancient Sardis nor
that old Lydian might."

This essay is addressed to a Sardian, Menemachus.
Cf. Sophocles, *Trachiniae* 1058.

Sardis in the Roman Poets

229. Horace, *Epistles* I.11.1–3. 1st c. B.C.

Quid tibi visa Chios, Bullati, notaque Lesbos,
quid concinna Samos, quid Croesi regia Sardis,
Zmyrna quid et Colophon, maiora minorane fama?

How did Chios strike you, Bullatius, and noble
Lesbos? What did you think of delightful Samos,
and of Sardis, royal home of Croesus? What of
Smyrna and Colophon? Did they measure up to
or fall short of their reputations?

The names are of cities and states of Asia Minor and
the Aegean. Horace reiterates his old theme that fulfill-
ment is internal.

230. Ovid, *Metamorphoses* 11.137–141. 1st c. B.C.

"vade" ait "ad magnis vicinum Sardibus amnem
perque jugum Lydum labentibus obvius undis
carpe viam, donec venias ad fluminis ortus."

Go to the river close to great Sardis and make your
way through the Lydian hills against the smooth-
flowing waters till you come to the river's source.

On the Pactolus see (*242*) through (*256*).

231. Ovid, *Metamorphoses* 11.150–152. 1st c. B.C.

nam freta prospiciens late riget arduus alto
Tmolus in ascensu clivoque extensus utroque
Sardibus hinc, illinc parvis finitur Hypaepis.

For looking out far and wide to the sea, Tmolus
soars steep and abrupt, stretched out on either
slope. On one side it reaches Sardis and on the
other to tiny Hypaepa.

Elsewhere in the *Metamorphoses* (6.15, 11.86) Tmolus
is referred to as Timolus.

232. Varro, *Menippean Satires EKATOMBH*
1st c. B.C.

Lydón fluens sub Sárdibus flumén tulit
Aurúm.

The Lydian river flowing beneath Sardis brought
gold.

V. Topography and Monuments

The sources are divided into two groups, those that pertain to geographical features and those which are relevant for specific monuments. Again, for the topography, the inscriptions are of great importance and reference should be made to L. Robert's forthcoming volume in this series. *Sardis* VII: 1 (1932) remains invaluable, and for topographical purposes attention may be directed to the useful index, p. 179.

GEOGRAPHY

General

233. Pliny, *Naturalis historia* 5.110.　　　1st c. A.D.

Lydia autem perfusa flexuosis Maeandri amnis recursibus super Ioniam procedit, Phrygiae ab exortu solis vicina, ad septentrionem Mysiae, meridiana parte Cariam amplectens, Maeonia antea appellata. celebratur maxime Sardibus in latere Tmoli montis, qui antea Timolus appellabatur, vitibus consito conditis; ex quo profluente Pactolo eodemque Chrysorroa ac fonte Tarni, a Maeonis civitas ipsa Hyde vocitata est, clara stagno Gygaeo.

Lydia, however, permeated by the labyrinthine wanderings of the river Maeander, stretches out beyond Ionia, adjacent to Phrygia to the east and Mysia to the north, and embracing Caria to the south. Lydia was formerly called Maeonia. It is most famous for Sardis, a city located on the flank of Mount Tmolus rich in vines, Tmolus previously called Timolus. The Pactolus, sometimes called Chrysorrhoas, flows from Tmolus as does the fountain of Tarnus. The city itself used to be called Hyde by the Maeonians and was famed for the Gygaean lake.

234. Strabo 13.4.5.　　　1st c. B.C.–1st c. A.D.

Αἱ δὲ Σάρδεις πόλις ἐστὶ μεγάλη, νεωτέρα μὲν τῶν Τρωικῶν, ἀρχαία δ' ὅμως, ἄκραν ἔχουσα εὐερκῆ· βασίλειον δ' ὑπῆρξε τῶν Λυδῶν, οὓς ὁ ποιητὴς καλεῖ Μῄονας, οἱ δ' ὕστερον Μαίονας, οἱ μὲν τοὺς αὐτοὺς τοῖς Λυδοῖς, οἱ δ' ἑτέρους ἀποφαίνοντες, τοὺς δ' αὐτοὺς ἄμεινόν ἐστι λέγειν. ὑπέρκειται δὲ τῶν Σάρδεων ὁ Τμῶλος, εὔδαιμον ὄρος, ἐν τῇ ἀκρωρείᾳ σκοπὴν ἔχον, ἐξέδραν λευκοῦ λίθου, Περσῶν ἔργον, ἀφ' οὗ κατοπτεύεται τὰ κύκλῳ πεδία, καὶ μάλιστα τὸ Καϋστριανόν· περιοικοῦσι δὲ Λυδοὶ καὶ Μυσοὶ καὶ Μακεδόνες. ῥεῖ δ' ὁ Πακτωλὸς ἀπὸ τοῦ Τμώλου, καταφέρων τὸ παλαιὸν ψῆγμα χρυσοῦ πολύ, ἀφ' οὗ τὸν Κροίσου λεγόμενον πλοῦτον καὶ τῶν προγόνων αὐτοῦ διονομασθῆναί φασι· νῦν δ' ἐκλέλοιπε τὸ ψῆγμα. καταφέρεται δ' ὁ Πακτωλὸς εἰς τὸν Ἕρμον, εἰς ὃν καὶ ὁ Ὕλλος ἐμβάλλει, Φρύγιος νυνὶ καλούμενος· συμπεσόντες δ' οἱ τρεῖς καὶ ἄλλοι ἀσημότεροι σὺν αὐτοῖς εἰς τὴν κατὰ Φωκαίαν ἐκδιδόασι θάλατταν, ὡς Ἡρόδοτός φησιν. ἄρχεται δ' ἐκ Μυσίας ὁ Ἕρμος, ἐξ ὄρους ἱεροῦ τῆς Δινδυμήνης, καὶ διὰ τῆς Κατακεκαυμένης εἰς τὴν Σαρδιανὴν φέρεται καὶ τὰ συνεχῆ πεδία, ὡς εἴρηται, μέχρι τῆς θαλάττης. ὑπόκειται δὲ τῇ πόλει τό τε Σαρδιανὸν πεδίον καὶ τὸ τοῦ Κύρου καὶ τὸ τοῦ Ἕρμου καὶ τὸ Καϋστριανόν, συνεχῆ τε ὄντα καὶ πάντων ἄριστα πεδίων. ἐν δὲ σταδίοις τετταράκοντα ἀπὸ τῆς πόλεώς ἐστιν ἡ Γυγαία μὲν ὑπὸ τοῦ ποιητοῦ λεγομένη, Κολόη δ' ὕστερον μετονομασθεῖσα, ὅπου τὸ ἱερὸν τῆς Κολοηνῆς Ἀρτέμιδος, μεγάλην ἁγιστείαν ἔχον. φασὶ δ' ἐνταῦθα χορεύειν τοὺς καλάθους κατὰ τὰς ἑορτάς, οὐκ οἶδ' ὅπως ποτὲ παραδοξολογοῦντες μᾶλλον ἢ ἀληθεύοντες.

Sardis is a great city and, though less old than Troy, is ancient nevertheless and with a well-fortified citadel. It was the royal city of the Lydians, whom the poet calls Maeonians; later authors call them Maeonians too, some associating them with the Lydians and others identifying them differently.

But it is better to call them the same people. Tmolus is located above Sardis, a delightful mountain which has an observation post on its summit, an exedra of white marble, a Persian work. From here are visible the plains all around, and especially the plain of the Cayster. Around about live Lydians, Mysians, and Macedonians. From Tmolus flows the Pactolus stream which in antiquity carried down a great amount of gold dust, from which, they say, the famed wealth of Croesus and his ancestors derived; but now the gold dust has failed. The Pactolus makes his way to the Hermus into which the river Hyllus also, now called the Phrygius, discharges. These three join with other less well-known streams and reach the sea near Phocaea, as Herodotus says. The Hermus rises in Mysia, flowing from the sacred mountain Dindymene through the Catacecaumene country into the land of Sardis and the adjacent plains, as has been said, to the sea. Below the city lies the plain of Sardis and those of Cyrus, the Hermus, and the Cayster, which are next to one another and are the best of all plains. Within forty stades of the city there is the Gygaean [lake], mentioned by Homer, and later named [Lake] Coloe, where the temple of Coloenian Artemis is located in all its holiness. They say that there at the festivals the baskets dance, for some reason that is beyond me, talking paradoxes rather than telling the truth.

For the geology and geography of Lydia see A. Philippson, *Topographische Karte des westlichen Kleinasien* (Gotha 1910) and cf. W. Warfield in *Sardis* I (1922) 175–180.

On the Catacecaumene cf. Xanthus *FGrHist* 765 F 13, and Strabo 12.8.18–19 (see *19*), 13.4.11.

For the sacred Mt. Dindymene cf. Herodotus 1.80 (see *115*); Arrian, *Anabasis* 5.6.4; Catullus 63.91; Virgil, *Aeneid* 9.618 and 10.252.

Acropolis

235. Arrian, *Anabasis* 1.17.3–6ff.　　　　2nd c. A.D.

Αὐτὸς δὲ ἐπὶ Σάρδεων προὐχώρει· καὶ ἀπέχοντος αὐτοῦ ὅσον ἑβδομήκοντα σταδίους Σάρδεων, ἧκον παρ' αὐτὸν Μιθρίνης τε ὁ φρούραρχος τῆς ἀκροπόλεως τῆς ἐν Σάρδεσι καὶ Σαρδιανῶν οἱ δυνατώτατοι, ἐνδιδόντες οἱ μὲν τὴν πόλιν, ὁ δὲ Μιθρίνης τὴν ἄκραν καὶ τὰ χρήματα. Ἀλέξανδρος δὲ αὐτὸς μὲν κατεστρατοπέδευσεν ἐπὶ τῷ Ἕρμῳ ποταμῷ· ἀπέχει δὲ ὁ Ἕρμος ἀπὸ Σάρδεων σταδίους ὅσον εἴκοσιν· Ἀμύνταν δὲ τὸν Ἀνδρομένους τὴν ἄκραν παραληψόμενον ἐκπέμπει ἐς

Σάρδεις· καὶ Μιθρίνην μὲν ἐν τιμῇ ἅμα οἷ ἧγε, Σαρδιανοὺς δὲ καὶ τοὺς ἄλλους Λυδοὺς τοῖς νόμοις τε τοῖς πάλαι Λυδῶν χρῆσθαι ἔδωκε καὶ ἐλευθέρους εἶναι ἀφῆκεν. Ἀνῆλθε δὲ καὶ αὐτὸς εἰς τὴν ἄκραν, ἵνα τὸ φρούριον ἦν τῶν Περσῶν· καὶ ἔδοξεν αὐτῷ ὀχυρὸν τὸ χωρίον· ὑπερύψηλόν τε γὰρ ἦν καὶ ἀπότομον πάντη καὶ τριπλῷ τείχει πεφραγμένον· αὐτὸς δὲ ἐπὶ τῇ ἄκρᾳ ναόν τε οἰκοδομῆσαι Διὸς Ὀλυμπίου ἐπενόει καὶ βωμὸν ἱδρύσασθαι. Σκοποῦντι δὲ αὐτῷ τῆς ἄκρας ὅπερ ἐπιτηδειότατον χωρίον, ὥρᾳ ἔτους ἐξαίφνης χειμὼν ἐπιγίγνεται καὶ βρονταὶ σκληραί, καὶ ὕδωρ ἐξ οὐρανοῦ πίπτει οὗ τὰ τῶν Λυδῶν βασίλεια· Ἀλεξάνδρῳ δὲ ἔδοξεν ἐκ θεοῦ σημανθῆναι ἵνα χρὴ οἰκοδομεῖσθαι τῷ Διὶ τὸν νεών, καὶ οὕτως ἐκέλευσε.

Alexander himself advanced toward Sardis. When he was about seventy stades from the city, the most important of the citizens of Sardis came to meet him and with them Mithrines, the commander of the troops that garrisoned the acropolis of Sardis. Mithrines surrendered the citadel and the treasure to him, and the burghers handed over the city. Alexander made camp near the Hermus, a river which is about twenty stades away from Sardis, but he sent Amyntas, son of Andromenes, to Sardis to occupy the acropolis. Mithrines he took with him, and honorably; and he allowed the Sardians and the rest of the Lydians to continue to use their ancestral laws and to be free. He climbed the acropolis where the Persian troops were garrisoned; and the place seemed to him very secure since it was very high and precipitous on all sides and encircled by a triple fortification. He planned to build a temple to Olympian Zeus on the acropolis and to set up an altar there. But as he was considering which part of the acropolis was most suitable a sudden storm broke, although it was summer. There were violent claps of thunder and rain poured down on the spot where the palace of the Lydians is located. Alexander interpreted this as a sign from the heavens as to where he ought to build the temple of Zeus, and he gave his instructions accordingly.

Pausanias, Nicias, and Asandrus were left to govern Lydia (7). The Argives were left to garrison the acropolis (8).

Ca. 334 B.C.

Mithrines reappears (3.16.5); and cf. Dio Chrysostom, *Orationes* 73.2.

Whatever may be meant by Alexander's "allowing the Sardians and the rest of the Lydians" to be free, under Attalus II the city was self-governing (*Sardis* VII: 1 [1932] 10–12 no. 4).

On shrines of Zeus in the Roman period see *Sardis* VII: 1 (1932) 38 no. 17.7, 47 no. 22.2.

(116) Herodotus 1.84.   5th c. B.C.

236. Lucian, *De mercede conductis* 13.   2nd c. A.D.

κεκράτηκας οὖν, ὦ μακάριε, καὶ ἔστεψαι τὰ Ὀλύμπια, μᾶλλον δὲ Βαβυλῶνα εἴληφας ἢ τὴν Σάρδεων ἀκρόπολιν καθῄρηκας, καὶ ἕξεις τὸ τῆς Ἀμαλθείας κέρας καὶ ἀμέλξεις ὀρνίθων γάλα.

Therefore, lucky man, you have vanquished and have won Olympian laurels. Better still, you have captured Babylon or taken the citadel of Sardis, and you shall have Amalthea's horn and shall squeeze the milk out of birds.

For Lucian, Sardis is an image of the highest achievement.

(64) Nicolas of Damascus, *FGrHist* 90 F 65 (4).
1st c. B.C.–1st c. A.D.

(118) Parthenius, *Love Stories* 22.   1st c. B.C.

(154) Plutarch, *De Herodoti malignitate* 24.
1st–2nd c. A.D.

237. Polyaenus 4.9.4.   2nd c. A.D.

Σέλευκος τὴν Σάρδεων ἄκραν ἐπολιόρκει, τοὺς ἐν αὐτῇ θησαυροὺς Θεοδότου φυλάσσοντος. τοῦτον θησαυροφύλακα Λυσίμαχος ἔταξε. μὴ δυνάμενος τὴν ἄκραν ἐχυρὰν οὖσαν ἑλεῖν ἐκήρυξε τάλαντα ἑκατὸν δώσειν τῷ κτείναντι Θεόδοτον.

Seleucus besieged the citadel of Sardis at the time when Theodotus, an appointee of Lysimachus, was in charge of the treasure there. When he was unable to take the acropolis, which was precipitous, he announced that he would give one hundred talents to the man who killed Theodotus.
In fear Theodotus surrendered the acropolis.

Ca. 281 B.C., perhaps prior to the battle of Corupedium.
For a daring escape from the acropolis at Sardis by Diodorus and his comrades see Polyaenus 6.49. For Orontes' maneuvers around Sardis see Polyaenus 7.14.2.
Sardis became an administrative center for the Seleucids (C. B. Welles, *Royal Correspondence in the Hellenistic Period* [New Haven 1934] nos. 18–19).
The Seleucids struck coins in Sardis in the third century; see E. T. Newell, *Coinage of the Western Seleucid Mints* (New York 1941) 242.

(119) Polyaenus 7.6.2–3.   2nd c. A.D.

(17) Strabo 13.4.6.   1st c. B.C.–1st c. A.D.

(122) Xenophon, *Cyropaedia* 7.2.1–4.
5th–4th c. B.C.

Gygaean Lake

(278) Herodotus 1.93.   5th c. B.C.

238. Homer, *Iliad* 2.864–866.

Μῄοσιν αὖ Μέσθλης τε καὶ Ἄντιφος ἡγησάσθην, υἷε Ταλαιμένεος, τὼ Γυγαίη τέκε λίμνη, οἳ καὶ Μῄονας ἦγον ὑπὸ Τμώλῳ γεγαῶτας.

Mesthles and Antiphus were the leaders of the Maeonians, the two sons of Talaimenes, whose mother was the Gygaean Lake. They led the Maeonians whose home was beneath Tmolus.

The geographical equation between Maeonia and Lydia is commonly made. On Maeonia and Maeonians see Eustathius 365.15ff.; Herodotus 1.7 (see *26*); Dionysius of Halicarnassus 1.27.1 (see *20*), 1.28.2; Hipponax F 3 (Masson); Strabo 13.4.5 (see *234*); and cf. *Iliad* 3.401, 4.142, 10.430, 18.291.

239. Homer, *Iliad* 20.389–392.

"κεῖσαι, Ὀτρυντεΐδη, πάντων ἐκπαγλότατ' ἀνδρῶν· ἐνθάδε τοι θάνατος, γενεὴ δέ τοί ἐστ' ἐπὶ λίμνη Γυγαίῃ, ὅθι τοι τέμενος πατρώϊόν ἐστιν, Ὕλλῳ ἐπ' ἰχθυόεντι καὶ Ἕρμῳ δινήεντι."

Son of Otrynteus, most feared of men, there you lie. Your death is here, though your birth was by the Gygaean Lake where is your ancestral estate close by the Hyllus rich in fish and the eddying Hermus.

On the Gygean Lake see also Strabo 13.4.5 (see *234*); Pliny, *Naturalis historia* 5.110 (see *233*); Eustathius 365.45ff; and cf. A. H. Sayce, *JHS* 1 (1880) 87; and G. M. A. Hanfmann, *BASOR* 177 (1965) 35–36, 186 (1967) 40–42, D. G. Mitten in Hanfmann, *BASOR* 191 (1968) 7–10.
The lake referred to by Nicolas *apud* Stephanus of Byzantium, s.v. *Torrhebos*, may also be the Gygaean.

240. Propertius 3.11.17–20.   1st c. B.C.

Omphale in tantum formae processit honorem,
    Lydia Gygaeo tincta puella lacu,
ut, qui pacato statuisset in orbe columnas,
    tam dura traheret mollia pensa manu.

Omphale the Lydian girl bathed in the Gygaean lake and advanced to such fame of beauty that he who had set up his pillars in the pacified world handled soft wool with calloused palms.

Evidently Omphale's beauty was increased by bathing in the Gygaean Lake.

Propertius interprets Heracles' pillars as columns set up in Roman fashion to commemorate military victories.

241. Quintus Smyrnaeus, *Posthomerica* 11.67–69.

4th c. A.D.

Εὐρύπυλος δὲ μενεπτόλεμος κτάνε φαίδιμον Ἑλλον,
τόν ῥα παρὰ λίμνη Γυγαίῃ γείνατο μήτηρ
Κλειτὼ καλλιπάρῃος.

The steadfast Eurypylus killed glorious Hellus whom his mother Cleito of the beautiful cheeks bore by the Gygaean Lake.

Cf. W. H. Roscher, *Ausfürliches Lexicon der griechischen und römischen Mythologie* (Leipzig 1884) 2031, s.v. *Hellos 1.*

(279) Strabo 13.4.7.

1st c. B.C.–1st c. A.D.

Pactolus

242. Dio Chrysostom, *Orationes* 78.31. 1st–2nd c. A.D.

καθάπερ, οἶμαι, φασὶ Κροίσῳ πρότερον τὸν Πακτωλὸν διὰ μέσων ἀφικνούμενον Σάρδεων ἕτοιμα χρήματα κομίζειν, πλείω φόρον τε καὶ δασμὸν ἢ ξύμπασα Φρυγία καὶ Λυδία καὶ Μαιονές τε καὶ Μυσοὶ καὶ ξύμπαντες οἱ νεμόμενοι τὴν ἐντὸς Ἁλυος.

Just as, I think, they say that in days gone by the Pactolus flowed through the middle of Sardis and brought riches for the taking for Croesus—a greater income and tribute than the whole of Lydia and Phrygia and the Maeonians and the Mysians and all who hold the territory this side the Halys yielded him.

On the Pactolus see also *Orationes* 33.23; Herodotus 5.101 (see *282*); Strabo 13.4.5 (see *234*).

The Pactolus rises on Tmolus (Pliny, *Naturalis historia* 5.110 [see *233*]; Dionysius Periegetes 831).

243. Horace, *Epodes* 15.17–20. 1st c. B.C.

et tu, quicumque es felicior atque meo nunc
superbus incedis malo,
sis pecore et multa dives tellure licebit
tibique Pactolus fluat . . .

And you, wherever you are in your state of happiness who now go about arrogant in my ill fortune, though you are rich in flocks and much land and though Pactolus flows for you . . .

The Pactolus as symbol of greatest wealth. Cf. Propertius 1.14.9–13.

244. Juvenal, *Satire* 14.298–300. 1st–2nd c. A.D.

sed cuius votis modo non suffecerat aurum
quod Tagus et rutila volvit Pactolus harena,
frigida sufficient velantes inguina panni
exiguusque cibus.

The man whose wishes would not have been satisfied by the gold which Tagus and Pactolus with its glittering sand provide must now make do with rags covering his chill loins and with an indigent crust.

245. Lucan, *Pharsalia* 3.209–210. 1st c. A.D.

Passaque ab auriferis tellus exire metallis
Pactolon, qua culta secat non vilior Hermus.

There the earth has allowed Pactolus to spring from gold-laden mines, where Hermus equally rich cuts through the ploughed fields.

246. Ovid, *Metamorphoses* 11.85–88. 1st c. B.C.

Nec satis hoc Baccho est, ipsos quoque deserit agros
cumque choro meliore sui vineta Timoli
Pactolonque petit, quamvis non aureus illo
tempore nec caris erat invidiosus harenis.

Nor is this enough for Bacchus. He also leaves their lands and with a livelier band of comrades he makes for the vineyards of his Tmolus and the Pactolus, though at that time this was not golden nor was it envied for its costly sands.

(230) Ovid, *Metamorphoses* 11.137–141. 1st c. B.C.

247. Philostratus, *Life of Apollonius* 6.37.

2nd–3rd c. A.D.

Δυοῖν δὲ λόγοιν ἐν Σάρδεσι λεγομένοιν, τοῦ μέν, ὡς ὁ Πακτωλός ποτε τῷ Κροίσῳ ψῆγμα χρυσοῦ ἄγοι, τοῦ δέ, ὡς πρεσβύτερα τῆς γῆς εἴη τὰ δένδρα, τὸν μὲν πιθανῶς ἔφη πεπιστεῦσθαι, χρυσία γὰρ εἶναί ποτε τῷ Τμώλῳ ψαμμώδη καὶ τοὺς ὄμβρους αὐτὰ φέρειν ἐς τὸν Πακτωλὸν κατασύροντας, χρόνῳ δέ, ὅπερ φιλεῖ τὰ τοιαῦτα, ἐπιλιπεῖν αὐτὰ ἀποκλυσθέντα.

There are two tales narrated in Sardis, one that the Pactolus at one time carried down gold dust to Croesus, and the other that the trees are older than the land. Apollonius said that the former story was trustworthy as being plausible enough, since at one time there had been golden sand on Tmolus and showers had carried it down into the Pactolus, sweeping it away. In time, however, as is customary in such matters, it was all washed away and the supply ceased.

248. Pliny, *Naturalis historia* 33.66.　　1st C. A.D.

fluminum ramentis, ut in Tago Hispaniae, Pado Italiae, Hebro Thraciae, Pactolo Asiae, Gange Indiae, nec ullum absolutius aurum est, ut cursu ipso attrituque perpolitum.

[It is found] in the silt of rivers, as in the Tagus in Spain, the Hebrus in Thrace, the Pactolus in Asia, and the Ganges in India. No gold is more pure, as this has been thoroughly polished by the rivers' flow and by friction.

249. Propertius 1.6.31–32.　　1st C. B.C.

at tu seu mollis qua tendit Ionia, seu qua
　　Lydia Pactoli tingit arata liquor . . .

Whether you go where soft Ionia extends itself or where the waters of Pactolus tinge the ploughed fields of Lydia . . .

250. Propertius 1.14.9–13.　　1st C. B.C.

nam sive optatam mecum trahit illa quietem,
　　seu facili totum ducit amore diem,
tum mihi Pactoli veniunt sub tecta liquores,
　　et legitur Rubris gemma sub aequoribus.

For if she spends the longed-for night with me, or passes the whole day in gentle love, then the waters of Pactolus come beneath my roof and the Red Sea's jewelry is mine.

See also 3.18.28.

251. Seneca, *Oedipus* 467–468.　　1st C. B.C.–1st C. A.D.

Divite Pactolos vexit te Lydius unda,
aurea torrenti deducens flumina ripa.

The Lydian Pactolus carried you on its rich waves, drawing the golden waters rapidly along its banks.

A hymn to Bacchus. See also *Phoenissae* 604 (see *260*).

252. Solinus 40.10.　　3rd C. A.D.

mons Lydiae Tmolus croco florentissimus: amnis Pactolus, quem aurato fluore incitum aliter Chrysorrhoam vocant.

The mountain of Lydia is Tmolus, abundant with saffron; the river is the Pactolus which, swirling rapidly with its floods of gold, some call the Chrysorrhoas.

On the Pactolus termed Chrysorrhoas see also Hyginus, *Fabulae* 191; Pliny, *Naturalis historia* 5.110 (see *233*); Eustathius, *Commentarii ad Homeri Iliadem* 20.385.

253. Sophocles, *Philoctetes* 391–395.　　5th C. B.C.

ὀρεστέρα παμβῶτι Γᾶ,
　μᾶτερ αὐτοῦ Διός,
ἃ τὸν μέγαν Πακτωλὸν εὔχρυσον νέμεις,
　σὲ κἀκεῖ, μᾶτερ πότνι᾽, ἐπηυδώμαν.

O Earth, you who dwell in the mountains and feed all men, mother of Zeus himself, you who supply great Pactolus rich in gold, to you, my Mother and Sovereign, I call.

(83) Tzetzes, *Historiarum variarum chiliades* 1:1, 1–5.　　12th C. A.D.

(232) Varro, *Menippean Satires EKATOMBH*.
　　　　　　　1st C. B.C.

254. Varro, *Menippean Satires: Lex Maenia* 7.
　　　　　　　1st C. B.C.

Non hos Pactolus aureas undas agens
Eripiet umquam e miseriis.

The Pactolus with its golden waters will never snatch these men from their miseries.

For Pactolus elsewhere in the Roman poets see Silius Italicus, *Punica* 1.159; Manilius, *Astronomicon* 5.530.

255. Virgil, *Aeneid* 10.139–142.　　1st C. B.C.

te quoque magnanimae viderunt, Ismare, gentes
vulnera derigere et calamos armare veneno,
Maeonia generose domo, ubi pinguia culta
exercentque viri Pactolusque inrigat auro.

Your courageous kinsfolk, Ismarus, saw you contriving wounds and arming missiles with poison, a noble warrior from a Maeonian house, where men work the rich fields and the Pactolus irrigates them with gold.

256. Xenophon, *Agesilaus* 1.30.   5th–4th c. B.C.

τῇ δὲ τετάρτῃ ἡμέρᾳ ἧκον οἱ τῶν πολεμίων ἱππεῖς.
καὶ τῷ μὲν ἄρχοντι τῶν σκευοφόρων εἶπεν ὁ ἡγεμὼν
διαβάντι τὸν Πακτωλὸν ποταμὸν στρατοπεδεύεσθαι.

On the fourth day the enemy cavalry arrived and
their captain told the leader of the baggage train to
cross the river Pactolus and make camp.

Ca. 395–394 B.C.
Tissaphernes' cavalry reach Sardis. See also *Hellenica*
3.4.22 (see *178*).

(121) Xenophon, *Cyropaedia* 6.2.11.   5th–4th c. B.C.

Tmolus

257. Euripides, *Bacchae* 461–464.   5th c. B.C.

Δι. οὐ κόμπος οὐδείς· ῥάδιον δ' εἰπεῖν τόδε.
     τὸν ἀνθεμώδη Τμῶλον οἶσθά που κλύων.
Πε. οἶδ', ὃς τὸ Σάρδεων ἄστυ περιβάλλει κύκλῳ.
Δι. ἐντεῦθέν εἰμι, Λυδία δὲ μοι πατρίς.

D. That's no great matter and to tell it is easy.
    Perhaps you know by hearsay of flowery
    Tmolus.
P. I know it; the encircling mountain that holds
    the city of the Sardians in its arms.
D. From there I come, and Lydia is my fatherland.

See also *Bacchae* 13, 55, 154, 234.
Tmolus lies behind (i.e., to the south of) Sardis; cf.
Herodotus 5.101 (see *282*); Polyaenus 7.14.2; Pliny,
Naturalis historia 5.110 (see *233*); Strabo 13.4.5 (see *234*).

(15) Eustathius, *Commentarii ad Homeri Iliadem*
366.15–20.   12th c. A.D.

(278) Herodotus 1.93.   5th c. B.C.

(8) Homer, *Iliad* 20.385.

(238) Homer, *Iliad* 2.866.

(14) Joannes Laurentius Lydus, *De mensibus* 4.71.
6th c. A.D.

258. Lycophron, *Alexandra* 1351–1353.   3rd c. B.C.

Αὖθις δὲ κίρκοι, Τμῶλον ἐκλελοιπότες
Κίμψον τε καὶ χρυσεργὰ Πακτωλοῦ ποτὰ
καὶ νᾶμα λίμνης . . .

Again the falcons have left Tmolus and Cimpsus
and the goldbearing stream of Pactolus and the
waters of the lake . . .

The falcons are the sons of Atys, and the lake the
Gygaean: so the scholiast. See also *Alexandra* 272.

(231) Ovid, *Metamorphoses* 11.150–152.   1st c. B.C.

259. Seneca, *Hercules Oetaeus* 371–373.
1st c. B.C.–1st c. A.D.

hospes Timoli Lydiam fovit nurum
et amore captus ad leves sedit colus,
udum feroci stamen interquens manu.

As a guest on Tmolus he fondled the Lydian
woman, and, taken by love, he sat by the swift
distaff twisting the damp thread with massive hand.

Seneca refers to the relationship between Hercules and
Omphale.

260. Seneca, *Phoenissae* 602–605.   1st c. B.C.–1st c. A.D.

hinc nota Baccho Tmolus attollit juga,
qua lata terris spatia frugiferis iacent
et qua trahens opulenta Pactolus vada
inundat auro rura.

Here Tmolus raises his ridges known to Bacchus
where wide plains of fruitful acres lie, and where
Pactolus moving his rich depths inundates the
fields with gold.

A possible kingdom suggested by Jocasta to Polynices.

261. Silius Italicus, *Punica* 5.9–11.   1st c. A.D.

Lydius huic genitor, Tmoli decus, aequore longo
Maeoniam quondam in Latias advexerat oras
Tyrrhenus pubem dederatque vocabula terris.

Trasimene's father, a Lydian and the pride of
Tmolus, had formerly brought the youth of
Maeonia to the shores of Latium by a long sea-
voyage. His name was Tyrrhenus and he gave his
name to the land.

Cf. *Punica* 4.738.

262. Silius Italicus, *Punica* 7.209–211.   1st c. A.D.

It monti decus, atque ex illo tempore dives
Tmolus et ambrosiis Ariusia pocula sucis
Ac Methymna ferox lacubus cessere Falernis.

Fame came to the mountain; and from that time
rich Tmolus and the goblets of Arimia with their

sweet wines and fiery Methymna have all yielded place to the Falernian vats.

263. Statius, *Thebaidos* 7.685–687.   1st c. A.D.

marcida te fractis planxerunt Ismara thyrsis,
te Tmolos, te Nysa ferax Theseaque Naxos
et Thebana metu juratus in orgia Ganges.

Swooning Ismara wept for you with broken wands, Tmolus and rich Nysa mourned for you, and Naxos, known to Theseus, and Ganges, sworn in fear to the Theban orgies.

> Places connected with Bacchus mourn the death of Eunaeus.

264. Strabo 13.1.23.   1st c. B.C.–1st c. A.D.

Ὑπέρκειται δὲ τῆς τῶν Ἀβυδηνῶν χώρας ἐν τῇ Τρωάδι τὰ Ἄστυρα, ἃ νῦν μὲν Ἀβυδηνῶν ἐστί, κατεσκαμμένη πόλις, πρότερον δὲ ἦν καθ᾽ αὑτά, χρυσεῖα ἔχοντα, ἃ νῦν σπάνιά ἐστιν ἐξαναλωμένα, καθάπερ τὰ ἐν τῷ Τμώλῳ τὰ περὶ τὸν Πακτωλόν.

Above the territory of Abydos in the Troad is Astyra, a city in ruins which now belongs to Abydos though formerly it was independent and had gold mines. These are now exhausted like those on Tmolus near the river Pactolus.

265. Strabo 13.4.13.   1st c. A.D.

Τῷ δὴ Καϋστριανῷ πεδίῳ μεταξὺ πίπτοντι τῆς τε Μεσωγίδος καὶ τοῦ Τμώλου, συνεχές ἐστι πρὸς ἔω τὸ Κιλβιανὸν πεδίον.

Adjacent to and to the east of the plain of the Cayster, which is located between the Mesogis and the Tmolus, is the plain of Cilbis.

266. Strabo 14.1.15.   1st c. B.C.–1st c. A.D.

καὶ μὴν καὶ ὁ Ἐφέσιος καὶ Μητροπολίτης ἀγαθοί, ἥ τε Μεσωγὶς καὶ ὁ Τμῶλος καὶ ἡ Κατακεκαυμένη καὶ Κνίδος καὶ Σμύρνα καὶ ἄλλοι ἀσημότεροι τόποι διαφόρως χρηστοινοῦσιν ἢ πρὸς ἀπόλαυσιν ἢ πρὸς διαίτας ἰατρικάς.

The Ephesian and Metropolitan wines are good; and Mesogis and Tmolus and the Catacecaumene and Cnidus and Smyrna and some other less famous places produce wine of distinction either for pleasure or for medicinal use.

> On the wine of Tmolus see also Pliny *Naturalis historia* 14.74; Vitruvius 8.3.12.

(190) Timotheus, *Persae* 116–118.   5th–4th c. B.C.

267. Virgil, *Georgics* 1.56–57.   1st c. B.C.

nonne vides, croceos ut Tmolus odores,
India mittit ebur, molles sua tura Sabaei?

Surely you see how Tmolus sends us saffron perfumes, India ivory, and the soft Sabaeans their frankincense?

Lexica

268. Stephanus of Byzantium, s.v. *Sardis*.   6th c. A.D.

Σάρδις, πόλις Λυδίας. ὁ πολίτης Σαρδιανός καὶ Σαρδιανή. τὸ κτητικὸν Σαρδιανικός καὶ Σαρδιανικὴ καὶ Σαρδιανός.

Sardis, a city of Lydia; the citizen Sardianus and Sardiane; the object Sardianicus and Sardianice and Sardianus.

> See also *Etymologicum magnum* s.v. *Sardis*; *Etymologicum Gudianum* s.v. *Sardis*.

269. Suidas, s.v. *Sardaios*.   10th c. A.D.

Σαρδαῖος ἀπὸ πόλεως Σάρδεων. καὶ Σάρδεις πόλις.

Sardaios from the city Sardeis. And Sardeis the city.

> In the lexicon see also the entries under Croesus (*4*), Alyattes (*1*), and Gyges (*1*); these are drawn very largely from Herodotus and Nicolas of Damascus.

RELIGIOUS STRUCTURES

The Altar of Artemis

270. Pausanias 7.6.6.   2nd c. A.D.

οἶδα δὲ καὶ ἄνδρα αὐτὸς Λυδὸν Ἄδραστον ἰδίᾳ καὶ οὐκ ἀπὸ τοῦ κοινοῦ τοῦ Λυδῶν ἀμύναντα Ἕλλησι· τοῦ δὲ Ἀδράστου τούτου χαλκῆν εἰκόνα ἀνέθεσαν οἱ Λυδοὶ πρὸ ἱεροῦ Περσικῆς Ἀρτέμιδος, καὶ ἔγραψαν ἐπίγραμμα ὡς τελευτήσειεν ὁ Ἄδραστος ἐναντίον Λεοννάτῳ μαχόμενος ὑπὲρ Ἑλλήνων.

I myself know that a Lydian, Adrastus by name, aided the Greeks, but privately and not at the instructions of the Lydian state. But the Lydians set up a bronze statue of Adrastus in front of the sanctuary of Persian Artemis, and they wrote an epigram saying that Adrastus died fighting for the Greeks against Leonnatus.

> Ca. 323–322 B.C.
> Adrastus evidently perished in the Lamian War.
> On Adrastus, see G. W. Elderkin, *AJA* 37 (1933) 389.
> The sanctuary was presumably at Sardis. On the later Artemis temple see *Sardis* II (1925); G. Gruben, *AM* 76 (1961) 155–196; and cf. *Sardis* VII:1 (1932) 19 no. 8.133.139. The recent excavations of the temple and precinct will be treated in a forthcoming report in this series.

271. Xenophon, *Anabasis* 1.6.6–7.   5th–4th c. B.C.

τοῦτον γὰρ πρῶτον μὲν ὁ ἐμὸς πατὴρ ἔδωκεν ὑπήκοον
εἶναι ἐμοί· ἐπεὶ δὲ ταχθείς, ὡς ἔφη αὐτός, ὑπὸ τοῦ
ἐμοῦ ἀδελφοῦ οὗτος ἐπολέμησεν ἐμοὶ ἔχων τὴν ἐν
Σάρδεσιν ἀκρόπολιν, καὶ ἐγὼ αὐτὸν προσπολεμῶν
ἐποίησα ὥστε δόξαι τούτῳ τοῦ πρὸς ἐμὲ πολέμου
παύσασθαι, καὶ δεξιὰν ἔλαβον καὶ ἔδωκα, μετὰ ταῦτα,
ἔφη, Ὀρόντα, ἔστιν ὅ τι σε ἠδίκησα; ἀπεκρίνατο ὅτι
οὔ. πάλιν δὲ ὁ Κῦρος ἠρώτα· Οὐκοῦν ὕστερον, ὡς
αὐτὸς σὺ ὁμολογεῖς, οὐδὲν ὑπ' ἐμοῦ ἀδικούμενος
ἀποστὰς εἰς Μυσοὺς κακῶς ἐποίεις τὴν ἐμὴν χώραν
ὅ τι ἐδύνω; ἔφη Ὀρόντας. Οὐκοῦν, ἔφη ὁ Κῦρος,
ὁπότ' αὖ ἔγνως τὴν σαυτοῦ δύναμιν, ἐλθὼν ἐπὶ τὸν
τῆς Ἀρτέμιδος βωμὸν μεταμέλειν τέ σοι ἔφησθα καὶ
πείσας ἐμὲ πιστὰ πάλιν ἔδωκάς μοι καὶ ἔλαβες παρ'
ἐμοῦ;

"My father gave me this man to be my subject. Then, at the instructions of his brother, as he said, he seized the acropolis of Sardis and made war on me. I fought back against him and brought it about that he thought it wise to stop warring against me; and I extended and received the right hand of friendship. Since that," he said, "Orontas, have I wronged you?" And he replied that he had not. Again Cyrus interrogated him, "Later, as you yourself admit, though in no way maltreated by me, did you not desert to the Mysians and do whatever damage you could to my country?" Orontas admitted that he had. "Then," said Cyrus, "when again you learnt your weakness, did you not go to the altar of Artemis and say you repented and did you not convince me and again give and receive tokens of trust from me?"

> Cyrus was satrap of Lydia (*Anabasis* 1.9.7.). For Lydia as satrapy see *Cyropaedia* 8.6.7.
> For an altar at Sardis on which Orontas might have taken his oath see *Sardis* II (1925) 3f; with which cf. A. von Gerkan, *Der Poseidonaltar bei Kap Monodendri* (Berlin 1915) 447–466.
> Preliminary publication of recent excavation of the altar appears in G. M. A. Hanfmann and J. C. Waldbaum, *BASOR* 199 (1970) 30ff, figs. 18, 19.

Temple of Cybele

272. Herodotus 5.102ff.   5th c. B.C.

καὶ Σάρδιες μὲν ἐνεπρήσθησαν, ἐν δὲ αὐτῇσι καὶ ἱρὸν
ἐπιχωρίης θεοῦ Κυβήβης, τὸ σκηπτόμενοι οἱ Πέρσαι
ὕστερον ἀντενεπίμπρασαν τὰ ἐν Ἕλλησι ἱρά. τότε δὲ
οἱ Πέρσαι οἱ ἐντὸς Ἅλυος ποταμοῦ νομοὺς ἔχοντες
προπυνθανόμενοι ταῦτα συνηλίζοντο καὶ ἐβοήθεον
τοῖσι Λυδοῖσι. καί κως ἐν μὲν Σάρδισι οὐκέτι ἐόντας
τοὺς Ἴωνας εὑρίσκουσι, ἑπόμενοι δὲ κατὰ στίβον
αἱρέουσι αὐτοὺς ἐν Ἐφέσῳ.

Sardis was burnt and the temple of Cybele there, the epichoric goddess. It was with this in mind that the Persians later burnt the temples of Greece. Then when the Persians west of the Halys heard of these things they gathered and came to the assistance of the Lydians. They found that the Ionians were no longer in Sardis, but they followed hard on their heels and overtook them in Ephesus.

The Ionians were routed (102). The Athenians left the Ionian cause which was joined by Caunus after the events at Sardis (103). Angered at the Athenians (105), Darius was persuaded by Histiaeus (106) to send him to Ionia (107). The governor of Sardis, Artaphrenes, was appointed to war against Ionia and Aeolic Cyme (123).

> The attack on Sardis took place ca. 499 B.C.
> On the pursuit see also 5.116, 5.122, 6.101, 7.8.
> For a possible replica of Cybele's temple in Sardis see D. G. Mitten in G. M. A. Hanfmann, *BASOR* 174 (1964) 39–42, with which cf. Hanfmann and J. C. Waldbaum, *Archaeology* 22 (1969) 268–269.
> On Cybele see Herodotus 1.80, 4.76; Sophocles, *Philoctetes* 391ff; Strabo 10.3.12; Lucian, *De dea Syria*; Catullus 63; Virgil, *Aeneid* 6.784ff; Pindar, *Pythian Odes* 3.78; Euripides, *Baccae* 59: *Helen* 1301ff; Ovid, *Fasti* 4.201ff; Pausanias 7.17.9. Cf. E. Laroche, E. Will, and R. D. Barnett in *Éléments orientaux dans la religion grecque ancienne* (Paris 1960) 95–128, 144; E. O. James, *The Cult of the Mother Goddess* (London 1959) 161ff; in Thasos, F. Salviat *BCH* 88 (1964) 239ff; in Cilicia, A. Dupont-Sommer and L. Robert, *La Déesse de Hiérapolis Castabala* (Paris 1964).

Fire Altar

273. Pausanias 5.27.5ff.   2nd c. A.D.

ἔστι γὰρ Λυδοῖς ἐπίκλησιν Περσικοῖς ἱερὰ ἔν τε
Ἱεροκαισαρείᾳ καλουμένῃ πόλει καὶ ἐν Ὑπαίποις, ἐν
ἑκατέρῳ δὲ τῶν ἱερῶν οἴκημά τε καὶ ἐν τῷ οἰκήματι
ἐστιν ἐπὶ βωμοῦ τέφρα· χρόα δὲ οὐ κατὰ τέφραν ἐστὶν

αὐτῇ τὴν ἄλλην. ἐσελθὼν δὲ ἐς τὸ οἴκημα ἀνὴρ μάγος καὶ ξύλα ἐπιφορήσας ἀνὰ ἐπὶ τὸν βωμὸν πρῶτα μὲν τιάραν ἐπέθετο ἐπὶ τῇ κεφαλῇ, δεύτερα δὲ ἐπίκλησιν ὅτου δὴ θεῶν ἐπάδει βάρβαρα καὶ οὐδαμῶς συνετὰ Ἕλλησιν· ἐπάδει δὲ ἐπιλεγόμενος ἐκ βιβλίου. ἄνευ τε δὴ πυρὸς ἀνάγκη πᾶσα ἀφθῆναι τὰ ξύλα καὶ περιφανῆ φλόγα ἐξ αὐτῶν ἐκλάμψαι.

The Lydians, who are called Persians, have religious precincts in the city of Hierocaesareia and at Hypaepa. Within each sanctuary there is a building and in the building there is an altar with ashes atop. But the color of the ashes is not normal. When the priest has entered the building and heaped up dry wood on the altar, he first puts a diadem on his head and then chants foreign incantations incomprehensible to Greeks to some god or other, reciting from a book. It is required that the wood be kindled without fire, and that bright flames gleam from the logs.

For a Persian altar at Sardis see A. Ramage in G. M. A. Hanfmann, *BASOR* 191 (1968) 11–13.

On Hierakome-Hierocaesareia see L. Robert, *Villes d'Asie Mineure* (Paris 1962) 39, 84, 266.

On Hypaepa see S. Wikander, *Feuerpriester in Kleinasien und Iran* (Lund 1946) 81–84; L. Robert, *Villes d'Asie Mineure* (Paris 1962) 381.

Metroon

274. Plutarch, *Themistocles* 31.   1st–2nd c. A.D.

Ὡς δ᾿ ἦλθεν εἰς Σάρδεις καὶ σχολὴν ἄγων ἐθεᾶτο τῶν ἱερῶν τὴν κατασκευὴν καὶ τῶν ἀναθημάτων τὸ πλῆθος, εἶδε καὶ ἐν Μητρὸς ἱερῷ τὴν καλουμένην ὑδροφόρον κόρην χαλκῆν, μέγεθος δίπηχυν, ἣν αὐτὸς ὅτε τῶν Ἀθήνησιν ὑδάτων ἐπιστάτης ἦν, ἑλὼν τοὺς ὑφαιρουμένους τὸ ὕδωρ καὶ παροχετεύοντας, ἀνέθηκεν ἐκ τῆς ζημίας ποιησάμενος· εἴτε δὴ παθών τι πρὸς τὴν αἰχμαλωσίαν τοῦ ἀναθήματος, εἴτε βουλόμενος ἐνδείξασθαι τοῖς Ἀθηναίοις, ὅσην ἔχει τιμὴν καὶ δύναμιν ἐν τοῖς βασιλέως πράγμασι, λόγον τῷ Λυδίας σατράπῃ προσήνεγκεν, αἰτούμενος ἀποστεῖλαι τὴν κόρην εἰς τὰς Ἀθήνας.

When he had arrived in Sardis and in his leisurely way was inspecting the arrangement of the sanctuaries and the quantity of the dedications, he saw in the temple of the Mother the statue called the Water-Carrier, a girl in bronze and two cubits high. When he had been the water commissioner in Athens he himself had had this made and had dedicated it from the fines he extracted when he caught individuals stealing and draining off the water. Whether he now was irritated at the capture of the statue or whether he wished to show the Athenians how much respect and influence he had in the king's affairs, he spoke to the satrap of Lydia asking him to send the statue back to Athens.

Ca. 470 B.C.

On Themistocles in Asia Minor see Diodorus Siculus 11.56.4ff. For a new approach to one of the so-called letters of Themistocles, thought of as written from Asia, see C. Nylander, *Opuscula Atheniensia* 8 (1968) 119–136.

On the authorities for Themistocles' flight to Xerxes, see *Themistocles* 27. On the restoration of stolen treasures, etc., see B. Perrin, *Plutarch's Themistocles and Aristides* (New York 1901) 254.

A new inscription, discovered at Sardis in 1963 and to be published by L. Robert in the volume of inscriptions in this series, mentions the Hellenistic Metroon, and was, in fact, inscribed on one of the Metroon's *parastades*. It is dated precisely to June 214/213 B.C. Cf. L. Robert, *Nouvelles inscriptions de Sardes* (Paris 1964) 58.

Synagogue

275. Josephus, *Antiquitates Judaicae* 14.235.   1st c. A.D.

Λούκιος Ἀντώνιος Μάρκου υἱὸς ἀντιταμίας καὶ ἀντιστράτηγος Σαρδιανῶν ἄρχουσι βουλῇ δήμῳ χαίρειν. Ἰουδαῖοι πολῖται ἡμέτεροι προσελθόντες μοι ἐπέδειξαν αὐτοὺς σύνοδον ἔχειν ἰδίαν κατὰ τοὺς πατρίους νόμους ἀπ᾿ ἀρχῆς καὶ τόπον ἴδιον, ἐν ᾧ τά τε πράγματα καὶ τὰς πρὸς ἀλλήλους ἀντιλογίας κρίνουσιν, τοῦτό τε αἰτησαμένοις ἵν᾿ ἐξῇ ποιεῖν αὐτοῖς τηρῆσαι καὶ ἐπιτρέψαι ἔκρινα.

Lucius Antonius, son of Marcus, proquaestor and propraetor, to the magistrates, council, and people of Sardis, greetings. Our Jewish citizens came to me and showed me that from the beginning they have had a private association in accordance with their ancestral laws and a private place where they decide their own business and resolve their differences. When they asked to be able still to do these things, I decided to take care of this and to allow them.

Cf. Josephus, *Antiquitates* 14.232.

For more precise reference to the synagogue at Sardis see *Antiquitates* 14.259. On the building itself see D. G. Mitten in G. M. A. Hanfmann, *BASOR* 170 (1963) 38–48, Mitten in Hanfmann, *BASOR* 174 (1964) 30–44, Mitten in Hanfmann, *BASOR* 177 (1965) 17–21, Mitten in Hanfmann, *BASOR* 182 (1966) 34–45, Hanfmann, *BASOR* 187 (1967) 9–50, Hanfmann, *BASOR* 191 (1968)

26–32, Hanfmann and J. C. Waldbaum, *BASOR* 199 (1970) 47–51; the building will be treated in detail by A. R. Seager in a forthcoming report in this series.

The Jewish community at Sardis may have been expanded by Antiochus (Josephus, *Antiquitates* 12.148–149): on which see A. T. Kraabel, *GRBS* 10 (1969) 86.

The Jews in Asia Minor successfully appealed to Augustus against the decisions of the city administrations (Josephus, *Antiquitates* 16.171).

For the Fountain of the Synagogue see *Sardis* VII: 1 (1932) 38, no. 17.7.

For inscriptions from the Synagogue see L. Robert, *Nouvelles inscriptions de Sardes* (Paris 1964) 37–57.

TOMBS

Abradatas

276. Xenophon, *Cyropaedia* 7.3.4–5ff.   5th–4th c. B.C.

καὶ νῦν γε, ἔφη, λέγεται αὐτοῦ ἡ γυνὴ ἀνελομένη τὸν νεκρὸν καὶ ἐνθεμένη εἰς τὴν ἁρμάμαξαν, ἐν ᾗπερ αὐτὴ ὠχεῖτο, προσκεκομικέναι αὐτὸν ἐνθάδε ποι πρὸς τὸν Πακτωλὸν ποταμόν. καὶ τοὺς μὲν εὐνούχους καὶ τοὺς θεράποντας αὐτοῦ ὀρύττειν φασὶν ἐπὶ λόφου τινὸς θήκην τῷ τελευτήσαντι· τὴν δὲ γυναῖκα λέγουσιν ὡς κάθηται χαμαὶ κεκοσμηκυῖα οἷς εἶχε τὸν ἄνδρα, τὴν κεφαλὴν αὐτοῦ ἔχουσα ἐπὶ τοῖς γόνασι.

And now, he said, they say that his wife has taken up his dead body and put it in the carriage in which she used to go about and has brought it here somewhere by the Pactolus river. And they say that his eunuchs and servants are digging a grave for the corpse on some ridge or other; and that his wife has adorned her husband with the things she had, and is sitting on the ground holding his head in her lap.
Cyrus rode over and joined Panthea (7.3.6). He commiserated with her (7.3.8ff). Panthea's death (7.3.14).

On Abradatas and Panthea in Lydia see *Cyropaedia* 6.3.35ff; 6.4.2ff; 7.1.15ff, 29ff. Cf. Zonaras, *Epitome* 3.22ff.

277. Xenophon, *Cyropaedia* 7.3.15.   5th–4th c. B.C.

ὁ δὲ Κῦρος ὡς ᾔσθετο τὸ ἔργον τῆς γυναικός, ἐκπλαγεὶς ἵεται, εἴ τι δύναιτο βοηθῆσαι. οἱ δὲ εὐνοῦχοι ἰδόντες τὸ γεγενημένον, τρεῖς ὄντες σπασάμενοι κἀκεῖνοι τοὺς ἀκινάκας ἀποσφάττονται οὗπερ ἔταξεν αὐτοὺς ἑστηκότες. [καὶ νῦν τὸ μνῆμα μέχρι τοῦ νῦν τῶν εὐνούχων κεχῶσθαι λέγεται· καὶ ἐπὶ μὲν τῇ ἄνω στήλῃ τοῦ ἀνδρὸς καὶ τῆς γυναικὸς ἐπιγεγράφθαι φασὶ τὰ ὀνόμ-

ατα, Σύρια γράμματα, κάτω δὲ εἶναι τρεῖς λέγουσι στήλας καὶ ἐπιγεγράφθαι ΣΚΗΠΤΟΥΧΩΝ.]

On learning what the woman had done, Cyrus was overcome and hurried over in case he might be able to help in any way. And when the three eunuchs saw what had happened, they too drew their daggers and killed themselves in exactly the place where she had instructed them to stand. It is said that the monument of the eunuchs is standing even to this day; and on the stele above they say the names of the man and wife are written in Assyrian letters. And it is said that below are three other stelai and written on them is THE STAFF-BEARERS.
Cyrus saw that the grave monument was raised over them all (16).

The tomb of Abradatas and Panthea may well be identified with the Persian tomb discovered on the flank of the acropolis facing Pactolus, on which see *Sardis* I (1922) 167ff; G. M. A. Hanfmann, *BASOR* 162 (1961) 31, 166 (1962) 28–30, Hanfmann and J. C. Waldbaum, *BASOR*, 199 (1970) 36f, figs. 27, 28.

The second part of this passage is difficult and seen by most editors as an interpolation. Dindorf (1857) described it as an "absurdum recentioris Graeculi additamentum." It is not, however, without archaeological interest, whatever the date of the confused interpolation.

On the Assyrian letters of the inscription on the stele above the tomb in the interpolated passage see C. Nylander, *Opuscula Atheniensia* 8 (1968) 122.

For staffbearers, perhaps court officials, cf. *Cyropaedia* 8.1.38, 8.3.15, *Anabasis* 1.6.11.

Alyattes

278. Herodotus 1.93.   5th c. B.C.

Θώματα δὲ γῆ ⟨ἡ⟩ Λυδίη ἐς συγγραφὴν οὐ μάλα ἔχει, οἷά γε καὶ ἄλλη χώρη, πάρεξ τοῦ ἐκ τοῦ Τμώλου καταφερομένου ψήγματος. ἓν δὲ ἔργον πολλὸν μέγιστον παρέχεται χωρὶς τῶν τε Αἰγυπτίων ἔργων καὶ τῶν Βαβυλωνίων· ἔστι αὐτόθι Ἀλυάττεω τοῦ Κροίσου πατρὸς σῆμα, τοῦ ἡ κρηπὶς μέν ἐστι λίθων μεγάλων, τὸ δὲ ἄλλο σῆμα χῶμα γῆς. ἐξεργάσαντο δέ μιν οἱ ἀγοραῖοι ἄνθρωποι καὶ οἱ χειρώνακτες καὶ αἱ ἐνεργαζόμεναι παιδίσκαι. οὖροι δὲ πέντε ἐόντες ἔτι καὶ ἐς ἐμὲ ἦσαν ἐπὶ τοῦ σήματος ἄνω, καί σφι γράμματα ἐνεκεκόλαπτο τὰ ἕκαστοι ἐξεργάσαντο. καὶ ἐφαίνετο μετρεόμενον τὸ τῶν παιδισκέων ἔργον ἐὸν μέγιστον. τοῦ γὰρ δὴ Λυδῶν δήμου αἱ θυγατέρες πορνεύονται πᾶσαι, συλλέγουσαι σφίσι φερνάς, ἐς ὃ ἂν συνοικήσωσι τοῦτο ποιεῦσαι· ἐκδιδοῦσι δὲ αὐταὶ ἑωυτάς. ἡ μὲν δὴ περίοδος τοῦ σήματός εἰσι στάδιοι ἓξ καὶ δύο πλέθρα, τὸ δὲ εὖρός ἐστι πλέθρα τρία καὶ δέκα· λίμνη δὲ ἔχεται τοῦ σήματος μεγάλη, τὴν λέγουσι Λυδοὶ ἀένναον εἶναι· καλέεται δὲ αὕτη Γυγαίη.

Lydia does not have many marvels worth mentioning like any other country, except the gold dust brought down from Tmolus. But there is one piece of work which is more enormous than any excepting those of Egypt and Babylon. There is there the tomb of Alyattes father of Croesus; its retaining wall is built of large stones, and the rest of the tomb is a mound of earth. The merchants, the craftsmen, and the prostitutes built it, and five markers on which written characters recorded the work contributed by each survived till my day atop the tomb. And when measured it appeared that the prostitutes' contribution was the largest. All the daughters of the Lydians work as prostitutes collecting dowries until they are able to marry; and they give themselves away. The circumference of the tomb is six stades and two plethra, and its breadth is thirteen plethra. A great lake is nearby the tomb which the Lydians say is ever full, and it is called Gygaean.

On the tomb of Alyattes see Hipponax F 42 (see *280*) (Masson); von Olfers, *AbhBerlAkad* (1858) 539–556; and G. M. A. Hanfmann, *BASOR* 170 (1963) 52–57. In the last century (Spiegelthal in von Olfers) the mound had a diameter at the base of the retaining wall of 355.2 meters, giving a circumference of 1,115.32 m. Its height was 61.46 m.

279. Strabo 13.4.7.   1st c. B.C.–1st c. A.D.

Περίκειται δὲ τῇ λίμνῃ τῇ Κολόῃ τὰ μνήματα τῶν βασιλέων. πρὸς δὲ ταῖς Σάρδεσίν ἐστι τὸ τοῦ Ἀλυάττου ἐπὶ κρηπῖδος ὑψηλῆς χῶμα μέγα, ἐργασθέν, ὥς φησιν Ἡρόδοτος, ὑπὸ τοῦ πλήθους τῆς πόλεως, οὗ τὸ πλεῖστον ἔργον αἱ παιδίσκαι συνετέλεσαν· λέγει δ᾽ ἐκεῖνος καὶ πορνεύεσθαι πάσας, τινὲς δὲ καὶ πόρνης μνῆμα λέγουσι τὸν τάφον. χειροποίητον δὲ τὴν λίμνην ἔνιοι ἱστοροῦσι τὴν Κολόην πρὸς τὰς ἐκδοχὰς τῶν πλημμυρίδων, αἳ συμβαίνουσι τῶν ποταμῶν πληρουμένων.

The tombs of the kings are located close by Lake Coloe. Directly opposite Sardis itself is the great mound of Alyattes built within a high retaining wall by the city's populace, as Herodotus says. Prostitutes contributed most of the work, and Herodotus says that all Lydian women prostituted themselves; some call the tomb itself a monument of prostitution. Some state that Lake Coloe is man-made to contain the floods which occur when the rivers overflow.

On prostitution in Sardis see Strabo 11.14.16; Strabo 12.3.36 with reference to Strabo 8.6.20; Athenaeus 12.515d–f (see *130*); and cf. S. Pembroke, *JWarb* 30 (1967) 4ff.

Gyges

280. Hipponax F 42.   6th c. B.C.

. . . δεύειε τὴν ἐπὶ Σμύρνης·
ἴθι διὰ Λυδῶν παρὰ τὸν Ἀττάλεω τύμβον
καὶ σῆμα Γύγεω καὶ † μεγάστρυ . . . στήλην
καὶ μνῆμα Τῶτος † μυτάλιδι πάλμυδος,
πρὸς ἥλιον δύνοντα γαστέρα τρέψας.

. . . by the road to Smyrna; go through Lydia past the mound of Attales, the tomb of Gyges . . . and the marker and memorial of Tos . . . turning your belly to the setting sun.

See O. Masson, *Les Fragments du poète Hipponax* (Paris 1962) 65, 129–134. This fragment is preserved by Tzetzes in *Anecdota Graeca Oxoniensia* (ed. J. A. Cramer) III 310, with which cf. Schol. Nicander *Theriaca* 633. For Tzetzes on Gyges see *Historiarum variarum chiliades* 1:3, 137–166; 7:120, 195–202.

Hipponax describes a westward journey past Sardis to the coast.

An Attales is mentioned by Nicolas (*FGrHist* 90 F 63), but Alyattes should likely be understood here.

Smyrna was a suburb of Ephesus (see Hipponax F 50 and Strabo 14.1.4).

On the tomb of Gyges see G. M. A. Hanfmann, *BASOR* 177 (1965) 27–34, 182 (1966) 27–30, C. H. Greenewalt, Jr., in Hanfmann, *BASOR* 186 (1967) 43–46; R. Gusmani, *InnsBeiKult* 14 (1968) 51.

For the stele cf. Athenaeus 13.573a, b quoting Clearchus of Soli. The text is far from clear. Some (A. Sayce, *JRAS* [1927] 710ff) conjecture a reference to the rock sculpture at Karabel, for which see Herodotus 2.106.

For the date of Hipponax and relation to the chronology of Sardis see *Marmor Parium* (*FGrHist* 239 F 42). He preserves many Lydian words (G. L. Huxley, *The Early Ionians* [New York 1966] 34, 111–112).

281. Nicander, *Theriaca* 630–635.   2nd c. B.C.

Ἄγρει μὰν ὀλίγαις μηκωνίσι ῥάμνον ἐΐσην
ἑρσομένην, ἀργῆτι δ᾽ ἀεὶ περιδέδρομεν ἄνθῃ·
τὴν ἤτοι φιλέταιριν ἐπίκλησιν καλέουσιν
ἀνέρες οἳ Τμώλοιο παραὶ Γύγαό τε σῆμα
Παρθένιον ναίουσι λέπας, τόθι Κίλβιν ἀεργοί
ἵπποι χιλεύουσι καὶ ἀντολαί εἰσι Καΰστρου.

Take the dewy Rhamnus which is similar to the little wild lettuces, always bedecking itself with white flowers. It is given the name of Good Companion by those who inhabit the flank of Parthenius near the tomb of Tmolus and of Gyges where work-free horses feed on Cilbis and where the Cayster rises.

On Tmolus as king, not mountain, see (Apollodorus) *Bibliotheca* 2.6.3.

Schol. *Theriaca* 634 describes Parthenius as the height of Lydia. On Cilbis the scholiast is equally enlightening, though cf. Pliny, *Naturalis historia* 5.115, Strabo 13.4.13.

For an illustration showing the tomb as a heroon see H. Omont, *Miniatures des plus anciens manuscrits grecs de la Bibliothèque Nationale du VIe au XIVe siècle*, 2nd ed. (Paris 1929) 38–39, pl. 66; on the manuscript see K. Weitzmann, *DO Papers* 14 (1960) 49.

SECULAR STRUCTURES

The Agora and Domestic Architecture

282. Herodotus 5.101.   5th c. B.C.

ἦσαν ἐν τῆσι Σάρδισι οἰκίαι αἱ μὲν πλεῦνες καλάμιναι, ὅσαι δ' αὐτέων καὶ πλίνθιναι ἦσαν, καλάμου εἶχον τὰς ὀροφάς. τουτέων δὴ μίαν τῶν τις στρατιωτέων ὡς ἐνέπρησε, αὐτίκα ἀπ' οἰκίης ἐπ' οἰκίην ἰὸν τὸ πῦρ ἐπενέμετο τὸ ἄστυ πᾶν. καιομένου δὲ τοῦ ἄστεος οἱ Λυδοί τε καὶ ὅσοι Περσέων ἐνῆσαν ἐν τῇ πόλι, ἀπολαμφθέντες πάντοθεν ὥστε τὰ περιέσχατα νεμομένου τοῦ πυρὸς καὶ οὐκ ἔχοντες ἐξήλυσιν ἐκ τοῦ ἄστεος, συνέρρεον ἔς τε τὴν ἀγορὴν καὶ ἐπὶ τὸν Πακτωλὸν ποταμόν, ὅς σφι ψῆγμα χρυσοῦ καταφορέων ἐκ τοῦ Τμώλου διὰ μέσης τῆς ἀγορῆς ῥέει καὶ ἔπειτα ἐς τὸν Ἕρμον ποταμὸν ἐκδιδοῖ, ὁ δὲ ἐς θάλασσαν· ἐπὶ τούτον δὴ τὸν Πακτωλὸν καὶ ἐς τὴν ἀγορὴν ἀθροιζόμενοι οἵ τε Λυδοὶ καὶ οἱ Πέρσαι ἠναγκάζοντο ἀμύνεσθαι. οἱ δὲ Ἴωνες ὁρῶντες τοὺς μὲν ἀμυνομένους τῶν πολεμίων, τοὺς δὲ σὺν πλήθεϊ πολλῷ προσφερομένους ἐξανεχώρησαν δείσαντες πρὸς τὸ ὄρος τὸ Τμῶλον καλεόμενον, ἐνθεῦτεν δὲ ὑπὸ νύκτα ἀπαλλάσσοντο ἐπὶ τὰς νέας.

Most of the houses in Sardis were of reeds and even those that were made of brick had reed roofs. When one of the soldiers set fire to one of these, the blaze immediately raced from house to house spreading through the whole city. When the city was burning, the Lydians and the Persians who were in the city were surrounded on every side since the fire was devouring the outer buildings. Since they had no way out of the city, they all rushed together into the agora, to the river Pactolus which brings down gold dust from Tmolus, flows through the middle of the agora, and joins the Hermus in the same way as the Hermus joins the sea. Thronging together into the agora by the Pactolus, the Lydians and Persians were obliged to defend themselves. As the Ionians saw some of the enemy defending themselves and others approaching in great numbers, they took fright and withdrew to the mountain called Tmolus. From there they made their way under cover of night to their ships.

Ca. 499 B.C.

The tactic of encircling the city with fire suggests very deliberate arson on the part of the Ionians.

For domestic architecture in Sardis see G. M. A. Hanfmann, *BASOR* 182 (1966) 18–22. The subject will be fully treated by Andrew Ramage in a forthcoming report in this series.

For the Roman Agora, see *Sardis* VII:1 (1932) 17, 19, no. 8.49, 128; 38, no. 17.11.

(29) Nicolas of Damascus, *FGrHist* 90 F 22.

1st c. B.C.–1st c. A.D.

Fortification Walls

(112) Ctesias of Cnidus, *FGrHist* 688 F 9 (4).

4th c. B.C.

(116) Herodotus 1.84.   5th c. B.C.

283. Polybius 7.15.6–7ff.   2nd c. B.C.

συνθεωρήσας δὲ τὸ κατὰ τὸν καλούμενον Πρίονα τεῖχος ἀφυλακτούμενον—οὗτος δ' ἔστι τόπος ὁ συνάπτων τὴν ἄκραν καὶ τὴν πόλιν—ἐγίνετο περὶ τὴν ἐλπίδα καὶ τὴν ἐπίνοιαν ταύτην. τὴν μὲν οὖν τῶν φυλαττόντων ῥᾳθυμίαν ἐκ τοιούτου τινὸς σημείου συν(έβη) θεωρῆσαι.

Seeing that the wall along the so-called Saw—the place which links the citadel with the lower city—was unguarded, he became hopeful and began to hatch plots involving this. He chanced to have noticed the sloppiness of the sentinels here from the following indication.

The place was very steep (8), and Lagoras noticed vultures sitting on the city wall showing it to be unguarded (9). He scouted the ground at night (10), found it suitable for ladders, and approached the king (11). The king was delighted (16.1), and Lagoras asked for the help of Theodotus and Dionysius (2), with whom plans were made (3). On a suitable night they picked fifteen men to take the ladders (4) and thirty others to attack from the outside the gate they would assault from the inside (5).

Events in the spring of 214 B.C.

Polybius visited Sardis (21.38.7) where he met the Galatian Chiomara (Plutarch, *Mulierum virtutes* 22 [258 E]; cf. P. A. Stadter, *Plutarch's Historical Methods* [Cambridge, Mass. 1965] 109). The date of his visit is uncertain (F. W. Walbank, *A Historical Commentary on Polybius* I [Oxford 1957] 5, 296).

On the assault cf. Cyrus' capture of the city in 547 B.C. (Herodotus 1.84 [see *116*]; Xenophon, *Cyropaedia* 7.2.1–4 [see *122*]; etc.) when the geography may well have been the same as in Achaeus' time.

The saddle connecting the acropolis with the city proper was called the Saw from its similarity to that instrument (cf. Polybius 1.85.7). See also *Sardis* I (1922) 16–25.

Like Lagoras (see *203*), Theodotus was a deserter from Ptolemy IV (Polybius 5.40.1–3).

284. Polybius 7.16.6ff.   2nd c. B.C.

δι—σχιλίους δὲ τοὺς κατόπιν ἀκολουθήσοντας τούτοις, οὓς συνεισπεσόντας ἔδει καταλαβέσθαι τὴν τοῦ θεάτρου στεφάνην, εὐφυῶς κειμένην πρός τε τοὺς ἐκ τῆς ἄκρας καὶ πρὸς τοὺς ἐκ τῆς πόλεως.

Two thousand men would follow behind these thirty, and their assignment was to dash through the gate and seize the crown of the theater, a position well situated both against the enemy in the acropolis and those issuing from the lower town.
All was in readiness (17.1) and at dawn the ascent began (2). Dionysius and Lagoras climbed the two ladders first (3) and their ascent, though visible to their own army, went unseen by the enemy (4).

On the archaeology of the acropolis see *Sardis* I (1922) 15–25; G. M. A. Hanfmann, *BASOR* 162 (1961) 32–39, 166 (1962) 35–40, 170 (1963) 31–37, 177 (1965) 8–10.

On the theater see *Sardis* I (1922) 31; and cf. *Sardis* VII:1 (1932) 11, no. 4.22.

285. Polybius 7.17.6ff.   2nd c. B.C.

ὅθεν ὁ βασιλεύς, θεωρῶν τὸ περὶ τὴν ὅλην παρεμ—βολὴν κίνημα, καὶ βουλόμενος ἀποσπᾶν ἀπὸ τοῦ προ—κειμένου τούς τε παρ' αὐτοῦ καὶ τοὺς ἐκ τῆς πόλεως, προῆγε τὴν δύναμιν καὶ προσέβαλε πρὸς τὰς ἐπὶ θά—τερα πύλας κειμένας, Περσίδας δὲ προσαγορευομένας.

And so when the king saw the hubbub in his own camp, he was anxious to channel the attention of his own troops and those of the enemy away from Lagoras' enterprise. Accordingly he led his army forward and attacked the gate at the other side of the town, the gate known as the Persian gate.

Achaeus in the acropolis could not understand what was happening (7), but sent a force to engage Antiochus (8). Aribazus, in command of the town, similarly opposed Antiochus (9). Lagoras crossed the Saw and attacked the designated gate (18.1). The gate was opened and the 2000 entered (3). The garrison left the Persian gate to oppose the intruder (4), but the Persian gate itself was then forced by Antiochus' men (5–6). Aribazus and his soldiers retreated to the acropolis (7) while Lagoras held the theater area (8). Antiochus' army now entered the city en masse, and the city was burnt and sacked (9).

Lagoras and his men evidently climbed the cliffs to the east of the saddle joining acropolis and lower town. Once over the wall they took the nearest gate: as there was no difficulty in seizing the theater, this gate may be assumed to have been close by. The gate which Antiochus attacked, the Persian gate, will then likely have been to the west.

On the technology of gates in antiquity see F. W. Walbank. *A Historical Commentary on Polybius* II (Oxford 1967) 64–65.

Antiochus' devastation of Sardis is now amply documented: see G. M. A. Hanfmann, *BASOR* 174 (1964) 25, 34, 182 (1966) 24–25, A. Ramage in Hanfmann, *BASOR* 177 (1965) 4, A. Ramage in Hanfmann, *BASOR* 191 (1968) 13–14.

286. Polybius 8.20.5–6ff.   2nd c. B.C.

παρεγένοντο πρὸς τὸν τῷ Καμβύλῳ διατεταγμένον τόπον, καὶ τὸ σύνθημα προσσυρίξας ὁ Βῶλις ἀπέδωκε, τῶν μὲν ἄλλων οἱ διαναστάντες ἐκ τῆς ἐνέδρας ἐπελά—βοντο, τὸν δ' Ἀχαιὸν αὐτὸς ὁ Βῶλις ὁμοῦ τοῖς ἱματίοις, ἔνδον τὰς χεῖρας ἔχοντα, συνήρπασε, φοβηθεὶς μὴ συννοήσας τὸ γινόμενον ἐπιβάλοιτο διαφθείρειν αὐτόν· καὶ γὰρ εἶχε μάχαιραν ἐφ' αὑτῷ παρεσκευασμένος.

When they had come to the place they had arranged with Cambylus, and when Bolis had given the signal with a whistle, those who jumped out of the ambush seized some of them while Bolis himself grabbed Achaeus by his clothes, in this way holding his hands inside his garments. For he was afraid that when he found out what had happened he might try to kill himself; for he had provided himself with a sword.
Antiochus showed Achaeus no mercy (8.21.3) and shortly thereafter the acropolis fell (8.21.9).

Achaeus had hoped to get to Syria (8.17.10).

Bolis was familiar with the topography of Sardis (8.15.4); on him and Cambylus see H. van Effenterre, *La Crète et le monde grec de Platon à Polybe* (Paris 1948) 295, 296.

The route they took down the acropolis was hazardous (8.20.3), as the citadel was said to be the most impregnable place in the world (8.20.12). Lucian (*De mercede conductis* 13 [see *236*]) reflects on its difficulty.

(**122**) Xenophon, *Cyropaedia* 7.2.1–4.   5th–4th c. B.C.

(**123**) Zonaras, *Epitome historiarum* 3.23B.

The Hellenistic Gymnasium

(**210**) Polybius 31.6.   2nd c. B.C.

Parks and Gardens

(**130**) Athenaeus, *Deipnosophistae* 12.515d–f.

2nd–3rd c. A.D.

287. Cicero, *De senectute* 59.   1st c. B.C.

Atque ut intellegatis nihil ei tam regale videri quam studium agri colendi, Socrates in eo libro loquitur cum Critobulo Cyrum minorem, Persarum regem, praestantem ingenio atque imperi gloria, cum Lysander Lacedaemonius, vir summae virtutis, venisset ad eum Sardis eique dona a sociis attulisset, et ceteris in rebus communem erga Lysandrum atque humanum fuisse et ei quendam consaeptum agrum diligenter consitum ostendisse.

And that you may appreciate that nothing seemed to Xenophon as worthy of a king as enthusiasm for agriculture, Socrates in that book tells the following tale in conversation with Critobulus. Cyrus the Younger, a Persian king who excelled in intelligence and in the glory of his empire, was visited at Sardis by the Spartan Lysander. Lysander, a man of great capacity, had brought him gifts from the allies, so that Cyrus was in many ways kindly and generous toward him and also showed him a certain carefully arranged pleasure-park.

For this kind of park or preserve see Xenophon, *Anabasis* 1.2.7, 2.4.14; *Oeconomicus* 4.13.

288. Diodorus 14.80.2.   1st c. B.C.

ἐπελθὼν δὲ τὴν χώραν μέχρι Σάρδεων ἔφθειρε τούς τε κήπους καὶ τὸν παράδεισον τὸν Τισσαφέρνους, φυτοῖς καὶ τοῖς ἄλλοις πολυτελῶς πεφιλοτεχνημένον εἰς τρυφὴν καὶ τὴν ἐν εἰρήνῃ τῶν ἀγαθῶν ἀπόλαυσιν. μετὰ δὲ ταῦτ' ἐπιστρέψας, ὡς ἀνὰ μέσον ἐγενήθη τῶν τε Σάρδεων καὶ Θυβάρνων, ἀπέστειλε Ξενοκλέα

τὸν Σπαρτιάτην μετὰ χιλίων καὶ τετρακοσίων στρατιωτῶν νυκτὸς εἴς τινα δασὺν τόπον, ὅπως ἐνεδρεύσῃ τοὺς βαρβάρους.

Overrunning the country as far as Sardis, he destroyed the gardens and the pleasure-park of Tissaphernes, which had been set out artfully and expensively with plants and all else that contributes to luxury and the quiet enjoyment of the good things. He then turned about, and when he was midway between Sardis and Thybarnae he sent Xenocles the Spartiate with fourteen hundred soldiers by night to a densely wooded place to ambush the Persians.
The Persians were ambushed and withdrew to Sardis in confusion (3–5).

The Spartan admiral, Agesilaus, ravaged Asia Minor, perhaps 395–394 B.C. Subsequently, the satrap Tiribazus lured Conon to Sardis and arrested him (14.85.4).

289. Xenophon, *Oeconomicus* 4.20ff.   5th–4th c. B.C.

οὗτος τοίνυν ὁ Κῦρος λέγεται Λυσάνδρῳ, ὅτε ἦλθεν ἄγων αὐτῷ τὰ παρὰ τῶν συμμάχων δῶρα, ἄλλα τε φιλοφρονεῖσθαι, ὡς αὐτὸς ἔφη ὁ Λύσανδρος ξένῳ ποτέ τινι ἐν Μεγάροις διηγούμενος, καὶ τὸν ἐν Σάρδεσι παράδεισον ἐπιδεικνύναι αὐτὸν ἔφη.

When Lysander came to him bringing the gifts from the allies, Cyrus is said to have been well disposed to him in many ways, as Lysander himself said in casual conversation with a stranger once in Megara. He also said that Cyrus showed him over his park in person.
Lysander much admired the regularity of the planning (21), which delighted Cyrus as it was his own work (22). Noting the brilliance of his appearance, Lysander could not believe that Cyrus indulged in manual labor (23), to which Cyrus commented on the benefits attaching to war and agriculture (24).

For gardens of the Roman period see *Sardis* VII:1 (1932) 31, no. 12.6.

The Royal Palace

(**124**) Bacchylides, *Epinicia* 3.32.   5th c. B.C.

(**148**) Aristotle, *Analytica Posteriora* 94a, b.

4th c. B.C.

(**34**) Herodotus 1.9.   5th c. B.C.

(**89**) Herodotus 1.34.   5th c. B.C.

(35) Nicolas of Damascus, *FGrHist* 90 F 47 (8).

1st c. b.c.–1st c. a.d.

(126) Nicolas of Damascus, *FGrHist* 90 F 68.

1st c. b.c.–1st c. a.d.

290. Pliny, *Naturalis historia* 35.172.   1st c. a.d.

Graeci, praeterquam ubi e silice fieri poterat structura, latericios parietes praetulere. sunt enim aeterni, si ad perpendiculum fiant. ideo et publica opera et regias domos sic struxere: murum Athenis, qui ad montem Hymettum spectat, Patris aedes Jovis et Herculis, quamvis lapideas columnas et epistylia circumdarent, domum Trallibus regiam Attali, item Sardibus Croesi, quam gerusian fecere, Halicarnasi Mausoli, quae etiam nunc durant.

Except where a structure could be built in stone, the Greeks preferred brick walls; for if they are constructed absolutely perpendicular, they last forever. Therefore they built public structures and royal palaces of this material: the wall at Athens which faces Hymettus, the temples of Zeus and Heracles at Patrae (though stone was used for the columns and entablature), the royal palace of Attalus at Tralles, and similarly the palace of Croesus at Sardis which they converted into a senate house, and that of Mausolus at Halicarnassus, structures which are still in existence.

The palace at Sardis has yet to be found, though archaic masonry on the acropolis (G. M. A. Hanfmann, *BASOR* 162 [1961] 37–39) may have been integral to a Mermnad palatial complex.

(3) Plutarch, *An seni respublica gerenda sit* 4 (785E).

1st–2nd c. a.d.

(154) Plutarch, *De Herodoti malignitate* 24.

1st–2nd c. a.d.

291. Vitruvius 2.8.9–10.   1st c. b.c.–1st c. a.d.

Itaque nonnullis civitatibus et publica opera et privatas domos etiam regias a latere structas licet videre . . . Croesi domus, quam Sardiani civibus ad requiescendum aetatis otio seniorum collegio gerusiam dedicaverunt.

[9] And so in some states it is possible to see public buildings and private houses alike and even palaces built of brick . . . [10] There is the palace of Croesus which the townsfolk of Sardis dedicated as a place for the citizens to relax in the leisure of their age. It had been the meeting place for the college of elders.

Vitruvius may be misunderstanding the term "gerusia" and may be meaning an old-age home; or he may be misunderstanding his Hellenistic source; or his source may have misunderstood the term γερουσία; or the translation may reflect what both meant.

For an Augustan "gerusia" in Sardis see *Sardis* VII:1 (1932) 18, no. 8.72; and cf. 38, no. 17.2.

The palace has yet to be detected. Presumably it guards the king lists of which Nicolas of Damascus (*FGrHist* 90 F 44 [7] [see *30*]) speaks so lightly. It may have stood until the city was razed by Antiochus.

The Treasury

(75) Dio Chrysostom, *Orationes* 78.32.   1st–2nd c. a.d.

(84) Herodotus 1.30.   5th c. b.c.

(77) Herodotus 6.125.   5th c. b.c.

Appendix: Near Eastern Sources

Assyrian

292. *The Rassam Cylinder.*

Guggu [Gyges], king of Lydia, a district of the other side of the sea, a distant place, whose name, the kings, my fathers, had not heard, Assur, the god, my creator, caused to see my name in a dream. "Lay hold of the feet of Assurbanipal, king of Assyria and conquer thy foes by calling upon his name." On the day that he beheld this vision, he dispatched his messenger to bring greetings to me. [An account of] this vision, which he beheld, he sent to me by the hand of his messenger, and made it known to me. From the day that he laid hold of my royal feet, he overcame, by the help of Assur and Ishtar, the gods, my lords, the Cimmerians, who had been harassing the people of his land, who had not feared my fathers, nor had laid hold even of my royal feet. From among the chieftains of the Cimmerians, whom he had conquered, he shackled two chieftains with shackles, fetters of iron, manacles of iron, and sent them to me, together with his rich gifts.

His messenger, whom he kept sending to me to bring me greetings, he [suddenly] discontinued,—because he did not heed the word of Assur, the god who created me, but trusted in his own strength, and hardened his heart. He sent his forces to the aid of Tushamilki, king of Egypt, who had thrown off the yoke of my sovereignty. I heard of it and prayed to Assur and Ishtar, saying: "May his body be cast before his enemy, may [his foes] carry off his limbs." The Cimmerians, whom he had trodden underfoot, by calling upon my name, invaded and overpowered the whole of his land. His son seated himself upon his throne, after him [*i.e.,* his death]. He sent me, by the hand of his messenger, [an account] of the evil which the gods, my helpers, visited upon him [in answer] to my prayers, and he laid hold of my royal feet, saying: "Thou art the king whom the god has favored [*lit.,* looked upon]. Thou didst curse my father and evil was visited upon him. I am [thy] slave, who fears thee, be gracious unto me and I will bear [*lit.,* draw] thy yoke."

Translated by D. D. Luckenbill, *Ancient Records of Assyria and Babylonia* II (Chicago 1927) 297–298.

The cylinders, more accurately named prisms, were inscribed and set up to commemorate royal building projects. The Rassam text commemorates the rebuilding of the palace at Nineveh.

On the date of the cylinder/prism (644–636 B.C.; in the eponymy of Shamash-daninanni) see Luckenbill, ibid. 290, 323.

On Cimmerians in Lydia see Herodotus 1.15 (see *52*); Strabo 14.1.40 (see *51*).

293. *Cylinder B.*

Gyges, king of Lydia, a district which is by the shore of the sea, a distant place the mere mention of the name of which my royal ancestors had not heard—Ashur, the great god who begat me, caused him to see my royal name in a dream. The day on which he saw this dream he sent his mounted messenger to ask my welfare. The Cimmerian, a wicked foe who had not feared my ancestors and who as for me had not caught hold of my royal feet . . . [*A adds*: he conquered].

Translated by A. C. Piepkorn, *Historical Prism Inscriptions of Assurbanipal* (Chicago 1933) 47.

On the date (648 B.C.) of this prism see D. D. Luckenbill, *Ancient Records of Assyria and Babylonia* II (Chicago 1927) 323; Piepkorn, ibid. 19.

294. *Cylinder E.*

. . . his [mes]senger wi[th a present] approached to ask my health to the border of my land. The people of my country looked at him and said to him, "Who are you, stranger, whose mounted messenger hitherto has never blazed a trail to the marches?" To Nineveh, the city of my lordship, [the people] brought him to me into my presence. The tongues of the East and of the West, which Ashur had poured into my hand—there was no master of his language, and [his] tongue remained strange, so that they could not understand his speech. From the boundary of his land . . . he brough[t] with him . . .

[*Remainder of column missing.*]

Translated by A. C. Piepkorn, *Historical Prism Inscriptions of Assurbanipal* (Chicago 1933) 17.

On the identification of the messengers as Gyges' see Piepkorn, ibid. 9.

295. *Building Tablet.*

Gyges, king of Lydia, a province on the other side the sea, a distant region, whose name the kings who went before me, my fathers, had not heard mentioned,—Assur, the god who created me, revealed the honored name of my majesty to him in a dream, saying: "Lay hold of the feet of his highness, Assurbanipal, king of Assyria, favorite of Assur, king of the gods, lord of all, and revere [*lit.*, fear] his kingship, implore [the favor] of his lordship. As of one doing homage [*lit.*, service] and paying tribute, let thy prayers come to him."

On the [same] day that he saw this dream, he sent his couriers to me to greet me [*lit.*, ask my peace], and the Cimmerians who had been disturbing his land, his hands took alive in battle. Together with his heavy tribute he sent them [*lit.*, had them brought] to Nineveh, my royal city, and kissed my feet.

Translated by D. D. Luckenbill, *Ancient Records of Assyria and Babylonia* II (Chicago 1927) 351–352.

This clay tablet commemorates the rebuilding of the Temple of Sin at Harran and contains selections from the royal archives.

Babylonian

296. The Nabonidus Chronicle.

In Nisan

Cyrus king of Persia levied his troops.
and crossed [?] the Tigris below Arbela. In Iyyar he [marched] to the land of Lydia[?] . . . .
he killed its king, he took its booty, he put a garrison of his own therein.

Afterwards his garrison and the king remained therein.

Translated by S. Smith, *Babylonian Historical Texts* (London 1924) 116.

On the identification as the land of Lydia see Smith, ibid. 101, and S. Smith, *Isaiah, Chapters XL–LV* (London 1944) 35–36, 135. For the Nabonidus Chronicle see Smith, *Babylonian Historical Texts* 98–123.

For other versions of the fall of Sardis see Herodotus 1.84 (see *116*); Parthenius, *Love Stories* 22 (see *118*); Ctesias, *FGrHist* 688 F 9 (4) (see *112*); Xenophon, *Cyropaedia* 7.2.2ff (see *122*); etc.

Persian

297. *PF 873 (Persepolis Fortification Tablets).*

$121\frac{1}{2}$ [BAR of] flour, supplied by Istimanka, Sardian men, blacksmiths, subsisting on rations [at] Kurra, whose apportionments are set by Irsena, received as rations. Eleventh and twelfth and thirteenth months, for a total period of 3 months, 22nd year.

9 men, each receives $4\frac{1}{2}$ BAR per month. Total 9 workers.

Translated by R. T. Hallock, *Persepolis Fortification Tablets* (Chicago 1969) 252. G. G. Cameron, by letter, informs me that the translation "blacksmiths" may be somewhat free since the verb which goes with the logogram for "iron" only means "strike."

These are regular monthly rations paid from the local Persepolis Treasury for work not too far from Persepolis.

298. *PF 1321 (Persepolis Fortification Tablets).*

6 QA [of] flour, supplied by Haturdada: Hamaratsa [?] and his 3 companions, fast messengers, [are] receiving each $1\frac{1}{2}$ QA.

He carried a sealed document of the king, and they went to Sardis.

28th year, second month.

Translated by R. T. Hallock, *Persepolis Fortification Tablets* (Chicago 1969) 374. These Persepolis texts, written in Elamite, deal largely with transfers of food commodities in the years 509–494 B.C.; for a larger statement of the subject matter of the texts see Hallock, ibid. 4–8.

Here we deal with travel rations.

299. *PF 1401 (Persepolis Fortification Tablets).*

4.65 BAR [of] flour Dauma received. 23 men [received] each $1\frac{1}{2}$ QA. 12 boys received each 1 QA.

He carried a sealed document of Artaphernes.

They went forth from Sardis. They went to Persepolis.

Ninth month, 27th year. [At] Hidali.

Translated by R. T. Hallock, *Persepolis Fortification Tablets* (Chicago 1969) 396. Travel rations.

On Hidali, a place between Susa and Persepolis, see Hallock, ibid. 40 n. 35. Artaphernes was presumably the satrap at Sardis.

300. *PF 1409 (Persepolis Fortification Tablets).*

3 QA [of] flour, supplied by Parru, Kammazikara the elite guide received, and gave [it] as rations to 2 Sardian men, *halapzi* makers. For 1 man [they are] receiving 1½ QA [of] flour.

They went from Susa to Sandupirzana [at] Maknan. He carried a sealed document of Parnaka. 22nd year. For 1 day.

Translated by R. T. Hallock, *Persepolis Fortification Tablets* (Chicago 1969) 397. Travel rations.
The Sardian workmen's job is not identifiable.

301. *DB I (Darius, Behistan, Column I) 12–17.*

Saith Darius the King: These are the countries which came unto me; by the favor of Ahuramazda I was king of them: Persia, Elam, Babylonia, Assyria, Arabia, Egypt, [those] who are beside the sea, Sardis, Ionia, Media, Armenia, Cappadocia, Parthia, Drangiana, Aria, Chorasmia, Bactria, Sogdiana, Gandara, Scythia, Sattagydia, Arachosia, Maka: in all, XXIII provinces.

Translated by R. G. Kent, *Old Persian* (New Haven 1953) 119.

The trilingual (Old Persian, Elamite, Akkadian) inscription of Behistan is set on the face of a cliff, difficult to approach, close by the main trade route from Baghdad to Teheran. On it see Kent, ibid. 107f.

The formula is repeated with modifications in DPe (Darius, Persepolis E) on which see Kent, ibid. 109, 136, and in DSm (Darius, Susa M) for which see Kent, ibid. 110–111, 145.

More detailed catalogues of states subservient to Darius, including and mentioning Sardis are DNa (Darius, Naqš-i-Rustam A) 15–30 on which see Kent, ibid. 109, 138, and DSe (Darius, Susa E) 14–30 for which see Kent, ibid. 110, 142.

On the identification of figures on the Persepolis reliefs as Sardians see G. Walser, *Die Völkerschaften auf den Reliefs von Persepolis* (Berlin 1966) esp. 86–88, reviewed by O. W. Muscarella, *JNES* 28 (1969) 280–285.

302. *DPh (Darius, Persepolis H) 3–10.*

Saith Darius the King: This is the kingdom which I hold, from the Scythians who are beyond Sog-

diana, thence unto Ethiopia; from Sind, thence unto Sardis—which Ahuramazda the greatest of the gods bestowed upon me. Me may Ahuramazda protect, and my royal house.

Translated by R. G. Kent, *Old Persian* (New Haven 1953) 137.

A trilingual inscription on two gold and two silver plates: on this see Kent, ibid. 109.

The inscription on the gold and silver plate known as DH (Darius, Hamadan) is almost identical; cf. Kent, ibid. 111f, 147.

For another copy of the Foundation Record of Darius the Great see G. G. Cameron, *Iran* 5 (1967) 7–10.

303. *DSf (Darius, Susa F) 35–55.*

The gold was brought from Sardis and from Bactria, which here was wrought. The precious stone lapis-lazuli and carnelian which was wrought here, this was brought from Sogdiana. The precious stone turquois, this was brought from Chorasmia, which was wrought here.

The silver and the ebony were brought from Egypt. The ornamentation with which the wall was adorned, that from Ionia was brought. The ivory which was wrought here, was brought from Ethiopia and from Sind and from Arachosia.

The stone columns which were here wrought, a village by name Abiradu, in Elam—from there were brought. The stone-cutters who wrought the stone, those were Ionians and Sardians.

The goldsmiths who wrought the gold, those were Medes and Egyptians. The men who wrought the wood, those were Sardians and Egyptians. The men who wrought the baked brick, those were Babylonians. The men who adorned the wall, those were Medes and Egyptians.

Translated by R. G. Kent, *Old Persian* (New Haven 1953) 144.

The building inscription for Darius' palace at Susa; for bibliography see Kent, ibid. 110. For the newly found complete examples of the building inscription see the *New York Times*, Sunday, March 9, 1970, and cf. now F. Vallat, *Revue d'Assyriologie* 64 (1970) 149–160; F. Vallat, *Syria* 48 (1971) 54–59.

On the presence of foreign workmen in Susa and Persepolis see G. G. Cameron, *Persepolis Treasury Tablets* (Chicago 1948) 11 and passim; G. Goossens, *NouvClio* 1 (1949) 32–44.

On craftsmen from Sardis active in Achaemenid circles see C. Nylander, *Iranica Antiqua* 6 (1966) 143, 145, 146.

On Ionian and Lydian workmen active in the Neo-Babylonian palaces see E. F. Weidner, *Mélanges Dussaud* 2 (1939) 923–935; W. F. Albright, *BiblArch* 5 (1942) 51; see also A. Goetze, *JCS* 16 (1962) 54.

304. *XPh* (Xerxes, Persepolis H) 13–28.

Saith Xerxes the King: By the favor of Ahuramazda these are the countries of which I was king ... [= DNa 18–22]; Media, Elam, Arachosia, Armenia, Drangiana, Parthia, Aria, Bactria, Sogdiana, Chorasmia, Babylonia, Assyria, Sattagydia, Sardis, Egypt, Ionians, those who dwell by the sea and those who dwell across the sea, men of Maka, Arabia, Gandara, Sind, Cappadocia, Dahae, Amyrgian Scythians, Pointed-Cap Scythians, Skudra, men of Akaufaka, Libyans, Carians, Ethiopians.

Translated by R. G. Kent, *Old Persian* (New Haven 1953) 151.
The Daiva inscription, for which see Kent, ibid. 112. The text is close, in parts, to that of DNa (Darius, Naqš-i-Rustam A).
On the relation between Old Persian Sparda- and Lydian Śfard-, see A. Meillet, *Grammaire du Vieux-Perse* (Paris 1915) 26 no. 52; E. Herzfeld, *AMIran* 3:2 (1931) 63–64.

Other

305. Old Testament, Obadiah 20.

And the captivity of this host of the children of Israel that are among the Canaanites even unto Zarephath, and the captivity of Jerusalem that is in Sepharad shall possess the cities of the South.

See *The Twelve Prophets*, Hebrew text, English translation and commentary, ed. A. Cohen (London 1961) 134.
Sepharad is Aramaic for Sardis: for which see A. T. Kraabel *GRBS* 10 (1969) 81 n. 2.

306. Historical record of the reign of Antiochus I.

... In that year [the 36th of the Seleucid era] the king left his court, his wife and the crown prince in Sapardu to keep a strong guard. He went to the province Ebir-nari and marched against the Egyptian army which was camped in Ebir-nari ...

In the 37th year, Antiochus and Seleucus. In the month of Adar on the 9th the governor of Akkad and the town magistrates of the king who went to Sapardu in the 36th year to the king returned to Seleucia, the royal city on the Tigris.

Translated by S. Smith, *Babylonian Historical Texts* (London 1924) 156; on the document and its date see Smith, ibid. 150–159.
The account is of the events of the years 276–274 B.C. Antiochus removed his queen and court to Sardis when Ptolemy II, Philadelphus, invaded Syria.
For the identification of Sapardu with Sardis see Smith, ibid. 152–153.

307. Polemo, *Physiognomonica* (G. Hoffmann in vol. I of R. Foerster's Teubner edition of *Scriptores Physiognomici*, 139).

I was a companion of the emperor while we were traveling from Thrace to Asia; the king had his armies and chariots with him, and that man was in his entourage. We passed through many cities until we reached the sea. Then we journeyed to Ionia, Sardis, lands of Lydia and Phrygia, and many places. After that we returned from Asia by way of islands in the sea. We came[1] to Rhodes. Then we traveled[2] in ships to Athens.

1. Verb corrupt here.
2. Slight textual difficulty in verb here.

Emended from the Arabic and translated by G. Bowersock.
On Polemo's journey with Hadrian and their visit to Sardis see G. Bowersock, *Greek Sophists in the Roman Empire* (Oxford 1969) 120–123.
Hadrian's journey took place in A.D. 123/4. His visit to Asia Minor, including Sardis, is otherwise known: cf. G. W. Weber, *Untersuchungen zur Geschichte des Kaisers Hadrianus* (1907) 123–148.

Index

Authors

Numbers refer to the serial numbers of the sources.

Subjects

For many major subjects, people, and historical events, the table of contents provides the chief means of indexing. The following index contains less significant subjects and supplementary details not included in the extensive cross-referencing in the text itself. The numbers refer to the serial numbers of the sources. Where a page number is given the reader is referred to a heading in the text.